The Risk Society at War

In the globalised world of the twenty-first century, security policy in Western societies is driven by a wish to prevent future threats from becoming reality. Applying theories of 'risk society' to the study of strategy, this book analyses the creation of a new approach to strategy. The author demonstrates that this approach creates new choices for policy-makers and challenges well-established truths within the study of security and strategy. He argues that since the seventeenth century the concept of strategy has served to rationalise new technologies, doctrines and agents. By outlining the history of the concept of strategy in terms of rationality, Rasmussen presents a framework for studying strategy in a time of risk and uses this framework to analyse how new technologies of war, pre-emptive doctrines, globalisation and the rise of the 'terrorist approach to warfare' can formulate a new theory of strategy.

MIKKEL VEDBY RASMUSSEN is Associate Professor in the Department of Political Science at the University of Copenhagen. He is the author of *The West, Civil Society and the Construction of Peace* (2003).

The Risk Society at War

Terror, Technology and Strategy in the Twenty-First Century

Mikkel Vedby Rasmussen

CAMBRIDGE
UNIVERSITY PRESS

CAMBRIDGE UNIVERSITY PRESS
Cambridge, New York, Melbourne, Madrid, Cape Town, Singapore, São Paulo

CAMBRIDGE UNIVERSITY PRESS
The Edinburgh Building, Cambridge CB2 2RU, UK

Published in the United States of America by Cambridge University Press,
New York

www.cambridge.org
Information on this title: www.cambridge.org/9780521687317

© Mikkel Vedby Rasmussen 2006

First published 2006

Printed in the United Kingdom at the University Press, Cambridge

A catalogue record for this book is available from the British Library

ISBN-13 978-0-521-86791-7 hardback
ISBN-10 0-521-86791-6 hardback
ISBN-13 978-0-521-68731-7 paperback
ISBN-10 0-521-68731-4 paperback

Contents

Acknowledgements

I developed the ideas for this book in order to answer questions. The new strategic agenda which was unfolded after the end of the Cold War, but perhaps most visibly after that terrible day we have come to know as 9/11, has created a great public interest in security issues. When I have been asked to tell about the strategic issues of today to my students at the University of Copenhagen, in public lectures or in the Danish media I found that I had to reassess traditional concepts of strategic studies and develop new understandings of strategic issues. This book is the result. Thus elements of the ideas in this book have been presented on numerous occasions and I thank everyone who challenged my ideas for unwittingly helping me to sharpen the argument and directing my attention to areas that needed further research.

Previous incarnations of Chapters 2 and 3 have been presented at seminars at the Department of Political Science, University of Copenhagen, and an early version of Chapter 3 was presented at a seminar at the Danish Institute for International Studies. Thanks to the participants for constructive comments.

I would also like to thank Anna Riis Hedegaard and Kristian Søby Kristensen for very effective research assistance in the first phase of research for this book; later, Kristian was very helpful with his comments on Chapter 4. Thanks to Ingvar Sejr Hansen for compiling the bibliography and to Robert Parkin for correcting the mistakes of a non-native English speaker in the final phase of writing the book.

I acknowledge that the section on 'risk strategies' in Chapter 2 is loosely based on my 'Reflexive Security: NATO and International Risk Society', *Millennium: Journal of International Studies* 30 (2001), 285–309. The section on the boomerang effect in Chapter 3 has appeared in a somewhat different version under the title *The Revolution in Military Affairs and the Boomerang Effect*, Report 2004: 6 from the Danish Institute for International Studies.

I am very grateful for the thorough and constructive reviews of the three anonymous reviewers who read the manuscript for Cambridge

University Press. Their comments have been very helpful in the final revisions. John Haslam, my editor at Cambridge, has given this book a warm welcome and I thank him for that.

Most of all however I would like to thank my wife Anne. The life we live with our children should be reason enough to thank her, but it was actually she who first introduced me to the concept of risk society and asked if that concept did not cover much of the new strategic agenda I was talking about. I hope she will not be disappointed when she reads the book.

Any mistakes or misconceptions in what follows are my sole responsibility.

1 Introduction

At the beginning of the twenty-first century, people fortunate enough to live in Western societies are probably more secure than at any point in the twentieth century. No system of alliances currently creates a mechanism of international obligations that might trigger a war in the way that European alliances triggered the First World War. An almost universal consensus on the values of liberal democracy and the free market means that no totalitarian ideology is threatening to bury the Western way of life in the way that fascism did in the Second World War and communism during the Cold War. Not only are there fewer political reasons for conflict at the beginning of the twenty-first century, but the military means, such as nuclear weapons, for fighting these conflicts are no longer on the hair-trigger alert that was maintained during the Cold War. Today it is hard for schoolchildren to imagine that their grandparents were taught to 'duck and cover' or that their parents worried about whether Russians loved their children enough not to want to unleash nuclear Armageddon. Thus, measured by the standards of the twentieth century, we are safer than we have ever been. However, the standards by which we measure our security have changed.

To understand the way today's measurement of danger differs from the twentieth century it is useful to distinguish between threats and risks.[1] A threat is a specific danger which can be precisely identified and measured on the basis of the capabilities an enemy has to realise a hostile intent. During the Cold War the Soviet Union with the Red Army's tanks and nuclear missiles constituted such a threat. The Soviet

---

[1] The distinction between threat and risk appears in many forms in the risk literature (Luhmann, for instance, writes about risk vs security and risk vs danger), but the main point is the distinction between a modern concept of computable dangers (threat) and a late modern, reflexive concept of risk. See Ulrich Beck, *World Risk Society* (Cambridge: Polity Press, 1999), 52–8, Niklas Luhmann, *Risk: A Sociological Theory*, trans. Rhodes Barrett (New York: Walter de Gruyter, 1993), 1–31 and Anthony Giddens, *The Consequences of Modernity* (Cambridge: Polity Press, 1990), 124–31.

threat could be assessed in terms of the Kremlin's ends and the means the Soviet Union had at its disposal to realise these ends. That did not mean that politicians or researchers agreed on the nature of the Soviet threat, but they debated the threat in terms of what could be measured in the belief that it was possible to defeat the threat and achieve security. Thus threats were understood in a means-end rational framework. This reflected the nature of the danger, but it was also the result of a process that began in the seventeenth century when modern strategy began to place warfare in a means-end rational context.

Today the Red Army is gone and the West faces the new dangers of a globalising world. Terrorism and the spread of weapons of mass destruction (WMD) are often-mentioned examples of this, but the introduction of new military technologies, the advent of new great powers and the introduction of new doctrines for the use of armed force should also be mentioned. This strategic agenda is about 'risks' rather than threats. From a risk perspective a danger is much less computable than from a threat perspective. A risk is a scenario followed by a policy proposal for how to prevent this scenario from becoming real. However, such a policy proposal does not aim to achieve perfect security: from a risk perspective the best one can hope for is to manage or pre-empt a risk; one can never achieve perfect security because new risks will arise as a 'boomerang effect' of defeating the original risk.

Where strategic studies have clearly defined the nature of threats, the nature of strategy in a time of risk has not yet been codified and placed in a system which can help researchers and the public to understand the dangers of the twenty-first century and help policy-makers to act upon these dangers. If one studies the practice of security policy since the end of the Cold War, however, the outline of the new risk rationality of strategy emerges. This book seeks to describe this new rationality of strategy.

Strategy is not the only field where 'risk' is redefining the terms of policy-making. A number of sociologists – Anthony Giddens, Ulrich Beck, John Adams and Niklas Luhmann foremost among them – use the term 'risk society' to describe how the citizens of Western countries have come to see their society's development as 'a theme and a problem for itself'.[2] It is the argument of this book that the emergence of the risk society has profound consequences for how Western societies measure how secure they are, and that 'risk-thinking' – or 'reflexive rationality' as the sociologists prefer to call it – is shaping the strategies by which

---

[2] Ulrich Beck, *Risk Society*, trans. Mark Ritter (London: Sage Publications, 1992), 8.

Western governments seek to achieve security. In risk society there is no such thing as perfect security. Thinking in terms of risk means measuring the present in terms of the future – and from the perspective of the first years of the twenty-first century, there is plenty to fear from the future.

Although the West is not faced with a hostile balance of power, threatening new actors are appearing on the strategic horizon. Al-Qaeda is widely regarded as the first example of a new breed of strategic agents, who are able to operate because globalisation makes the world easily accessible to terrorists as well as traders. In time, other groups may follow al-Qaeda's example and form transnational terrorist networks. These networks may form coalitions with other non-state actors or with states, thus creating a new type of 'hostile coalition' that may produce conflict even though the balance of power between states may continue to be benign. Forming coalitions with non-state actors may also be a way for revisionist states to destabilise the balance of power in their favour. Furthermore, al-Qaeda is often presented as an example of a new ideological challenge to Western society. It is a challenge different from that posed by fascism or communism, however, because Western politicians and publics believe al-Qaeda to be of a different rationality than they are – these terrorists act because of their religious beliefs, not any national interests.

The confrontation with terrorism demonstrates how information and communication technologies have revolutionised the way the West, especially the United States, wages war. In Afghanistan and Iraq, the US armed forces have shown the effectiveness of a military machine with a global reach. However, they have also demonstrated that this 'revolution in military affairs' (RMA) is not living up to the promise of clean, fast and unproblematic wars. Instead of perfecting war, technological innovation is opening up new possibilities for warfare, which in all likelihood will change warfare in the twenty-first century.

Technological innovations, the rise of new types of enemy and the way they are seen to challenge Western values define the strategic environment in the twenty-first century. To many people, the collapse of the World Trade Center on 11 September 2001, following al-Qaeda's attack on New York and Washington, is an iconic image that summarises the fears of a new age. While schoolchildren may no longer fear nuclear Armageddon, they do ask teachers and parents about the possibility of another 9/11. Children might return reassured to the playground once they have been told that the likelihood of a terrorist attack in their neighbourhood is small. And compared to the threats that Polish children faced in 1939 or American children faced during the Cuban Missile

Crisis in 1962, our children have little to fear. While this argument may reassure children, it does not seem to work on their parents because comparisons to the threats of the past do not work in a society that defines itself in terms of risk. 'Risks are not "real", they are "becoming real"', Joost van Loon notes.[3] In the twentieth century, threats were regarded like stocks: they were measurable and finite. One could count the number of Waffen SS divisions and defeat them in battle, or measure the number of Soviet nuclear warheads and deploy an equal number as a deterrent. Risks are flows. When assessing a risk, what matters is not so much what happens but what may happen, because, van Loon goes on, 'as soon as risks become real, say an act of terrorism destroying the financial heart of New York, they cease to be risks and become a catastrophe or at least an irritation. Risks have already moved elsewhere: to the anticipation of further attacks, economic decline or worldwide war.'[4]

A risk is a scenario followed by a policy proposal for how to prevent this scenario from becoming real. For this reason, a success cannot be measured with any degree of finality because success depends on creating a reality different from what one feared would happen. However, if one prevents a scenario from becoming real, the result will probably be to create new risks, which then rise to the top of the agenda. The theoretical outcome of this process is that risks are infinite because they multiply over time since one can always do more to prevent them from becoming real. Following 9/11, security specialists began to focus on society's vulnerability to further terrorist attacks. It soon became apparent that the non-specific nature of risk means that anything, anywhere is at risk. Since risks are infinite while government resources are not, the central feature of dealing with the new risks is judgement. Policy-makers must choose which risks they most need to prevent and which they have to accept. Discussing their judgement requires a debating culture based on premises very different from the premises of the national security debates during the Cold War.

Does the fact that Western societies regard strategic danger in terms of risk show that the world has become dominated by risk-type dangers, thus necessitating a risk world-view to make sense of it all; or is it the case that it is the world-view of Western societies that has changed, the world itself having changed little? In other words, is risk a social construction or a rational response? In the risk literature there is a great

---

[3] Joost van Loon, *Risk and Technological Culture: Towards a Sociology of Virulence* (London: Routledge, 2002), 2.
[4] Ibid.

deal of debate about precisely this question.[5] It should be noted that this debate is not really about the actual analysis of present Western society, but rather how this analysis should be carried out. Of course, one should be a little suspicious when the answer to a question does not really have consequences. Perhaps the question is being asked in the wrong way. In fact, I believe that the question of 'world' vs 'world-view' can be resolved if one approaches it less philosophically and more sociologically. Thus I suggest studying risk as a form of rationality.

Max Weber defined rationality in terms of the way actions make sense to the agents who carry them out. 'For Weber one type of action is distinguished from another by the meanings which the actors themselves attach to their actions,' Ann Swidler explains, 'rather than the objective characteristics of an action as they would be seen by an outside observer.'[6] Thus in Swidler's reading of Weber, rationality defines the idea of action. Doing certain things makes sense only because a given rationality defines the means, ends or values according to which you act. Perhaps Weber's most famous example of how rationality defines the idea of action is how means-end rationality makes bureaucracy work. The way bureaucrats deal with the morning post, conduct meetings, inform their ministers, draft laws and answer citizens' letters makes sense only because of the means-end rationality of the way the rules of bureaucratic procedure are defined. Without bureaucracy, government would be much simpler – for those who govern, at least. There is no inherent need for a government to go through all these elaborate procedures in order to govern, but government makes sense to the bureaucrat and is legitimate in modern society only if it is conducted with regard to means-end rationality.

Modern Western society has been shaped by how bureaucratisation has introduced means-end rationality into both public administration and business, as well as by how industrialisation has transformed modes of production, a process of modernisation that is also apparent in the strategic realm. The concept of strategy created a means-end rational approach to the use of armed force. Strategy came into being in the seventeenth century as a way of making sense of guns. How were guns

[5] For a social constructivist approach to the study of risk, see François Ewald, 'Insurance and Risk', in Graham Burchell, Colin Gordon and Peter Miller (eds.), *The Foucault Effect: Studies in Governmentality* (Hemel Hempstead: Harvester Wheatsheaf, 1991), 199. In *World Risk Society*, Ulrich Beck seems to argue that the new rationality is a reaction to the realities of risk society. Later, he insists that one can approach risk from a social constructivist as well as a realist position, 133–52.

[6] Ann Swidler, 'The Concept of Rationality in the Work of Max Weber', *Sociological Inquiry* 43 (1973), 38.

and muskets to be used in battle, and how were armies to be organised in order to utilise this new technology fully? Strategy was to make sense of this 'revolution in military affairs' by linking it to the development of the modern state. The new military technologies were to be put to use by the governments of the new sovereign states. Carl von Clausewitz famously defined warfare as the use of armed force as a means of politics. From this perspective, strategy is the modern idea of what going to war is all about. Strategy makes sense of the relationship between the technologies by means of which wars are fought, and of the doctrines that define the aims of the campaigns and the nature of the enemies one fights. Since precisely which technologies are useful and who is being fought have changed a number of times since the seventeenth century, strategy has become a means of continuously rationalising the use of armed force in order to identify the technologies, doctrines and agents that constitute either a source of insecurity or a means to security.

Thus, if one regards strategy as a form of rationality, it soon becomes apparent that this definition of the relationship between technologies, doctrines and agents is a creation of modern Western society, such that when Western society changes, so does the idea of armed force. Today the idea of using armed force is changing because Western society has adopted a new risk rationality that fits the new kind of global modernity and the new kinds of threats that globalisation is creating. Focusing on strategy as a part of social development allows one to look at 'strategies' other than military strategy. This is important because the creation of a risk society has led to a proliferation of strategic practices. Businessmen have strategies, and countless self-help books suggest strategies for a better life. These and other strategic practices inspire governments to draw up security strategies in new ways. As we shall see, there are clear parallels between the 'precautionary principle' used in environmental policy and doctrines of pre-emption such as those advocated by President Bush.

The similarity between certain aspects of environmental policy and strategy is one example of how studying strategy as a form of rationality makes it possible to link current policy debates on a number of civilian issues with strategic theory and the future of strategic practice. Stephen Kalberg notes that Weber used rationality to 'guide him to critical historical watersheds':[7] rationality is used in this book for precisely that purpose. The concept of risk as the new guiding principle of strategy makes it possible to connect a number of events, policy initiatives and

---

[7] Stephen Kalberg, 'Max Weber's Types of Rationality: Cornerstones for the Analysis of Rationalization Processes in History', *American Journal of Sociology* 85 (1980), 1,172.

technological developments, which would otherwise seem random and unconnected. The Iraq war, the revolution in military affairs, terrorism, pre-emptive doctrines and the increased legalisation of warfare are not isolated incidents and developments, but part of a new concept and practice of strategy. This is especially important since more traditional strategic studies are right to point out that many, if not most, of the elements of today's strategy are the same as those that prevailed during the twentieth century. However, the risk framework allows one to see how these well-known elements are being put together in a new way with the addition of other elements that are peculiar to the twenty-first century.

Rationality offers a new approach to strategy, and the study of strategic rationality helps to explain the curious fact that most studies of strategy are not really interested in how technology, terrorism and other factors are reshaping the strategic environment. Most definitions of strategy, as well as most students of strategic studies who are using them to analyse contemporary issues, regard strategy as a function of political ends and military means. The idea of using armed force is believed to have been defined once and for all by Clausewitz. The nature of politics and armed force is regarded as a given, a universal condition that is valid for all societies, governments and groups at all times. The concept of strategy also involves establishing a clear hierarchy of issues, saying what is important and what is not. The topics of terrorism and technology are not very high on that list. Mainstream strategic studies do not dismiss their temporary importance, nor do they refrain from analysing them, but most realist students of strategic studies (probably the largest group of researchers within the discipline) carefully emphasise that terrorism, technological innovation and related issues are not creating a new strategic reality: they are merely an interlude until the threats that made the twentieth century dangerous return. However, while academics wait, policy-makers are busy dealing with new strategic challenges in new ways. In doing so, they are defining a new strategic rationality that renders many, if not most, of the traditional strategic maxims irrelevant.

In focusing on rationality, this book does *not* ask why, for example, the US government decided to invade Iraq in 2003. Instead, I ask how US decision-makers arrived at the idea that invading Iraq would make the United States more secure; and I also ask how the invasion made sense – or not – to the American public and world public opinion, how the Iraq war utilised new technologies and how the idea of the war was framed by pre-emptive doctrines. In other words, this is a study of strategic ideas rather than specific policies or interests. As such, this book is about the context and consequences of actions rather than the actions themselves.

This means that the technological expert, the international lawyer or anyone meticulously noting the latest newspaper 'revelation' about what went on in Prime Minister Blair's or President Bush's cabinet in the run-up to the Iraq war might find some of the arguments superficial. While no author likes to disappoint his readers, my aim in writing this book has been to describe the development of a new strategic rationality. This means connecting and comparing a number of issues, such comparisons necessarily being more superficial than specific case studies.

The book begins by arguing the case for studying strategy in terms of rationality. In Chapter 2, the history of the concept of strategy is outlined in order to argue that the history of strategy is a history of rationality. Since the early modern period, strategy has been a way of rationalising technologies, doctrines and agents in order for strategists to guide governments on how to deal with security issues. A pivotal figure in the history of strategy is Carl von Clausewitz, who turned his experience of 'total war' during the Napoleonic wars into an analysis of the means-end rationality of modern war. Clausewitz' definition of warfare is still the guiding star of strategic studies, but the practice of warfare in the early twenty-first century is increasingly escaping means-end rational explanations. Thus the chapter offers a critique of the basic assumptions of mainstream strategic studies and suggests that studying strategy in terms of risk rationality is one way to make strategic studies more relevant to contemporary issues.

In the second chapter, three characteristics of a reflexive rationality for dealing with risk are presented. These three characteristics – management, the presence of the future and the boomerang effect – are used for structuring the analysis of the rest of the book. The following chapters deal with one of the building blocks of strategy in turn – first technology, then doctrines and finally agents. In each chapter, the three characteristics of risk politics are used to structure the analysis, in order to demonstrate the explanatory power of risk theory and to show that individual elements of strategy are subject to similar considerations. This serves to show that risk is not merely relevant for a single element of strategy (doctrines, for example), but that risk politics changes strategy as such.

Chapter 3 is about technology. 'Military transformation', or the 'revolution in military affairs' (RMA), is high on Western military agendas, but most researchers treat transformation as a technical issue. While the technology itself may be a technical issue that is rather too complicated for social scientists, the RMA is very much a social phenomenon, since it is a narrative of change and risk which provides a means of rationalising new technologies in ways that make them manageable for policy-makers. Thinking of military force in terms of the RMA means defining military capabilities in terms of technology trends, that is, in terms of future capabilities that have not yet been developed. It also means defining the capabilities of friends and foes in relation to their stake in the future RMA. From this perspective, one might regard the RMA as the culmination of a process that began with the introduction of gunpowder weapons in the seventeenth century. As already noted, strategy began as a way of rationalising these new technologies; now the latest military technologies offer a means of perfecting the means-end rational approach to warfare. Information and communication technologies promise near-perfect information about the battlefield, thus making it possible to apply the right means to the right ends. However, although the perfect battle may be possible, the perfect war is not. One boomerang effect of the RMA is that the Western ability to design battles leads to 'asymmetrical strategies'. Another is the fact that the increased amounts of information which the RMA provides make Western societies believe that they can fight clean and cost-free wars. Thus the RMA may actually make Western societies more prone to use armed force, as well as more vulnerable to casualties when they do use it. The RMA makes it easier to fight wars, but harder to justify the death and destruction that wars still bring. Defeating a Western RMA force is thus a matter of imposing as many risks as possible on this force by running high risks oneself. Western forces can prevail in such a contest of risk-taking only by showing their willingness to accept casualties. The result is not more rational and cleaner warfare, but rather what two perceptive Chinese colonels term 'unrestricted warfare'.

Chapter 4 is about doctrines, by which I mean the fundamental principles that guide the use of armed force. The fundamental principle that is the focus of this chapter is the concept of pre-emption. This is as old as warfare itself, but as an idea which should guide strategy it gained, depending on one's point of view, fame or notoriety during the 2002 debates about the invasion of Iraq. President Bush argued that the United States could not remain secure in a globalising world if it did not pre-empt threats. This argument is surprisingly similar to that used by environmentalists when arguing for the precautionary principle. This illustrates that the strategic agenda has become much more like 'normal' policy areas than it used to be. Military strategy has actually been rather slow in adopting pre-emptive doctrines. The chapter thus shows how environmental policy and crime control have become dominated by such doctrines. When it comes to military strategy, however, the problems of the burden of proof and democratic legitimacy that haunt pre-emptive principles in other policy areas become acute. It is very difficult to produce mechanisms to make governments accountable for the judgements they make about when risks are so great that they need to be pre-empted. Judgement is the central concept in this discussion. Policymakers have to judge whether to act on a risk on the basis of scenarios that present the risks involved in acting as well as in not acting. Only if parliaments are careful to define benchmarks by which to judge such actions are they able to maintain democratic control of strategy while leaving room for the executive to operate in an unpredictable environment.

Chapter 5 is about agents. Strategic studies traditionally regard armed conflict as an activity between states or state-like units. When Clausewitz defined war as a means of politics, he meant that war was an instrument of the state. In the early twenty-first century, this principle describes an increasingly smaller part of the strategic practice that Western governments engage in. This chapter thus seeks to unpack the notion of agency. Clausewitz defined war in terms of politics and politics in terms of the state, thus providing the same answer ('the state') to the questions of 'who is waging war?', 'who is allowed to wage war?', 'who are they waging war against?' and 'how do the soldiers waging war regard their own role?' Separating these questions, it becomes apparent that they cannot all be answered with 'the state' any longer. In fact, the areas of armed conflict still defined in terms of the state have been so tightly regulated by what I term 'the UN approach' to warfare that great-power war is no longer a legitimate means of changing the international order. This 'bureaucratisation of warfare' challenges the basic premise of many modern writings on strategy, namely that states conduct international politics in the knowledge that they can ultimately resort to war. Not only are international law and international organisations playing a more important part in defining the legitimate means and ends of war, but Western societies no longer expect to be fighting wars against only other states. Answering the question of who they may fight, they no longer answer 'states like us', because that is forbidden, but increasingly see their enemies as different in organisation and rationality. Al-Qaeda is both a symbol and a potent example of this new type of enemy. It is an interesting fact about risk societies that they not only fear their enemies but also fear identifying them, because identifying an enemy opens up new and unforeseen boomerang effects in a world where social groupings of any kind are connected in new and numerous ways across state borders. Identifying enemies and fighting them are widely regarded as risks, but it is a risk that some people in risk societies are willing to embrace. Most writings on Western attitudes to war focus on the 'post-heroic' nature of contemporary Western society and therefore conclude that we are not prepared to fight wars. The focus on risk suggests that some people are. While most people in risk societies fear risk, some turn fear into fascination. This is why 'extreme sports' proliferate and why some people are willing to risk their lives working for non-governmental organisations (NGOs) like Médecins Sans Frontières or special forces units. Because of the RMA, Western military forces need few people actually to risk the horrors of close combat. What Western armed forces need in larger numbers are people willing to manage the situation on the ground after victory has been achieved, thus actually fusing the roles of the humanitarian NGO and the special forces. The challenge for Western armed forces is how to integrate these very different types of risk-takers into stabilisation forces.

Finally, I conclude that the building blocks of strategy – technology, doctrines and agents – are changing, as is the conceptual framework of strategy. Strategy is no longer a question of defeating concrete threats in order to achieve perfect security; it has instead become a way of managing risks. This means that traditional strategic studies have little to say about the new dimensions of strategy. This also means that strategy has become more important than ever. The debates on the Iraq war, 'the war on terror', the West's relationship with the Muslim world, the interpretation of the rise of Chinese power, the proliferation of weapons of mass destruction and other important strategic issues of the early twenty-first century show that Western societies no longer agree on the ends of strategy and can disagree fiercely on how to achieve security. Thus in risk societies, strategy has become important for more issues than ever before, at the same time as traditional strategic studies have less and less to say about the problems of the present. The risk framework offers one way of conceptualising today's strategic issues.

2 Strategy, strategic studies and risk

Strategy rationalises the use of armed force in order to identify the technologies, doctrines and agents that constitute a source of insecurity or a means for achieving security. This is not the way in which strategy is usually defined. There are, of course, many definitions of strategy, but most writers on the subject would probably agree that it is 'a bridge between military means and political goals'.[1] The bridge metaphor illustrates how the concept of strategy is a way of thinking about the connection between military means and political ends, but the history, as well as the future, of this way of thinking is as irrelevant for this kind of strategic analysis as the engineering of a bridge is to those who simply use it. However, there is a reason to take a closer look at 'the bridge' itself, because strategy is not merely a convenient term to describe the link between politics and military force. It was the concept of strategy, and the political and social conditions that created it, that established this link in the first place. The history of how military force came to be understood in terms of politics reveals that 'strategy' has been the conceptual switchyard by which the technologies, ideologies and social blueprints of modernity have been adopted in warfare. The definition adopted in this book on strategy has thus been calibrated as a way of studying strategy as a system of thought leading to action, rather than specific actions, as in standard definitions.

The history of strategy is a history of rationality. Max Weber described the history of modern society as a process defined by rationality. This was no simple process, and Weber made no effort to present it as such. The different meanings that Weber gave to rationality show the different elements that he believed constituted modernisation.[2] These elements will guide our discussion of the history of strategy.

---

[1] John Baylis and James Wirtz, 'Introduction', in John Baylis et al. (eds.), *Strategy in the Contemporary World: An Introduction to Strategic Studies* (Oxford: Oxford University Press, 2002), 3. The authors list a number of well-known definitions of strategy that can all be subsumed under their definition (ibid., 4).

[2] The three concepts of rationality in Weber are taken from Swidler, 'Max Weber'. See also Kalberg, 'Weber's Types of Rationality'.

First, Weber focused on 'rationalism' as the practical attitude of an individual 'which sees and judges the world consciously in terms of the worldly interests of the individual ego'.[3] In terms of strategy, rationalism describes the fact that theories of strategy, from Machiavelli's *The Prince* onwards, are most often the work of practical men intended to guide the actions of even more practical men in positions of military or political responsibility. It is in the first sense that strategy is most often dealt with, as the strategy of a campaign or the 'grand strategy' of a government, but Weber's approach to rationality suggests that there are two more ways to view strategy, namely as a mode of thought or paradigm rather than as a practical matter.

Secondly, Weber studied the process of 'rationalisation', whereby ideas from other periods or the interests of defunct social classes and other historical inconsistencies were eliminated in the systematisation of the ideas constituting modernity. Hence the recurrent description of history as a machine that relentlessly made society more and more modern. Systematisation was necessary because modernity meant change, that is, the steady introduction of new technologies, new modes of organisation etc., which individuals and organisations somehow needed to systematise in order to be able to act purposefully. From Jomini to Bernard Brodie, an important aspect of strategy has been to give meaning to new technologies, logistical principles or political ambitions that made the use of force a different matter from what it had been before. In studying rationalisation, Weber focused on the individuals (e.g. religious leaders) who formulated the ideas about how to manage change. He believed that they functioned like 'switchmen', guiding history down new tracks. The most important 'switchman' in the history of strategy is probably Carl von Clausewitz, who was able to systematise the most important elements of Western strategic thinking. Focusing on Clausewitz thus enables one to understand strategic practice in the same way that Weber studied Calvin to learn about Protestant ethics. At a time when the practice of modern warfare was being created, Clausewitz systematised Western military thought and thus contributed to constituting the strategic application of force in relation to the nation state.

Thirdly, Weber showed how modern, means-end rationality was different from other types of rationality. The academic discipline of strategic studies clearly shows this preference for the means-end rational, which is the present incarnation of Clausewitz' dictum that war is the 'continuation of politics with the addition of other means'.[4] But contrary

---

[3] Weber, quoted in Swidler, 'Max Weber', 35.
[4] Carl von Clausewitz, *On War*, edited and translated by Michael Howard and Peter Paret (Princeton, NJ: Princeton University Press, 1976 (1832–4)), 605.

to Weber, the dominating realist approach to strategic studies does not take account of the fact that means-end rationality is not a universal law. Quite the contrary, the concept of universality itself is a product of the means-end rationality of modernity. In late modern society, means-end rationality no longer applies to strategy in the way it used to. This chapter therefore ends by claiming that the reflective rationality of risk is now guiding Western security strategies and outlining a way to study this rationality by focusing on the concepts of management, the presence of the future and the boomerang effect. However, first I would like to focus on how, in Weber's second understanding of the concept of rationality, strategy rationalised the concept of the technologies, doctrines and agents that came to be seen as sources of insecurity or as means for achieving security.

Stratos and modernity

The term 'strategy' is a neologism derived from the Greek *stratos*, 'army'.[5] Literally *stratos* means 'host', an entirely appropriate term for the Greek citizen armies, where the hoplites came together in times of danger around a host or general. The general's conduct of operations was referred to as an art. The Romans thus spoke of *ars belli*. In his discourses on Livy, Machiavelli adopted this term, writing of the *arte della guerra*, and it was this art of war which came to be debated in early modern Europe after the publication of Machiavelli's discourses.[6] War was an 'art' because, in an age of limited wars, the outcome of war was believed to depend exclusively on the results on the battlefield, which in their turn were believed to depend on the creative genius of the general. He embodied the drama of war because, as the 'host' of soldiers in the double meaning of being their leader in battle and the leader of their country (as he in fact often was at this time, where European princes still led their armies into battle), the conduct of war could be reduced to his abilities.

---

[5] This description of the history of strategy is based on Edward N. Luttwak, *Strategy: The Logic of War and Peace* (Cambridge, MA: Belknap Press, 2001), 267–9, and Martin van Creveld, *On Future War* (London: Brassey's, 1991), 95–7. On the Greek way of warfare, see Victor David Hanson, *Why the West Has Won: Carnage and Culture from Salamis to Vietnam* (London: Faber and Faber, 2001). On Machiavelli's conception of strategy, see Felix Gilbert, 'Machiavelli: The Renaissance of the Art of War', in Peter Paret (ed.), *Makers of Modern Strategy: From Machiavelli to the Nuclear Age* (Oxford: Clarendon Press, 1998).

[6] Niccolò Machiavelli, *Discourses on Livy* (Oxford: Oxford University Press, 1997). See also Niccolò Machiavelli, *Art of War*, ed. Christopher Lynch (Chicago, IL: University of Chicago Press, 2003).

In pre-modern and early modern times, writing on war meant relaying what the Greeks called *strategike episteme* or *strategon sophia*, meaning the general's knowledge and wisdom respectively. Such works, like Caesar's *Gallic Wars*, took their point of departure in the experience of a particular general: by reading his story, future generals could learn a trick or two. The purpose of such books was to mediate knowledge across time. The bloody practice of war was not believed to be changing, and thus by knowing how battles had been fought in the past, one would be able to win the battles of the future. Thus Machiavelli dedicated *The Prince* to Lorenzo de' Medici because he believed that this particular prince could be given no better introduction to him as a future advisor than a work on 'the actions of great men, learned by me from long experience with modern things and a continuous reading of ancient ones'.[7] This conception of knowledge meant that Machiavelli could turn to Livy for information on how to fight wars in spite of the very different nature of the Roman and Florentine societies and the very different armies that they were able to field. These differences were insignificant to Machiavelli, who believed that wisdom was to be gained from studying the past because the future, he imagined, would not be radically different. One might even argue that one's best hope for the future was to revive the glorious past of the classical period. At a time when the future was not believed to be of a radically different reality but was rather simply a repetition of the past, the way to acquire knowledge of the world was to apply the experience of the past to new problems.

However, things did not, in fact, stay the same. In early modern Europe, strategy became a conceptual tool used to deal with a world in which things had ceased to stay the same. Thus strategy introduced modern rationality as a way to make sense of a new type of warfare, and military men used this understanding to train for these wars and prevail in them. In this view, war was a science rather than an art. Warfare was guided by reason and technology rather than genius and valour. Actually, Machiavelli was already arguing against the tide of modernity when he spent several pages of his discourses complaining about the 'common opinion' that, had modern artillery existed in antiquity, it would have broken the ranks of the Roman legionaries, and Rome would not have conquered the world. In other words, Machiavelli argued against the view that developments in military technology had actually created new conditions for warfare which needed to be rationalised into new, systematic thoughts on how war was best fought. Just like the opponents of the 'revolution in military affairs', Machiavelli argued

---

[7] Niccolò Machiavelli, *The Prince* (Chicago, IL: University of Chicago Press, 1998), 3.

that it was the soldiers' character that was the true key to victory. The implication of this argument was that the Italians should not look for a technological solution for their military backwardness, but instead reform their social institutions and strengthen their values in order to breed citizen-soldiers on the Roman model.[8]

This argument soon became untenable. The technology and doctrines of war were changing, as was the nature of the agents who were fighting wars. Contemporary armies were the largest that Europe had seen since Roman times, but this did not mean that Livy or Vegetius could guide their deployment in the way that Machiavelli imagined. While his call for discipline and civic virtue played an important part in stimulating the military reforms undertaken by Maurice of Nassau and others,[9] these values were placed in a modern, rational setting that was alien to Livy. Now, discipline was used to harness new weapons technologies because the effective use of the musket demanded well-drilled infantry and elaborate logistical arrangements. Discipline became a part of the rationalisation of the new technologies in the same way as Machiavelli's statements on values and politics came to be seen as ways of ensuring a means-end rational conduct of war; politics were to be guided by interests rather than, for example, religious values. War was no longer an art, but a science. Because of the advances of science, modern armies were equipped with guns and able to organise logistically so as to fight a very different kind of war from those that Caesar had fought in Gaul. Generals would no longer learn all they needed to know about campaigning by reading about the Gallic wars. But perhaps more importantly, the people of the Enlightenment no longer believed in the finality of knowledge as Machiavelli had. They did not believe that Livy or Vegetius had lived in a time comparable to their own. The world was being made anew, and in such times of change, central concepts are freed from their normal boundaries.

Guns were revolutionising the ways battles were being fought. In his *Theory and Practice of Modern Wars* of 1598, Robert Barret has a civilian armchair strategist reminding an English army captain that the longbow had served England well for hundreds of years and therefore should not be scrapped in favour of guns.[10] 'Sir,' the captain replies, 'then was then,

[8] Machiavelli, *Discourses*, 195–200.
[9] Gunther E. Rothenberg, 'Maurice of Nassau, Gustavus Adolphus, Raimondo Montecuccoli, and the "Military Revolution" of the Seventeenth Century', in Peter Paret (ed.), *Makers of Modern Strategy: From Machiavelli to the Nuclear Age* (Oxford: Clarendon Press, 1998), 34–5.
[10] The 'armchair strategist' was quite right about the longbow: see Clifford J. Rogers, '"As If a New Sun had Arisen": England's Fourteenth-Century RMA', in MacGregor Knox and Williamson Murray (eds.), *The Dynamics of Military Revolution, 1300–2050* (Cambridge: Cambridge University Press, 2001), 15–34.

and now is now. The wars are much altered since the fiery weapons first came up.'[11] People who follow the present debate on the revolution in military affairs will find this exchange very familiar; but today the claim of radical, fundamental change is made every time a new brand of toothpaste is introduced. In 1598, to argue that the old ways had little bearing on the present and no bearing on the future represented a completely new way of conceiving your place in history. The fact that people like Barret argued that 'modern war' was different in practice as well as in theory from past ways of warfare illustrates that the modern theme of continuous transformation was being introduced, and 'fiery weapons' proved an example of this.

However, as Geoffrey Parker has argued, guns did not change warfare by themselves. The sovereign states being formed in this period were able to muster the resources to field the standing armies that were needed to deploy muskets in tight formations, firing volley upon volley against the enemy's formations. And only the new central governments were able to generate the resources to sustain, support and supply such armies, as well as to invest in fortresses and other defensive technologies, which were at least as important as massed formations in early modern war.[12] In order to drill soldiers to fire volleys, one needed standing armies, while in order to conduct sieges of the new fortresses or to defend them, governments needed professionals. Strategy served to define the curriculum for the training of this new, more professional officer corps by providing the intellectual foundation for the belief that principles of war existed, which, in the words of Martin van Creveld, 'could be discovered, laid down in a "system", and taught in the military academies that were just beginning to open their doors'.[13]

Clausewitz

Joly de Maizeroy, who was writing about military matters in France before the Revolution of 1789, seems to have been the first to use the term 'strategy'.[14] At the time of the French Revolution, the concept of strategy had become so fully fledged that people wrote about 'strategy', and even those who, like Jomini, still referred to 'the art of war' understood the use of armed force within the modern, rational paradigm of strategy. 'Strategy is the key to warfare,' Jomini stated in his

[11] Quoted in Geoffrey Parker, *The Military Revolution: Military Innovation and the Rise of the West, 1500–1800* (Cambridge: Cambridge University Press, 1996), 18.
[12] Parker, *The Military Revolution*. See also Charles Tilly, *Coercion, Capital and European States: AD 990–1990* (Oxford: Basil Blackwell, 1990).
[13] Creveld, *On Future War*, 96.   [14] Ibid.

first maxim, his second being: 'all strategy is controlled by invariable scientific principles'.[15]

It was the wars that followed the French Revolution that led to the most systematic presentation of what strategic thought was all about, and the man who wrote it was Carl von Clausewitz. Clausewitz is the greatest writer on strategy because he realised that the Napoleonic wars were an extreme version of how wars would be fought in the future, and from this historical vantage point he was able to observe the rationalisation as well as the rationality of modern war. He wrote about this experience in strategic terms.

Today it may be hard to appreciate how cataclysmic the twenty years of war that followed the French Revolution seemed to people in Europe at that time. Like the world wars of the twentieth century, the Napoleonic wars betrayed the idea that the world had put its most violent days behind it and that the conflicts of the future would be limited and regulated. Clausewitz describes how the wars of the *ancien régime* were limited in scope by the balance of power and increasingly fought without undue harm being done to the civilian population. Clausewitz wrote:[16]

Not only in its means . . . but also in its aims, war increasingly became limited to the fighting force itself. Armies, with their fortresses and prepared positions, came to form a state within a state, in which violence gradually faded away. All Europe rejoiced at this development. It was seen as a logical outcome of enlightenment. This was a misconception. Enlightenment can never lead to inconsistency.[17]

The experience of the Napoleonic wars illustrated to Clausewitz that the very logic of politics, which led to limited war among governments that were in agreement on the desirability of upholding the existing social and political order in Europe, led to 'total war' when the revolutionary government in France turned against the status quo. 'Austria and Prussia tried to meet this with the diplomatic type of war . . . They soon discovered its inadequacy,' Clausewitz dryly remarks.[18] The Age of Reason did not lead to an Age of Peace; instead it lead to the realisation that war was governed by reason. Clausewitz' famous dictum, that 'war is merely the continuation of policy by other means', was the result of this insight.[19] Realising that rationalisation does not lead to the abolition of war but to making war more rational, Clausewitz sought to describe war's rationality. Raymond Aron described Clausewitz' approach thus:

---

[15] Quoted from John Shy, 'Jomini', in Peter Paret (ed.), *Makers of Modern Strategy: From Machiavelli to the Nuclear Age* (Oxford: Clarendon Press, 1998), 146.
[16] Clausewitz, *On War*, 590–1.
[17] Ibid., 591.   [18] Ibid.   [19] Ibid., 81.

In the manner of Max Weber, Clausewitz interprets all action in war, at least that of the commander, down to the lowly level of the foot patrol, with reference to the means-end relationship. In this sense, he acknowledges the tactical and strategic decision to be *Zweckrational* in essence.[20]

In Weber's terms, Clausewitz believed that war had been through a process of rationalisation and that the end result was the modern concept of war. Clausewitz believed that rationalisation led modern man to be guided by 'intentions' rather than 'feelings'. 'Savage peoples are ruled by passion,' Clausewitz stated, 'civilized people by the mind.'[21] In his view, the Enlightenment optimists, like Immanuel Kant, made the mistake of concluding that doing away with passion would lead to a very limited use of force, or perhaps even perpetual peace.[22] The Napoleonic wars showed Clausewitz that a means-end rational view of politics provided ample reason for going to war. In fact, politics could make wars total because politics could mobilise the nation's entire resources for war, while political or national ideologies did not place the same restraint on warfare as the kings' shared world-view had. Hence Clausewitz believed that the process of rationalisation had to be supplemented by a description of the modern rationality that now defined war.

The Napoleonic wars proved to Clausewitz that, while war had its own 'grammar', its overall logic was decided by politics.[23] War was a means that served political ends. This made war different from other kinds of violence, according to Clausewitz. A fight in a bar was not war because drunken people beating each other up seldom serves the political purposes of a government. As a Prussian nationalist, Clausewitz believed that the policy of the state was the result of the 'will of the people', translated into certain state interests. War was one means to realise these interests, and thus war was 'a true political instrument, a continuation of policy intercourse, carried on with other means'.[24] This statement should be seen against the devastating background of the Napoleonic wars, where war, in Clausewitz' words, 'had broken loose in all its elemental fury'.[25] In fact, Clausewitz told his readers that the Napoleonic wars were neither a

---

[20] Raymond Aron, 'Reason, Passion, and Power in the Thought of Clausewitz', *Social Research: An International Quarterly of the Social Sciences* 39 (1972), 601.

[21] Having said this, Clausewitz did point out that means-end rationality had its limits. War was guided by means-end rationality, but it also invoked passions. 'It would be an obvious fallacy', Clausewitz concluded, 'to imagine war between civilized peoples as resulting merely from a rational act.' Clausewitz, *On War*, 76.

[22] Immanuel Kant, 'To Perpetual Peace: A Philosophical Sketch', *Kant's Political Writings*, trans. H. B. Nisbet and ed. H. Reiss (Cambridge: Cambridge University Press, 1970 (1795)). See also Michael Howard, *War and the Liberal Conscience* (New Brunswick, NJ: Rutgers University Press, 1978).

[23] Clausewitz, *On War*, 605.   [24] Ibid., 87.   [25] Ibid., 593.

momentary lapse into barbarism nor the final act of incivility before the progress of reason and civilisation ended war forever. On the contrary, Clausewitz argued that the Napoleonic wars were the logical conclusion of the rationalisation of society. Or, as Clausewitz put it: 'Enlightenment can never lead to inconsistency.' When means-end rationality came to define the conduct of governments, then total war was exactly what should be expected. Means-end rational war had come into its own, and one should regard the Napoleonic wars as the beginning of a new kind of war suitable for the modern age. 'At least when major interests are at stake,' he concluded, 'mutual hostility will express itself in the same manner as it has in our own day.'[26]

However, Clausewitz assumed that most wars would not be total, because the political ends that governments pursued were mostly limited and therefore the military resources they employed to reach their ends would be limited too.[27] What Clausewitz offered in *On War* was a guide to navigate a future in which wars were potentially total – and that guide was strategy. Clausewitz defined strategy as 'the use of engagements for the object of war', and in this rather technical definition, the understanding of the means-end rational strategic paradigm is clear.[28] Henceforth strategy would be defined as the relationship between political ends and military means, a relationship that set the standard for how to think about war and peace. Clausewitz summed it up in this way:

No one starts a war – or rather, no one in his senses ought to do so – without first being clear in his mind what he intends to achieve by that war and how he intends to conduct it. The former is the political purpose; the latter its operational directive.[29]

The twentieth century and strategic studies

Today the discipline of strategic studies has developed its own grammar, but the logic by which the academic study of strategy operates is that pointed out by Carl von Clausewitz. As one passionate advocate of the virtues of traditional strategic studies puts it, 'Clausewitz rules, OK?'[30] When one reviews different definitions of strategy, it soon becomes clear that indeed he does. One of the founders of strategic studies after the end of the Second World War, Bernard Brodie, stated that, 'above all, strategic theory is a theory of action'.[31] What Aron said of

---

[26] Ibid.   [27] Ibid., 80–1.   [28] Ibid., 128.   [29] Ibid., 579.
[30] Colin Gray, 'Clausewitz Rules, OK? The Future is the Past – with GPS', *Review of International Studies* 25 (December 1999), 161–82.
[31] Bernard Brodie, *War and Politics* (London: Cassell, 1974), 452.

Clausewitz is true of present-day strategic studies in general: it deals in praxeologies.[32] Hence strategic studies is based on rationalism in Weber's terms, as it seeks to devise concepts and doctrines that can be used to guide action. Strategic studies has served to rationalise ways of dealing with new technologies, policies and powers. Perhaps the most clear-cut example of this has been how the US strategic community dealt with the invention of the nuclear bomb by, in Weber's terms, rationalising its use in terms of doctrines of deterrence. In the words of one observer, the mission of the strategists at RAND and other intellectual communities inside and outside the US government was to 'try to impose the order of the rational life on the almost unimaginably vast and hideous maelstrom of nuclear war'.[33]

How fundamentally strategic studies is based on the thinking of Clausewitz becomes clear in the way means-end rationality features in definitions of strategy. Richard Betts argues that 'strategies are chains of relationships among means and ends',[34] while Lawrence Freedman defines the means as military and the ends as political: 'strategy is about the pursuit of political ends with military means in the international environment'.[35] Barry Posen defines grand strategy as a 'political-military means-end chain'.[36] Even Basil Liddell Hart, who most unkindly dismissed Clausewitz as someone who 'had acquired a philosophical mode of expression without developing a truly philosophical mind',[37] could not manage to formulate a definition of strategy that transcended the means-end rational logic explained by Clausewitz. By defining strategy as the 'the art of distributing and applying military means to fulfil the ends of policy', Liddell Hart indirectly showed that *On War* is more than the work of one man, it reflects the way Western thought on military and security matters works.[38]

Strategic studies follows a Clausewitzian logic because Clausewitz was right in claiming that the Napoleonic wars were a blueprint for the

---

[32] Aron, 'Reason, Passion, and Power in the Thought of Clausewitz', 600.

[33] Fred Kaplan, *The Wizards of Armageddon* (New York: Simon and Schuster, 1983), 73. See also Lawrence Freedman, 'The First Two Generations of Nuclear Strategists', in Peter Paret (ed.), *Makers of Modern Strategy: From Machiavelli to the Nuclear Age* (Oxford: Clarendon Press, 1998), 735–78; Raymond Aron, 'The Evolution of Modern Strategic Thought', in *Problems of Modern Strategy*, The Institute for Strategic Studies (London: Chatto and Windus, 1970), 13–46.

[34] Richard K. Betts, 'Is Strategy an Illusion?', *International Security* 25 (2000), 6.

[35] Lawrence Freedman, 'Indignation, Influence and Strategic Studies', *International Affairs* 60 (1984), 210.

[36] Barry Posen, *Sources of Military Doctrine: France, Britain, and Germany between the World Wars* (Ithaca, NY: Cornell University Press, 1984), 13.

[37] B. H. Liddell Hart, *Strategy* (London: Penguin, 1954), 339–40.

[38] Ibid., 321.

future. The two centuries that followed saw the further development of modernity and a rationalisation of the use of armed force. Zygmunt Bauman points out that the idea of violence as a means which could be put at the service of any government policy reached its terrible apogee in the Holocaust, when Germany unleashed the resources of an industrial society to wage total war on an ethnic group rather than on another state.[39]

Strategic studies came into being following the Second World War because a number of academics found that 'strategy is not receiving the scientific treatment it deserves either in the armed services or, certainly, outside them'.[40] During the war, the British armed forces had developed what they called 'operational analysis' in order to calculate how their limited resources could best be put to maximum strategic effect against the Germans. In Weberian terms, by quantifying means and ends they were able to rationalise warfare. In the course of the war, operational analysis was exported to the US, where it was adopted with such vigour that in 1946 Winston Churchill observed that, 'when American military men approach some serious situation they are wont to write at the head of their directive the words "over-all strategic concept"'.[41] Thus there was a demand within the US armed forces for strategic analysis. There was also a political demand for civilian strategic analysis, which could be used to strengthen civilian control over the military. In this sense too, strategy was to bridge the military and political worlds. To meet this demand a number of the academics, like Brodie, who had been employed in the 'operational research' units, turned to think tanks like RAND to use their analytical skills on the problems of the Cold War, chiefly on how to use nuclear weapons strategically.[42] Like Clausewitz, they wanted to establish a science of war in order to determine whether the total war they had just witnessed provided a blueprint for the future. The prospect of it being so was all the more terrible since a new conflict (the Cold War) was on its way and the development of nuclear weapons meant that, if this conflict turned into a hot, shooting war, then the consequences would be very dire indeed. 'The issues that face us', the

---

[39] Zygmunt Bauman, *Modernity and the Holocaust* (Cambridge: Polity Press, 1989).
[40] Bernard Brodie, 'Strategy as a Science', *World Politics* 1 (1949), 468.
[41] Winston S. Churchill, *Sinews of Peace*, 5 March 1946, Westminster College, Fulton Missouri, the Churchill Center, http://www.winstonchurchill.org (26 May 2000), §7.
[42] Kaplan, *Wizards of Armageddon*, 52. The way Herman Kahn calculated the time-span after which the United States would get back on track after a nuclear war is a supreme example of this, a calculation so rational in the face of the horror of a nuclear war that it did in fact seem utterly irrational and thus served as the blueprint for the movie *Dr Strangelove*. Herman Kahn, *On Thermonuclear War* (Princeton, NJ: Princeton University Press, 1961), 40–95. I shall return to Dr Kahn and Dr Strangelove in Chapter 6.

US National Security Council concluded, in its NSC-68 report of 1950, 'are momentous, involving the fulfilment or destruction not only of this Republic but of civilization itself.'[43] NSC-68 was itself instrumental in expanding the agenda of strategy from dealing with military issues only to a focus on 'national security'. Bernard Brodie explained the new strategic concepts which followed from the focus on national security as follows:

Whether we are discussing security policy in the broad sense or more specifically military strategy – or even tactics – we are discussing problems involving economy of means, *i.e.*, the most efficient utilization of potential and available resources to the end of enhancing our security.[44]

According to Brodie, security policy was 'grand strategy' and covered 'the total preparation for war as well as the waging of it'.[45] At a time when the absence of war did not mean peace, the concept of security served to include civilian life in strategic considerations.[46] The fact that the nation was mobilised, in every sense of the term, for conflict would not, of course, have been news to Clausewitz – this was the type of warfare that the Napoleonic wars had shown the beginnings of. However, Clausewitz would probably have been surprised that the government was able to direct such large elements of civilian life and that the standard of living of a society had turned out to be an important weapon in fighting the Cold War. This level of mobilisation showed the differences between the autocratic night-watch state in which Clausewitz lived and the democratic welfare state of the mid-twentieth century: the increased level of mobilisation during the Cold War was not the result of a different conception of strategy.

Not only did civilian life become part of strategy in the twentieth century: the term 'strategy' itself has been increasingly used by civilians. The US strategic studies community, especially the part associated with

---

[43] National Security Council, 'A Report to the National Security Council by the Executive Secretary on United States Objectives and Programs for National Security', 14 April 1950, reprinted in D. Merrill (ed.), *Documentary History of the Truman Presidency, vol. VII: The Ideological Foundations of the Cold War – the 'Long Telegram,' the Clifford Report, and NSC 68* (Landham, MD: University Publications of America, 1996), 330.

[44] Brodie, 'Strategy as a Science', 478.

[45] Ibid., 477, including note 30.

[46] On the introduction of the concept of 'national security' after the Second World War, see Robert Latham, *The Liberal Moment: Modernity, Security, and the Making of Postwar International Order* (New York: Columbia University Press, 1997); Mikkel Vedby Rasmussen, *The West, Civil Society and the Construction of Peace* (London: Palgrave, 2003), 112–24; Ole Wæver, 'Security: A Conceptual History for International Relations', unpublished paper presented at the 12th Nordic Political Science Congress, Uppsala, 19–21 August 1999.

RAND, sought to develop a scientifically rigorous approach to strategy by using game theory. Game theory focuses on strategies. In the words of Fred Kaplan, game theory is a 'mathematically precise method of determining rational strategies in the face of critical uncertainties'.[47] As such, game theory suited the strategic agenda perfectly, but one wonders whether it was the world of political ends and military means that inspired game theorists to adopt the term 'strategy', or whether they developed their own strategic concepts. One might speculate that, in writing the first introduction to game theory in the 1940s, John von Neumann and Oskar Morgenstern were influenced by the military jargon that fills the language of a nation at war.[48] In general, the use of military metaphors had increased greatly following the First World War.

Communist and fascist writers especially were fond of using military metaphors. Arguing that communists should first focus on taking over civil society rather than the state apparatus, the Italian communist Antonio Gramsci 'likened civil society to the labyrinthine trench systems of modern warfare'.[49] Gramsci referred to the communist onslaught on civil society as a 'war of position' against the 'fortresses and earthworks' of capitalist society.[50] While the left regarded society as a battlefield on which the armies of different classes fought one another, the right wanted to turn the nation into one big army. Indeed it would only be a slight exaggeration to argue that fascism and nazism were in fact military metaphors in the shape of ideologies, because they sought to translate the perceived community of the trenches into a political project for the entire nation. Following Germany's defeat in the First World War, people on the German right simply refused to accept defeat and carried on the war in the politics of the Weimar Republic. In 1918 Franz Schauwecker argued that 'the proper war is only just beginning, the real war . . . for this peace is the continuation of war through other means, each goes to his own front'.[51] But of course to communists and fascists war was never just a metaphor, it soon translated into actual warfare against other nations or, as Trotsky described it, to an 'organised civil war'[52] against 'races' or 'classes' within the state itself.

The totalitarian ideologies of the twentieth century reveal a phenomenon that was also found in liberal democracies: mobilisation for total

---

[47] Kaplan, *Wizards of Armageddon*, 65.
[48] John von Neumann and Oskar Morgenstern, *Theory of Games and Economic Behaviour* (Princeton, NJ: Princeton University Press, 1944).
[49] John Keane, *Civil Society: Old Images, New Visions* (Cambridge: Polity Press, 1998), 15.
[50] Ibid.
[51] Schauwecker quoted in Christopher Coker, *War and the 20th Century* (London: Brassey's, 1994), 124.
[52] Trotsky quoted in ibid., 12.

war profoundly influenced the public demand for government intervention.[53] The Labour Party won the 1945 British general election, among
other reasons because it realised that the electorate wanted the resources
the government had used to fight the war to be used to create a welfare
state. 'People are ready for great changes,' Labour argued in a 1942
report; 'the War has accustomed them to innovation. It would be folly
not to take advantage of a mood which enables those changes to be made
by consent.'[54] Thus Labour believed that a new society was 'being
forged on the anvil of war'.[55] Later in the twentieth century war would
not only be regarded as a catalyst for social change: changing certain
social conditions would be regarded as 'war' in its own right. 'War' was
used to signify a substantial and determined government commitment to
overcome social ills, as in the case of the 'war on poverty' or the 'war on
drugs'. Such 'wars' do, of course, have strategies for how they are to be
'won'. In 1990, President George Bush Sr thus presented a 'National
Drug Control Strategy' as a 'clear blueprint for [winning] the war on
drugs'.[56]

Martin Shaw argues that the 'diffusion of strategic language to the
non-military state and private corporate spheres can be seen as a part of
the general expansion of state and corporate activities'.[57] While, as we
have seen, Shaw is right that the concept of strategy is essentially military
in origin, he is wrong to neglect the fact that it developed as one of the
processes that created modern, means-end rationality. Shaw is criticising
a number of sociologists[58] for using the concept of strategy to explain
social behaviour (for example, among the rural poor and other people
operating in a high-risk environment), arguing that 'strategy analysis is
flawed, as a freestanding method, in the field of its origin, it cannot

---

[53] For analyses of how profoundly European societies were transformed by the total wars
of the twentieth century, see Clive Emsley, Arthur Marwick and Wendy Simpson (eds.),
War, Peace and Social Change in Twentieth Century Europe (Buckingham: Open University Press, 1989). On the not-so-liberal policies even of Western democracies in the
interwar years, see Mark Mazower, *Dark Continent: Europe's Twentieth Century* (London:
Allen Lane, 1998).

[54] The Labour Party, *Labour Looks Ahead*, abridged edition of *The Old World and the New
Society* (London: The Labour Party, 1942), 6.

[55] Ibid., 4.

[56] George H. W. Bush, *Remarks at a White House Briefing on the National Drug Control
Strategy*, 5 September 1990, George Bush Presidential Library, http://bushlibrary.tamu.
edu/ (1 March 2004), §1.

[57] Martin Shaw, 'Strategy and Social Process: Military Context and Sociological Analysis',
Sociology 24 (1990), 466.

[58] Graham Crow, 'The Use of the Concept of "Strategy" in Recent Sociological Literature', *Sociology* 23 (1989), 1–24; D. H. J. Morgan 'Strategies and Sociologists:
A Comment on Crow', *Sociology* 23 (1989), 25–9.

simply be transferred to any and every other field of social life'.[59] However, while the concept may be of recent import in sociological analysis, strategy thinking is already present in 'any and every other field of social life'. The description of the development of the concept of strategy presented above suggests three reasons for this.

First, strategy is the politico-military version of the process of rationalisation that describes the development of modern society as such. Thus what is known as a strategy in military matters may be known as industrialism or bureaucracy in other social spheres, but it is the same rationality. Secondly, strategy developed in concert with the concept of 'sovereignty' because the concept of strategy served to describe the need for the development of 'sovereign' states able to generate the funds to exploit the 'military revolution' of the sixteenth century. As the terms of sovereignty changed with the introduction of nationalism in the wake of the French Revolution, so did the concept of strategy change to explain how a national polity used military force. Clausewitz' analysis of total wars served this purpose. However, over time the liberalisation of modern society meant that individuals came to be seen as more 'sovereign' in their actions. Anthony Giddens argues that 'modernity confronts the individual with a complex diversity of choices and, because it is non-foundational, at the same time offers little help as to which options should be selected'.[60] Faced with numerous choices – from sexual preferences to profession and wardrobe – the modern individual needs a strategy for how to fit these choices into a coherent narrative of who he or she is. This is especially true since the end of the Second World War, which suggests that the use of 'strategy' outside the military sphere increased because the actions of individuals came to resemble the state units that the concept of strategy was originally developed to describe. One result of this is the guides to business strategy and the self-help books that overflow the bestseller lists in most Western countries. These are the Clausewitzs on relationship strategies and the Jominis on how to succeed in the corporate world. Thus it is not really the case that strategy was exported; rather, other spheres of action were imported into the 'strategic world'. This should not be regarded as an expansion of the zone of state domination, as Shaw argues, but rather as a liberalisation permitting individuals to pursue their individual life strategies.

---

[59] Shaw, 'Strategy and Social Process', 472. For a summary of the 'strategy debate' in British sociology, see Claire Wallace, 'Reflections on the Concept of "Strategy"', in David Morgan and Liz Stanley (eds.), *Debates in Sociology* (Manchester: Manchester University Press, 1993), 94–117.

[60] Anthony Giddens, *Modernity and Self-Identity: Self and Society in the Late Modern Age* (Cambridge: Polity Press, 1991), 80.

Thirdly, the very point of the concept of strategy is that it shows the connection between the military and the political sphere. War did not have its own logic according to Clausewitz, who regarded armed force as an additional means of statecraft. Governments seek to achieve security using the same rationality as in realising other political or social goals. If the strategies by which governments, organisations or individuals *within* society seek to realise their goals change, then one must assume that this will also influence the conduct of military strategy. And this is exactly what is happening now.

The end of the Cold War and strategic studies

Today there is more strategic thinking than ever before, but traditional strategic studies is describing fewer and fewer strategic practices. Following the end of the Cold War, 'the spectre of peace' haunted strategic studies.[61] Since strategic studies developed as a way to rationalise the Cold War, it was only fair to ask whether the discipline had any relevance for the post-Cold War world – was it rational to follow its prescriptions?

Cold-War strategic studies was based on a focus on states as rational actors and thus defined a research programme 'concerned primarily with the choices of alternative strategies for states'.[62] This focus places the mainstream of Strategic Studies firmly within the realist school of International Relations. While Strategic Studies has come to include other approaches, the discipline's centre of gravity is still the realist research questions analysing the choices of states when it comes to war and peace. With some notable exceptions,[63] these questions about the rational choices of states still define the discipline. In order for strategy to continue to be relevant, the future does not need to be like the Cold War, the Second World War or any other of the conflicts of the past by which students of strategic studies define their discipline. Still, the realists seem to have recalibrated strategic studies for the post-Cold War world by assuming that many of the defining characteristics of the post-Cold War world are transitory. In Colin Gray's words, 'if there is a

---

[61] Richard K. Betts, 'Should Strategic Studies Survive?', *World Politics* 50 (1997), 7.

[62] Joseph S. Nye and Sean M. Lynn-Johns, 'International Security Studies: A Report of a Conference on the State of the Field', *International Security* 12 (1988), 7.

[63] See, for example, the work of Martin van Creveld and Christopher Coker. Scholars like Michael Howard and Lawrence Freedman, who are more inclined to a historical approach to questions of strategy, may subscribe to the focus on states from time to time, but they are not prisoners of it to the same extent as the realists who make deductive arguments.

golden rule in world politics it is to the effect that bad times return'.[64] While the Cold War has ended, the argument goes, new conflicts will arise and traditional strategic thinking will be needed to deal with them. This is a strong argument for the rationalism of strategy: strategy will still be needed to guide 'princes'. Andrew Bacevich would like strategic studies to guide US decision-makers to a post-Cold War security policy, just as Bernard Brodie and his colleagues had guided a previous generation of decision-makers in the early days of the Cold War. 'A revival of Strategic Studies', Bacevich argues, 'may thus make it possible for the United States in this new era to conduct itself with the foresight and steadfastness appropriate to a Great Power.'[65] But in this case foresight seems to mean looking determinedly over your shoulder to the past. It is telling that many of the central contributions to this debate have titles that indicate a cyclical conception of time. Thus Colin Gray argues that 'the future is the past – with GPS',[66] while John Mearsheimer expects the European security environment to go 'back to the future'.[67] The most important part of their argument is not that progress is impossible in world affairs. Instead their actual claim is that, although the most important political issues of the post-Cold War period (democratic peace, the workings of security communities, globalisation, micro-chip technology, terrorism etc.) are important in their own right, from a historical perspective they are actually non-issues not worthy of much strategic consideration because the really significant possibility remains interstate war, sometime in the future. Thus they see no reason to tinker with the strategic paradigm inherited from the Cold War strategists and Clausewitz.

In arguing in this way, Colin Gray, John Mearsheimer and others are in fact not learning very much from the past. Their past is a theoretical construct based on a realist conception of history as guided by repeated great-power conflicts. What they should learn from history in general and military history in particular is that how conflicts are fought, by whom and for what reasons change over time.[68] No one knew this better than Clausewitz, who himself wrote *On War* in order to explain the new conditions of warfare that the Napoleonic wars had shown the existence of. While Clausewitz believed warfare to be guided by a universal

---

[64] Colin Gray, 'Villains, Victims, and Sheriffs: Strategic Studies and Security for an Interwar Period', *Comparative Strategy* 13 (1994), 354.
[65] Andrew J. Bacevich, 'Strategic Studies: In from the Cold', *SAIS Review* 13 (1993), 23.
[66] Gray, 'Clausewitz Rules, OK?'
[67] John J. Mearsheimer, 'Back to the Future: Instability in Europe after the Cold War', *International Security* 15 (1990), 5–56.
[68] Creveld, *On Future War*.

means-ends **rationality**, he knew that societies and technologies change and therefore **believed** that 'every age had its own kind of war'.[69] By declining to discuss the dangers of the age on their own terms, many if not most realist scholars practising strategic studies are in danger of forgetting that elements of the twentieth-century strategic reality may be peculiar to that century and therefore not constitute a universal standard of what to expect, and fear, for the future. The future might actually not be like the past.

Put in Weberian terms, traditional strategic studies insists that rationality stays the same, while ignoring the need to rationalise new developments. The history of the concept of strategy shows how it has been about rationalising new developments. From its early modern beginnings, it has been about making sense of change. It did this by placing questions of technology, doctrines and agents into a means-end rational framework. Since Clausewitz defined strategy in terms of the relationship between political ends and military means, the means-end rational approach to strategy has become more and more rigid. The ambition to conduct a scientific study of strategy has thus resulted in realists ignoring the processes of rationalisation. Having defined strategy not only in terms of means-end rationality, but a certain type of means (national armed forces) and a certain type of ends (national interests), realists, and thus most of strategic studies, have closed themselves conceptually from rationalising the rise of new technologies, doctrines and agents. Instead of using rationality to explain new phenomena, traditional strategic studies uses rationality to explain why new phenomena are of little consequence.

By defining the issues of today as less important, realists are in danger of betraying the *raison d'être* of strategic studies as a theory of action. While decision-makers are dealing with the problems of new technologies, globalisation, the spread of weapons of mass destruction and the rise of transnational strategic actors like al-Qaeda, realists are arguing that, for all their topicality, these issues are in fact of less significance than the prospect of Russian revanchism or of a revitalisation of German power in Europe or the rise of Japanese or Chinese power in Asia. By focusing determinedly on the past as a blueprint for the future, realists are excluding the possibility that bad times may come in a new form. By insisting that any claim of change is a utopian claim of progress, Gray, Mearsheimer and other central realist figures in strategic studies have actually closed their eyes to the threat that is always the most dangerous: the unexpected.

[69] Clausewitz, *On War*, 593.

The events of 11 September 2001 did not fit the bill of realist strategic studies, but instead of studying how transnational military actors would function in international security policy, many students of strategic studies castigated the US government for declaring a 'war on terrorism'.[70] Again, the titles of some of the realist analyses of the strategic impact of 9/11 say it all: 'Beyond Bin Laden', 'The Continuity of International Politics', 'World Politics as Usual after September 11'.[71] 'The tendency has been', Audrey Kurth Cronin notes, 'to fall back on established bureaucratic mind-sets and prevailing theoretical paradigms that have little relevance for the changes in international security that became obvious after the terrorist attacks.'[72] It is symptomatic of the fixation on the return of great-power conflict that 'The Third World War?' is the title of an article by Lawrence Freedman on 'the war on terrorism'.[73] Perhaps Freedman knows that only by answering this question positively can terrorism be a truly serious threat in the eyes of those who set the agenda for strategic studies. He wants to demonstrate, however, that other types of conflict are important and concludes that, 'instead of gearing up its security policy to deal with strong, but for the moment, hypothetical "peer competitors", the US must take more seriously the problems of weak states and the conflicts they engender'.[74]

Peer competitors are not 'hypothetical' for Barry Posen. He argues that the 'war on terror' should awaken US policy-makers to the fact that their country needs a coherent 'grand strategy'.[75] However important the fight against al-Qaeda may be, the true significance of the war on terror to Posen is the way the conflict highlights present US problems in getting priorities straight in dealing with traditional issues.[76] By insisting that al-Qaeda is a 'political organization' murdering people for 'political reasons', Posen is placing al-Qaeda's use of violence within a

[70] Michael Howard, speech at the Conference New Policies for a New World, RUSI, unpublished, London, November 2001.
[71] Colin Gray, 'World Politics as Usual after September 11: Realism Vindicated', in Ken Booth and Tim Dunne (eds.), *Worlds in Collision* (London: Palgrave, 2002), 226–34; Stephen M. Walt, 'Beyond Bin Laden: Reshaping US Foreign Policy', *International Security* 26 (2001), 57–78; Kenneth N. Waltz, 'The Continuity of International Politics', in Ken Booth and Tim Dunne (eds.), *Worlds in Collision* (London: Palgrave, 2002), 348–53.
[72] Audrey Kurth Cronin, 'Behind the Curve: Globalization and International Terrorism', *International Security* 27 (2002), 30.
[73] Lawrence Freedman, 'The Third World War?', *Survival* 43 (2001), 61–88.
[74] Ibid., 80. See also, Lawrence Freedman, *The Revolution in Strategic Affairs*, Adelphi Paper 318, International Institute for Strategic Studies (Oxford: Oxford University Press, 1998).
[75] Barry R. Posen, 'The Struggle Against Terrorism: Grand Strategy, Strategy and Tactics', *International Security* 26 (2001), 39–55.
[76] Ibid., 51–5.

Clausewitzian, means-end rational framework.[77] By implication al-Qaeda can be dealt with as a state, albeit one that is organised in a different way, and by categorising al-Qaeda as such, Posen is clearly indicating that more powerful political entities, such as China, are of greater concern. One must assume that it is for the benefit of such future, state-based threats that Posen believes that the US needs to get its grand strategy right.

By basing strategic thinking on the enduring lessons of the past, realists have failed to recognise the threats we shall endure in the future. Since realists dominate the discipline, this has serious consequences for the entire research programme of strategic studies. This seems to prove Phillip Windsor right in his assertion that 'strategic thinking is now in a state of confusion and disarray'[78] because 'it does still depend largely on the assumption that strategic considerations are causal rather than consequential in nature. It is still part of the process of Weber's rationalization; and much of the effort represents an attempt to pour the old wine of strategic thinking into new, smaller, and intellectually fragile bottles.'[79] Windsor does not believe that the present means-end rationality-based strategic thinking (realist or otherwise) has adequate answers to the questions posed by the new technologies, doctrines and security agents of the post-Cold War world. In order to reinvigorate strategic thinking, students of strategy will either turn to dealing with the moral issues of force, Windsor argues, or else they must rephrase strategic questions in terms of 'international sociology'. And what will a strategic studies discipline based on such an 'international sociology' be all about in Windsor's view? 'What it does mean is an attempt to examine the utility, or otherwise, of force within the complex interaction of international and social questions that characterizes the present world.'[80] The focus of the realists on the past displays a lack of imagination, an unwillingness to recognise the possibility that the practices which strategy describes are changing, and that one needs to rethink strategic studies in order to understand the ramifications of these changes.

It has been argued that this lack of imagination is a reason to leave the study of strategy altogether. From this point of view, strategic studies is conceptually narrowing the possibilities for escaping a logic of confrontation and conflict in world affairs.[81] Instead of searching for new

---

[77] Ibid., 39.
[78] Phillip Windsor, *Strategic Thinking: An Introduction and Farewell*, ed. Mats Bredal and Spyros Economides (Boulder, CO: Lynne Reinner, 2002), 172.
[79] Ibid., 174.
[80] Ibid., 180.
[81] Bradley S. Klein, *Strategic Studies and World Order: The Global Politics of Deterrence* (Cambridge: Cambridge University Press, 1994); R. B. J. Walker, 'The Subject of

approaches to strategy, Bradley Klein argues that one should 'search for a post-modern politics of peace'.[82] However, as argued above, post-modern or late modern politics seems to be dominated by strategic thinking. It would therefore hardly make sense for students of strategy to abandon the concept. What is required is what Wright Mills termed 'the sociological imagination', that is, the ability to see a social activity, in this case strategy, in the context of the society that is engaging in it.[83] If one adopts this sociological approach to strategy, then the fact that strategic thinking is used outside politico-military institutions offers an opportunity for a more imaginative strategic studies. The strategies by which new technologies, insecurity and new social agents are being dealt with by governments and individuals in social spheres not normally dealt with by strategic studies might be a better way of understanding the new strategic thinking. Leaving strategy at a time when a plethora of other social practices are being guided by strategic thinking would mean overlooking the importance of the connection between how society as such deals with 'strategic issues' and how armed force is being dealt with. Furthermore, it seems that post-modern politics is far from peaceful. The issue is not one of choosing between an inherent violent modernity and an inherently peaceful post-modernity, but rather of identifying how new technologies, doctrines and enemies make post-modern conflicts different from modern ones. Thus Charles Moskos is probably right when he argues that 'one key difference between Modern and Postmodern societies lies in the character of the threats they face and the ways they perceive them'.[84] It is very doubtful indeed that peace would be the only outcome of finding 'alternative conceptualizations of human community at levels both below and beyond that of the modern state'.[85] As the ethnic conflicts of the former Yugoslavia and the actions of al-Qaeda show, the politics of intra-state or extra-state entities can lead to some very unpeaceful strategies. Appreciating that the problems of human conflict are not just made up by strategic studies is an all-important first step in the direction of studying the challenges posed by new technologies, doctrines and agents.

Security', in Keith Krause and Michael C. Williams (eds.), *Critical Security Studies* (Minneapolis, MN: University of Minnesota Press, 1997), 61–81.

[82] Bradley S. Klein, 'After Strategy: The Search for a Postmodern Politics of Peace', *Alternatives* 13 (1988), 293–318.

[83] C. Wright Mills, *The Sociological Imagination* (New York: Oxford University Press, 1959).

[84] Charles C. Moskos, 'Toward a Postmodern Military: The United States as a Paradigm', in Charles C. Moskos, John Allen Williams and David R. Segal (eds.), *The Postmodern Military: Armed Forces After the Cold War* (Oxford: Oxford University Press, 2000), 16.

[85] Klein, 'After Strategy', 313.

Risk strategies

Sociologists are realising that there is more strategic thinking going on than ever before. As noted above, sociologists are using the concept of strategy to describe the everyday activity of families, rural poor or any other social groups who have to navigate a high-risk environment.[86] Graham Crow notes that 'a central theme of this literature is the unpredictability of the environment in which these enterprises operate, and the rationality of risk-minimisation in such circumstances'.[87] The use of strategy to minimise risk has become the central theme for a growing body of sociological studies. These studies of 'risk society' demonstrate that means-end rationality is no longer the guiding strategic choice in the 'civilian world'. Instead a reflexive rationality is guiding actors who have no secure ends to choose between but who have to balance risks.

Deborah Lupton explains that students of risk 'see risk as having become a central cultural and political concept by which individuals, social groups and institutions are organized, monitored and regulated'.[88] Ulrich Beck is perhaps the best-known student of risk society. He defines risk as 'a systematic way of dealing with hazards and insecurities induced and introduced by modernization itself'.[89] Along with Anthony Giddens, Beck argues that modernity has become 'reflexive' because the sovereign, modern individual is constantly faced with the consequences of his or her own actions. What is true on the individual level is also true on the level of society itself. Beck first stated the case for risk society on the basis of his reflections on the debate over the environment in the 1980s. Since, Beck argues, pollution is the invariable outcome of modern, industrial society, in discussing the dangers of pollution, the Germans were in fact debating the consequences of their own lifestyle. There can be no modernity without pollution, but on the other hand many people argue that the present rate of pollution is unsustainable for the ecosystem. Beck concludes that 'society becomes a theme and a problem for itself'.[90] Since Beck's early writings, the concept of risk has been expanded into an analysis of what Beck and Giddens both believe to be a new phase of modernity: late or reflexive modernity. They regard the spread of risk-analysis and other rationales for calculating and dealing with risk as a sign that individual and social strategies are changing fundamentally:

---

[86] Wallace, 'Reflections on the Concept of "Strategy"', 95.
[87] Crow, 'The Use of the Concept of "Strategy"', 6.
[88] Deborah Lupton, *Risk* (London: Routledge, 1999), 25.
[89] Beck, *Risk Society*, 21.   [90] Ibid., 8.

Under the surface of risk calculation new kinds of *industrialized, decision-produced incalculabilities and threats* are spreading within the globalization of high-risk industries, whether for warfare or welfare purposes. Max Weber's concept of 'rationalization' no longer grasps this late modern reality, produced by successful rationalization. *Along with the growing capacity of technical options [Zweckrationalität] grows the incalculability of their consequences.*[91]

Beck argues that reflexivity is the end point of the process of rationalisation that Weber identified. Society has become identical with a complex web of rational and technological systems. However, these systems become 'a theme and a problem' in themselves because they no longer constitute a means to an end – in other words, rationalisation no longer furthers means-end rationality. The process of systematising responses to modernity continues, but it no longer produces means-end rationality. Instead, individuals and organisations adopt reflexive strategies in order to deal with the risks produced by their own existence.

The literature on risk society deals with the very issues that rock the belief in existing strategic studies' explanations: the advent of new technologies, new ways or doctrines for dealing with the hazards of life, and the rise of new political agents because of globalisation. While sociologists seem to produce theories that are useful in explaining international security strategies, they mostly fail to engage with these issues themselves. As Martin Shaw points out,[92] sociologists who are so perceptive about domestic changes fall back surprisingly often on sweeping generalisations and old concepts of state power when it comes to discussing international affairs.[93] Perhaps it takes the vantage point of strategic studies to realise how much a risk society is dealing with the same set of problems that characterises international society in general. In any case, there is no ready-made blueprint for applying the risk literature to strategic studies. However, I would argue that a thorough reading of the literature suggests that risk strategies are characterised by what I term 'management', 'the presence of the future' and 'the boomerang effect'. Below I describe how these characteristics constitute a reflexive rationality for dealing with risks.

---

[91] Ibid., 22.

[92] Martin Shaw, 'The Development of "Common Risk" Society: A Theoretical Overview', in Jürgen Kuhlmann and Jean Callaghan (eds.), *Military and Society in 21st Century Europe: A Comparative Analysis* (London: Transaction Publishers, 2000), 20.

[93] For example, Giddens, *The Consequences of Modernity*, 55–78; Ulrich Beck, *What Is Globalization?* (Cambridge: Polity Press, 2000), 87–113. Beck is a prolific writer on international affairs in the German and international press. However, the purpose of this study is not to survey the views of Professor Beck or any other theorist of risk society.

Management

Michel Foucault argues that the constitutive metaphor of modern governance ('governmentality') is the ship: from the seventeenth century onwards, politics has been about guiding the ship of state to a safe harbour.[94] In risk society, that safe harbour has disappeared from the horizon. As captains navigate by observing celestial bodies, so did modern governments in the twentieth century navigate by means of plans. The modern approach to governance is epitomised in 'the plan', whether in terms of architecture, social policy, economics or, indeed, warfare. A plan told the story of the problems that faced a government, or a business or a person for that matter, at a given moment and the means by which these problems could be eliminated in favour of a brighter future. The concept of planning demonstrates that, for all the upheavals and changes that constituted modernity, the basic trend in modern governance was about giving upheavals meaning and change a sense of direction. This was what government economists did with their charts of economic output and employment, and what Freudian psychologists did with their functionally similar charts of stages of personal development. In this way, experts gave people a sense of what Anthony Giddens terms 'ontological security': a coherent narrative of what happened now, what one could expect from the future, and the idea that you, or your nation, could choose what developmental path to follow.[95] But, according to Giddens, the current phase of modernity does not allow people to know what to do or what to expect. In his words, 'to live in the universe of high modernity is to live in an environment of chance and risk'.[96] The defining narrative of late modernity is not about plans for perfection, but about choosing the lesser evil. Thus John Adams argues that 'the starting point of any theory of risk must be that everyone willingly takes risks'.[97] One has no choice but to take risks: the questions are, how many risks and of what kind?

Adams criticises traditional, modern concepts of risk for aiming at producing plans that eliminate risk. They see risk as a product of deficient procedures that allow 'human error' to occur and systems to malfunction, but Adams' point is that every procedure has its own

[94] Michel Foucault, 'Governmentality', in *Essential Works of Foucault 1954–1984, vol. III: Power*, ed. James D. Faubion (New York: The New Press, 2000). See also Graham Burchell, Colin Cordon and Peter Miller (eds.), *The Foucault Effect: Studies in Governmentality* (London: Harvester Wheatsheaf, 1990).
[95] Giddens, *Modernity and Self-Identity*, 36.
[96] Ibid., 109.   [97] John Adams, *Risk* (London: Routledge, 1995), 16.

deficiencies. Most accidents occur because of a 'human error' (who else is there to make them?), but the point is that training human operators better cannot eliminate these 'errors'. The error is not anyone's error in particular but contingent: you might prevent the individual accident, but the level of accidents will be constant. There is no plan for safety. You choose the system of risk you prefer rather than aim at a universe of safety that does not exist.[98]

If problems have to be managed rather than definitely solved, then the most important political objective is to maintain freedom of action. Knowing that new risks will arise, a government needs to retain resources to deal with the next problems, and the next, and the next. The 'governmentality' of risk society, Mitchell Dean argues,[99] is therefore about 'the security of governmental mechanisms themselves'.[100] The most important task of government is to make government itself possible by letting its 'methods' transform with the times. Ulrich Beck calls this the 'politics of politics'.[101] According to Beck, one might thus distinguish between 'rule-directed' politics and 'rule-altering' politics.[102] The notion of 'rule-altering' politics is one example of Beck's belief in social constructivism as a reflexive social practice that is characteristic of risk society. If one defines a social construction as socially instituted rules of action, 'rule-altering' politics may be defined as constructivist politics. Risk society is open to 'rule-altering' politics because of risk's 'origin in decision-making'.[103] In a risk society you choose the risks you take, rather than eliminate them altogether. 'Risks are revealed as systematic events,' Beck argues, 'which are accordingly in need of general political regulation.'[104]

---

[98] Ibid., 52–3.
[99] Mitchell Dean, *Governmentality: Power and Rule in Modern Society* (London: Sage Publications, 1999), 176–97. Dean argues that the focus on governmentality, or management, goes beyond Beck's conception of society. He points to the fact that in *Risk Society* it is never entirely clear whether risks are 'real' or socially constructed. Later, Beck argues that they are in fact both: see his *World Risk Society*, 133–52. This argument places him in a school of social constructivism not unlike John Searle's: see John R. Searle, *The Construction of Social Reality* (London: Penguin Books, 1995). A constructivist reading of Beck has always been possible, and Beck seems to have come to understand his project in that way. Given Beck's focus on politics – which is strangely absent in Dean's account of Beck's thoughts – governmentality provides a way to conceptualise Beck's ideas of a new rationality of government, rather than a departure from his analysis.
[100] Dean, *Governmentality*, 194.
[101] Ulrich Beck, 'The Reinvention of Politics: Towards a Theory of Reflexive Modernization', in Ulrich Beck, Anthony Giddens and Scott Lash, *Reflexive Modernization: Politics, Tradition and Aesthetics in the Modern Social Order* (Cambridge: Polity Press, 1994), 35.
[102] Ibid., 34–6.   [103] Beck, *World Risk Society*, 50.   [104] Ibid., 51.

In risk society, politics is no longer about initiating a social, economic or political process and bringing an end to a particular problem, as Foucault's ship metaphor implied. Governments no longer master ends, only means. Politics is about managing the process. In Foucault's metaphor, the rationale of government is to keep the ship of state afloat. In these circumstances, processes become projects,[105] as governments come to identify political success in terms of their ability to manage processes of transformation. In order to manage them, events are placed in the context of a certain political project. Political discourse is therefore constituted by 'definitional struggles over the scale, degrees and urgency of risks'.[106] An important political technique in this discourse is what Beck terms 'symbolical politics': the art of producing closure where there is none.[107]

The presence of the future

To someone involved in a road accident, traffic is no longer a risk. An accident is a concrete event that has occurred and left the scars to prove it, whereas '"risk" is defined', according to John Adams, 'by most of those who seek to measure it, as the product of the probability and utility of some *future* event'.[108] Since risks are about what might happen to you, the identification of risk entails a strategy for how to avoid the identified risk from becoming reality. Insurance is all about calculating the probability for a risk to become an actual event. This illustrates how thinking in terms of risk makes future dangers an object of action. An unfortunate occurrence, like your house burning down, is not just a result of bad luck or divine wrath, but something you have a responsibility to prevent and the opportunity to insure yourself against. As such, insurance makes an event a possibility because you have to either prevent it or secure yourself against its effect by taking out an insurance policy.[109] But insurance can only be general. No one knows whether your house is going to burn down: one can only calculate the probability that a house like yours might burn down. By taking out fire insurance, you are making the general probability a potential reality in your life, a reality which you have to deal with. But, as insurance agents know, people have different 'risk cultures': some people will accept a lot of risk, while others are very risk-averse.[110]

---

[105] I owe this phrase to Bertel Heurlin.   [106] Beck, *Risk Society*, 46.
[107] Ibid., 57.   [108] Adams, *Risk*, 30.
[109] Ewald, 'Insurance and Risk', 199–200.   [110] Adams, *Risk*, 67–8.

Giddens uses the insurance industry and the stock market as examples of institutionalised systems of 'risk-profiling',[111] but 'risk-profiling' is no longer limited to insurance or the stock market: such profiling strategies are increasingly part of personal choices and government policies. As Giddens himself points out, people are increasingly faced with all kinds of risks which they have to manage. For example, choosing to quit smoking is to make a 'life-plan' on the basis of the probability that smoking will kill you.[112] In fact, you may live to be a hundred and happily puff your cigar all the while. Lung cancer statistics are general statements, they are not necessarily applicable to you. Still, people choose to make the statistics applicable to them by using them as a guide to what will happen to them if they do not quit smoking. Another example of 'risk-profiling' is the way in which social services determine whether a child should be placed in the care of foster parents rather than live with its natural parents. No one can know exactly what will happen to the child in question, but based on the life of the particular family and their own experience, social workers draw up a scenario for the child's future. In order to prevent this scenario from becoming a reality, they decide that it should be placed in the care of someone else.

Thus thinking in terms of risks results in a 'colonisation of the future'.[113] Since risks are the consequences of actions yet to be made, Ulrich Beck argues that 'the concept of risk reverses the relationship of past, present and the future'.[114] In attempting to avoid risk, one is defining present problems by their perceived future consequences. At present, global warming is making an impact that is easily dismissed as the usual fluctuations of the weather. It is the scenario for the consequences that global warming may have on the world's ecosystem that constitutes a threat, a threat real enough to place global warming high on the international political agenda. In Beck's words, 'future events that have not yet occurred become the object of current action':[115] governments are compelled to act on the causes of global warming. A cause, however, is supposed to be identified in terms of its effect. At present there is no effect, only the scenario of what may happen. In this way scenarios make risks, in Beck's phrase, a 'real virtuality'.[116] The very causality of political discourse is thus circumvented. It is not present actions that are to produce future results, but perceived future results that produce present actions.

---

[111] Giddens, *Modernity and Self-Identity*, 119.   [112] Ibid., 124–8.
[113] Ibid., 111.   [114] Beck, *World Risk Society*, 137.
[115] Ibid., 52.   [116] Ibid., 136.

Thus the focus on risk leads to pre-emptive actions. Children are forcibly removed from parents who are believed to be standing in the way of their development; environmental laws are passed to prevent ills that might, or might not, occur in the future; people stop smoking to prevent themselves from contracting cancer; and so on. Because you act on the basis of a 'real virtuality', you cannot know whether what you are seeking to prevent will happen, but on the other hand you cannot wait to find out either. The knowledge that you might be able to prevent something bad from happening gives you a responsibility for the future, a duty to protect the future from the present. However, fulfilling your duty may turn out to be a risk in itself. When you begin contemplating the scenarios of the consequences of your pre-emptive action they will surely present new risks, and you will soon realise that every avenue open to you seems to lead to new risks – and then you might not be able to act at all. If the agent undertaking this particular action is a government rather than a person, this inability to act might be reinforced by a reflexive decision-making process in which each department involved presents a new risk to the suggested course of action. Beck refers to this as the 'risk trap': policy-makers become paralysed because every action holds a new risk.[117] While reflecting on risks makes some people overly cautious, others may become overambitious when faced with many risks. They risk falling in a 'pre-emptive trap' by acting on every scenario, thus ending by being caught in so many unintended consequences of their actions that they may have very few political resources left to manage these, or indeed any future risks. In both cases the mismanagement of pre-emptive strategies makes it difficult to manage risks, but the scenario for the risk that gives rise to the question of action in the first place is agreed upon. However, the calculability of risks also means that people with equal rights can reject the scenario altogether. Perhaps one could term this the 'John Lennon doctrine': just imagine something completely different. In any case, the quality of individuals or governments in risk societies is determined by their ability to present scenarios that are credible to every or most 'risk cultures' and to act upon them in ways that produce new options rather than lead to risk traps or pre-emptive traps.

The boomerang effect

'Risks display a social *boomerang effect* in their diffusion', Beck argues.[118] In risk society, the strong may still do what they can, but the weak must

---

[117] Ibid., 141.   [118] Beck, *Risk Society*, 37.

not suffer alone any longer. The strong suffer with the weak because in reflexive society no one can escape the consequences of their actions. Beck's example is that pollution may give asthma to the daughter of the company president as well as to the son of a worker. '*Perpetrator and victim*', Beck argues, 'sooner or later become *identical.*'[119] For that reason, he argues that 'risk society is by tendency also a self-critical society'.[120] The best strategy for someone endangered with pollution is thus to establish a scenario for the broader consequences of their particular plight. It is for this reason that the politics of risk societies is centred around 'definitional struggles over the scale, degrees and urgency of risks'.[121] But there are more 'boomerang effects' than the unintended consequences that the perpetrator of certain social ills will sooner or later have to face up to.

First, the identification of risk can have a boomerang effect. Thus Lupton argues that 'risk meanings and strategies are attempts to tame uncertainty, but often have the paradoxical effect of increasing anxiety about risk through the intensity of their focus and concern'.[122] Shooting the messenger may be a lot more convenient than confronting a risk scenario, but the messenger may also be ignored because the level of risk that individuals, groups and governments are prepared to accept differs. What one may regard as a very dangerous scenario may be an acceptable risk to others. Talking about a risk and demanding action may thus open rifts by pointing to differences in perceptions that would otherwise have not become apparent.

Secondly, differences in 'risk culture' can be used strategically either by one side taking risks that the other side is not prepared to take, or by the 'risk-taker' exporting risks to the risk-averse. If you are prepared to accept risks that your competitors are not, then you will forge ahead as they stop at the brink while you take the leap. However, you might also choose to lure your competitor with you over the brink and thus make him subject to the same risks as yourself, but because he is more risk-averse than you he will not be able to bear them. In a risk-averse world, the risk-taker is king. But his reign lasts for only so long. At some point averseness to risk will become a 'theme and a problem in itself' for the risk-averse – then they will have to either accept defeat or prove that they are willing to take risks. One risk they might accept is to remove the 'risk-taker' and the risk that his risk-taking has come to constitute.

Thirdly, the literature on risk deals intensively with 'risk compensation', which describes the situation in which a reduction of risk leads

---

[119] Ibid., 38.   [120] Beck, 'Reinvention of Politics', 11.
[121] Beck, *Risk Society*, 46.   [122] Lupton, *Risk*, 13.

to more risky behaviour. An example of risk compensation, according to John Adams, is the way the use of seat belts actually makes driving more risky. While a seat belt certainly makes your chances of surviving a road accident much greater, mandatory use of seat belts also means that drivers expect to survive road accidents and therefore seem to drive more recklessly. Thus, according to Adams, mandatory seat-belt laws may decrease the percentage of people killed on the road, but the number of people involved in an accident in fact goes up because seat belts make drivers more irresponsible, thus resulting in more accidents.[123]

Conclusions

The history of strategy is the history of rationalising new technologies, doctrines and agents. The people of the Renaissance turned to the Romans in order to make sense of how to deal with the introduction of guns, professional armies and the sovereign state. Later the advent of total war and the nation state laid a similar requirement on the conceptualisation of the relationship between politics and the use of force. This time Clausewitz was able to present a concept of strategy that reflected the Enlightenment's focus on reason and means-end rationality. The man the strategic literature presents almost as a Moses figure, who emerged from the Napoleonic wars with the tablets on war, was in fact just someone who tried his best to understand the consequences of the modern way of warfare. Clausewitz' success in doing so was matched only by his failure to secure a commission to carry out his ideas on the battlefield. By making Clausewitz' means-end rational dictum a universal description of the past, while also believing it to be a guide to the future, many of the realist students of strategic studies are forgetting the most important lesson of Clausewitz' work: 'every age had its own kind of war'.

New technologies, doctrines and agents seem to be defining a new kind of war, but at present realists insist on using the concepts of a bygone age to describe them. The history of strategy is entering a new chapter, and we need new concepts to write about it. Realists, and with them much of strategic studies, still regard the society on behalf of which governments pursue strategy as a modern, industrial society. However, society has changed into a risk society, where information technology and globalisation are creating a framework for people acting by reflexive rationality. Such risk societies make policy differently from modern society. This does not mean that strategic studies does not serve a

---

[123] Adams, *Risk*, 113–34.

purpose any longer: on the contrary, the need to study strategies is as great as ever before because a society dominated by a concern for risk is much more 'strategic' than modern society ever was. It is from sociological insights into the logic of these reflexive strategies that strategic studies must acquire new insights into what constitutes late modern strategy. Presenting the literature on risk society, I have argued that late modern risk strategies are characterised by management, the presence of the future and the boomerang effect. In the next three chapters, I shall investigate whether these categories can be used to obtain new insights into how new technologies, doctrines and agents are constituting a new type of strategy.

3   Technology: the revolution in military affairs

One day in the autumn of 2001, a Predator drone flew above the mountains of Afghanistan, gathering intelligence on the operation of US special forces below. The Predator is an Unmanned Aerial Vehicle (UAV) piloted by specialists from well behind the front line, but back in Washington the President was following the live feed from the Predator, which gave him as much information as if he had been flying a reconnaissance plane above Afghanistan, and certainly better than what was available to the soldiers on the ground below.[1] Had the Predator been of the new version equipped with Hell-Fire missiles, which the US armed forces were introducing in the Afghanistan campaign, then the Commander-in-Chief could have taken part in the battle himself by remote control. George Bush's Predator experience was probably mostly a gimmick set up to illustrate the power of the new military technologies to the President, but in the near future he will immediately be able to plug into any US military operation by means of the so-called Global Information Grid, a US military network linking all platforms at all times.[2] This is an example of how information and communication technology is fundamentally changing the technological aspects of strategy, a transformation that is often referred to as a 'revolution in military affairs', or RMA for connoisseurs of military acronyms. The link between the President and the Predator is also an example of what the critics of the RMA describe as hype at best or a rebirth of militarism at worst. In the eyes of the critics, the RMA is promising a remote-controlled, high-tech, airborne war that makes war seem risk-free when in fact it is not.

RMA provides an understanding of the strategic possibilities created by the application of information and communication technologies to warfare. The proponents of the RMA identify precision-strike, more effective logistics and vastly increased information about what is going

---

[1] Bob Woodward, *Bush at War* (New York: Simon and Schuster, 2002), 117.
[2] Joint Doctrine and Concepts Centre, *Strategic Trends* (Swindon: JDCC, 2003), 4:10.

on on the battlefield as key factors in a new form of warfare. RMA enthusiasts like to present current technological developments like the Predator as the beginning of a process that will reshape warfare completely. However, the way in which the concept of the RMA has shaped the Western and US strategic discourse in the 1990s suggests that it does not represent a sudden and fundamental change in the state of strategic affairs, as opposed to their evolution. In fact, the RMA is a description of a process rather than an event. As such, it serves the same conceptual function that strategic concepts have provided since the dawn of the modern age: to define the nature of warfare in a universe of continuous transformation. Thus when generals and politicians are promoting the RMA, they are actually arguing for a redefinition of political goals in the light of the new military methods being created by information and communication technologies. The introduction of new technologies and new policies may be an incremental process, but the *result* is actually revolutionary because it breaks down the means-end rational understanding of war that used to define strategy.

This chapter will examine how the new military technologies are redefining war in terms of risk. It will do this by focusing on the three characteristics of risk society described in the introduction: management, the presence of the future and the boomerang effect. First, I investigate how management of the new technologies is becoming pivotal to Western strategy at the same time as the increased information that these technologies provide is making the management of battle possible in ways it has never been before. This should lead to the perfect Clausewitzian battle, but in fact it leads to the opposite. Secondly, I look at how the prospect of new methods of fighting war makes scenarios for the future central to defence planning. The presence of the future is clear in the shift to a 'capability-based approach' to defence planning and central to how the capabilities of both enemies and allies are evaluated. Thirdly, I analyse the 'boomerang effects' of the RMA, whose critics are arguing that the new technologies are introducing a new calculus of war, which, in Martin Shaw's words, is making 'risk-transfer militarism' possible. Taking my point of departure in the risk literature's notion of 'risk compensation', I argue that while war has indeed become easier, it has also made it politically much harder to justify its horrors. Focusing on what the risk literature terms 'risk-taking', I argue that when the West is waging war on the premise of lower risks, then the best counter-strategy is to be willing to take risks. One of the best analyses of this situation has been made by two Chinese colonels, whose work I shall deal with in some detail. The chapter ends with a conclusion.

Management

The 'revolution in military affairs' or RMA is focusing Western strategy increasingly on managing wars by creating political and military contingencies rather than by seeking decisive battles. Furthermore, the development of new weapons and strategies means that how wars are fought is no longer a given condition, but a process that needs to be managed if one wants to gain a strategic edge. The risk literature regards what I term 'management' as a departure from the modern mode of governance based on plans identifying the ends and providing the means. Students of risk society argue that such coherent narratives no longer guide policy. Instead of directing the development of society, policy is now focused on retaining the means for government to function in a time of profound change. The RMA is one such narrative of change and risk. It defines the causes of change, the challenges that change poses to defence policies, and ways of managing military power in the new environment. Thus where the RMA perhaps started as a focus on new technology, it has become a focus on a new way of conducting strategy.

First, I deal with how the RMA has become a way of conceptualising new goals and benchmarks for the US armed forces following the end of the Cold War. In other words, this part is about managing the RMA. The second part of the chapter is about how the RMA makes strategy about management. Although it makes the perfect Clausewitzian battle possible, means-end rational Clausewitzian thinking is far from perfect with the kind of information about the battlefield that the RMA provides.

Managing the revolution

Perhaps it should be no surprise that the Soviet Union was the first state to sense that a military revolution was under way.[3] First, it was directed against themselves – the kind of thing that focuses one's attention. Following its failure in Vietnam, the American military had to rethink how to fight and win wars with a smaller, professional army. The US armed forces focused on technology to make up for the lack of drafted

[3] On the development of RMA in the US military, see Steven Metz, 'The Next Twist of the RMA', *Parameters* (Autumn 2000), 40–53; Freedman, *The Revolution in Strategic Affairs*, 19–32; Williamson Murray and MacGregor Knox, 'Thinking About Revolutions in Warfare', in Knox and Murray (eds.), *The Dynamics of Military Revolution, 1300–2050* (Cambridge: Cambridge University Press, 2001), 1–5.

Americans after the ending of conscription when compared to the abundance of Russian conscripts, and they began to develop strategies for fighting 'AirLand Battle'. The doctrine for AirLand Battle was actually rather similar to the concept of 'battle in depth', which the Soviet military developed during the Second World War.[4] It was a way to conceptualise the front as a box rather than a line, a box within which a number of operations take place at the same time, with superior firepower being used to suppress opposing forces. Secondly, because they were educated in a materialist conception of history, Red Army officers thought of military history in terms of revolutions based on material foundations. Marshal Nikolai Ogarkov, Chief of the Soviet General Staff from 1977 to 1984, therefore argued that precision-guided munitions, cruise missiles and stealth bombers 'made it possible to sharply increase (by at least an order of magnitude) the destructive potential of conventional weapons, bringing them closer, so to speak, to weapons of mass destruction in terms of effectiveness'.[5] Ogarkov tried to reform the Red Army along similar lines, but the 'military technical revolution' was in the end just one more area in which the Soviet Union could not keep pace with the US military build-up in the 1980s.[6]

The 1990–1 Gulf war showed the power of the new technology and how it could be used for 'battle in depth'. At the time, Western public opinion had become used to thinking of war either in terms of the nuclear stand-off between the Soviet Union and the West, which made war unthinkable, or in terms of the failure of British, French, American and Soviet forces in low-intensity conflicts in the Third World, which seemed to suggest that military power always failed to deliver the results that the politicians wanted. Against this background, the sweeping effectiveness and precision of US forces in the battle for Kuwait did indeed seem revolutionary. Following an air campaign, which for the first time enabled the public to watch the terrible effectiveness of

---

[4] H. Willmott, *The Great Crusade: A New Complete History of the Second World War* (New York: The Free Press, 1989), 366. See also, Condoleezza Rice, 'The Making of Soviet Strategy', in Peter Paret (ed.), *Makers of Modern Strategy: From Machiavelli to the Nuclear Age* (Oxford: Clarendon Press, 1998), 648–76.

[5] Quoted in Murray and Knox, 'Thinking About Revolutions in Warfare', 3.

[6] This military build-up is widely credited as one factor, if not the decisive one, for the Soviet capitulation in the Cold War. Normally researchers focus on the way the 'Star Wars' programme faced the Soviet leadership with a technological challenge it could not meet. The 'military technical revolution' in the West should have been a much more urgent matter for the Kremlin, however, because it could offset Soviet conventional superiority within a short period of time, as opposed to the longer time horizon of the Strategic Defense Initiative.

precision-guided munitions on television, American and allied troops destroyed what was, at least numerically, the world's fourth largest army with minimal losses. Thus after the Gulf war the use of military force no longer seemed either unthinkable or ineffective. On the contrary, after the public had followed the precision strikes of the US Air Force on television, the US military had to fight the perception that it could strike more precisely and far more humanely than it actually could at the time. In turn, the advertised precision made people regard collateral damage in general and civilian casualties in particular as something avoidable for which the military should be held responsible. Civilian casualties thus became the centre of almost any press briefing of any conflict in the years to come.

Following the Gulf war, Andrew Marshall, who, as the director of the Office for Net Assessment at the Pentagon, had followed the Soviet debate on the supposed US military revolution, began to argue that a military revolution might actually be under way after all. Like the battle of Cambrai in 1917, where tanks were used for the first time, Marshall argued that the Gulf war was 'a first trial of new technology and new ways of operating'.[7] Marshall's ideas squared well with what people had seen on their television screens. Thus even before he became Secretary of Defense, William Perry concluded that, 'in Operation Desert Storm the United States employed for the first time a new class of military systems that gave American Forces a revolutionary advance in military capability'.[8] Ten years later Marshall was described as 'the Yoda of the Rumsfeld Defense Department' because at that point the idea of a revolution in military affairs which he launched in the early 1990s had become the basis for how the Pentagon was approaching strategy in the twenty-first century.[9] The RMA became one of those acronyms so beloved by military professionals and eagerly put to use by commentators who were trying to explain to the public how military force was being used in a new way.

In the beginning, however, the RMA was by no means a banner that everyone in the US military wanted to fly over the Pentagon. As Vice Chairman of the Joint Chiefs of Staff from 1994 to 1995, it was Admiral Bill Owens' job to implement Marshall's vision, but after resigning his post he concluded:

---

[7] Andrew W. Marshall, *Some Thoughts on Military Revolutions*, Second Version, Office of the Secretary of Defense, Director of Net Assessment, Washington, DC (1993), 3. See also Murray and Knox, 'Thinking About Revolutions in Warfare', 4.
[8] William J. Perry, 'Desert Storm and Deterrence', *Foreign Affairs* 70 (1991), 66.
[9] Bill Keller, 'The Fighting Next Time', *New York Times*, 10 March 2002.

It is my sad judgement that the Revolution in Military Affairs is in serious trouble today. Efforts to enact reforms and to create new structures that will deliver on the promise of the information revolution have stalled as a result of the distraction of world events, poor planning, insufficient budget priority, and behind-the-scenes bureaucratic opposition to the dramatic organizational and cultural changes required to put these new technologies to work for us as fully as possible.[10]

The true effects of the RMA would be realised only by integrating services and platforms in a new way. The result was a very predictable battle between 'revolutionaries' and the 'establishment' that shaped the two ways in which RMA was described in the 1990s. On the one hand was what Paul Hirst called the 'Wired Magazine version of the RMA',[11] which described a clear, clean, computerised version of the armed forces, which the 'revolutionaries' believed could be created sometime in the future if only they received the funds.[12] At present, however, the revolutionaries' vision could be criticised for its 'virtuality' exactly because the vision itself was mostly a piece of science fiction.[13] On the other hand were the accounts of the RMA that focused on the bureaucratic politics of the Pentagon. In this view, the RMA served little practical purpose but could be used by the 'military-industrial complex' to fire up the imagination of members of Congress in order to secure funds for military spending in the absence of a real enemy. By telling the story this way, the outcome of the struggle between revolutionaries and the establishment was given in advance: interservice rivalry and military conservatism would bury any revolutionary technologies or concepts.[14] Neither the 'Wired magazine' nor the 'Pentagon bureaucracy' versions were wrong, but neither was able to capture what perhaps was the most important aspect of the RMA.

The Gulf war had shown that information technology could generate more precise and effective armed forces, but following the collapse of the Soviet Union the US military had no enemy against which to use

---

[10] Bill Owens (with Ed Offley), *Lifting the Fog of War* (New York: Farrar, Straus and Giroux, 2000), 208.

[11] Paul Hirst, *War and Power* (Cambridge: Polity Press, 2001), 92.

[12] See, for example, Bruce Sterling, 'War is Virtual Hell', *Wired* (March–April 1993), www.wired.com (21 July 2000); Bob Riddell, 'Doom Goes to War', *Wired* (April 1997), www.wired.com (21 July 2000).

[13] James Der Derian, 'The Art of War and the Construction of Peace', in Morten Kelstrup and Michael C. Williams (eds.), *International Relations Theory and the Politics of European Integration: Power, Security and Community* (London: Routledge, 2000), 72–105.

[14] Asked by the journal *Foreign Policy* whether Secretary Rumsfeld would succeed in transforming the US military, three retired generals answered, 'No'. Moises Naim and Michael O'Hanlon, 'Reinventing War', *Foreign Policy* (November/December 2001), 39–41. Cf. Keller, 'The Fighting Next Time'.

these military means. This is why the '*Wired* magazine' version of the RMA seems so virtual. This narrative is all about identifying new, smart technological means, but there is an absence of an end for which to use them. Similarly, in the other version of the RMA story, the Pentagon bureaucracy stifled innovation because innovation seemed derived from any other purpose than to serve as a bargaining chip in the Washington political game. However, in the course of the 1990s the RMA gradually became a way of understanding the rationality of the armed forces without there being a clearly defined enemy like the Soviet Union. The revolution became its own justification. Military innovation ceased to be about harnessing the means to defeat an enemy and became instead a case of what Ulrich Beck would term 'rule-altering politics'.[15] The RMA became a way to define the rationale of strategy.

In the final years of the Clinton administration and during that of George W. Bush, the RMA was no longer about means and ends but about contingency. New military technology no longer merely provided better methods of fighting the Red Army and thus boosting the military credibility of US Cold War aims. Now, the RMA was believed to be redefining the rules of the military game as such. While they were working together at the Pentagon, Bill Owens and Joseph Nye therefore argued that 'the information revolution' was changing the nature of power in general and of military force in particular. 'The character of US military forces is changing, perhaps much more rapidly than most appreciate,' they argued, 'for, driven by the information revolution, a revolution in military affairs is at hand.'[16] Thus mastering the technological 'means' becomes an 'end' in itself. At this point the relationship between means and ends is no longer defined by means-end rationality; rather, means and ends become conditioned by the changing nature of military force. The RMA is the condition for the US military as it enters the twenty-first century, just as the Soviet Union had been the condition for the development of US armed forces during the Cold War. In 1997, the Chairman of the Joint Chiefs, General John Shalikashvili, described the RMA as the reference point of the armed forces in much the same way as his predecessors had described the Red Army: 'warfare is changing with the growth of technological change, and we must not only stay abreast of it, but dominate it'.[17]

---

[15] Beck, 'Reinvention of Politics', 34–6.
[16] Joseph S. Nye, Jr., and William A. Owens, 'America's Information Edge', *Foreign Affairs* 75 (1996), 23.
[17] *Quadrennial Defense Review Report*, May 1997 (Washington, DC: Department of Defense, 1997), Preface.

The RMA has changed the rules regarding the programmes for which a service can obtain funding.[18] The development is quite similar to the early days of the Cold War, when the Navy and the Army were struggling to obtain funds at a time when the rules of nuclear deterrence said that conventional forces mattered little, so that most of the new funding was going to the Air Force. Now, the services have to formulate their funding requests and strategic thinking in terms of the RMA. For example, during the Cold War the US Army could always point to the number of Soviet tanks in order to argue the need for new equipment and use what was known about Soviet strategy in planning its own use of force. Now, in the absence of any 'peer competitor' like the Soviet Union against which to benchmark itself, the US Army is creating an 'objective force' as a way of benchmarking itself against the RMA.[19]

In the political world, the RMA has become one of these processes of change that politicians promise to harness for the good of their votes, like globalisation or progress in medical technology. In 2000, Vice President Al Gore told the graduates of West Point that the US military would continue to win wars only if politicians like the Vice-President himself, who was about to run for President, were able 'to transform today's armed forces into tomorrow's Information Age force'.[20] Al Gore's opponent, George W. Bush, took up the challenge by campaigning on the Clinton administration's inability to live up to the challenge of the RMA, in much the same way as his role-model, Ronald Reagan, had campaigned against President Carter's inability to maintain a strong military against the Soviet Union. At The Citadel, a military academy in Charleston, Bush spoke of 'a revolution in the technology of war', which meant that 'power is increasingly defined, not by mass or size, but by mobility and swiftness'. Building on these revolutionary changes, Bush promised that if he became president he would work to 'replace existing programs with new technologies and strategies'.[21] In the next presidential campaign, Bush's challenger, Senator John Kerry, made a similar claim: 'As President, I will build a modern military, with the best troops and the most modern equipment and

---

[18] For an overview of US defence spending after the Cold War, see Cindy Williams (ed.), *Holding the Line: US Defense Alternatives for the Early 21st Century* (Cambridge, MA: The MIT Press, 2001).
[19] United States Army, *White Paper: Concepts for the Objective Force* (2002).
[20] Al Gore, *Remarks by Vice President Al Gore, US Military Academy Commencement*, West Point, 27 May 2000, Clinton Presidential Materials Project, http://searchclinton. archives.gov/ (3 May 2004), §23.
[21] George W. Bush, *A Period of Consequences*, The Citadel, Charleston, SC, 23 September 1999, www.vote-smart.org (12 April 2005), §35, §39.

technology.'[22] Because of the US experience in Iraq, Kerry's focus was on guerrilla warfare ('fighting unconventional forces in unconventional ways'),[23] but the argument that the conditions for the use of armed force were changing and that only the Democrats could be trusted to lead the US through that transition was the mirror image of the sitting president's argument when he was campaigning for the presidency four years earlier.

When Donald Rumsfeld became Secretary of Defense in 2001, the term 'RMA' seemed a somewhat quaint 1990s' concept that referred only to technological innovation and thus did not adequately capture how the very rationality of the use of armed force was changing in the United States. In the words of Rumsfeld's first Quadrennial Defense Review (QDR), 'transformation has intellectual, social and techno-logical dimensions'.[24] The QDR therefore refers to 'military transform-ation' rather than 'RMA', while Secretary Rumsfeld himself argues that 'we need to change not only the capabilities at our disposal but also how we think about war'.[25] But military transformation means the same thing as the RMA: the ways and means for fighting are changing. The very parameters not only of the challenges that the US military has to meet, but also of how one meets such challenges effectively are changing. Thus by embracing the concept of the RMA, the US armed forces are betting all their chips on a particular hand in the poker game of history. They do so, however, while being ahead in the game by a very large margin. With a defence budget of US$400 billion in 2004, of which 72 billion were for procurement,[26] the United States can be reasonably sure that its military might will not be surpassed any time soon. But in contrast with the 1980s, when the Reagan administration increased defence spending in order to increase the pressure on the Soviet Union, the US is not raising the stakes in order to call the opposing side's bluff. This time, it is paying to invent a whole new military game. If one can afford it, this is a quintessential strategy of government in risk society: to maintain one's ability to pursue the policies one wants to pursue by

---

[22] John Kerry, *Remarks of Senator John Kerry on Strengthening Our Military*, 3 June 2004, Independence, MO, http://johnkerry.com (4 June 2004), §34.

[23] *John Kerry for President*, http://johnkerry.com (3 May 2004).

[24] *Quadrennial Defense Review Report (QDR)*, 30 September 2001 (Washington, DC: Department of Defense, 2001), 29.

[25] Donald Rumsfeld, *21st Century Transformation of US Armed Forces*, National Defense University, Fort McNair, Washington, DC, Thursday 31 January 2002 (Washington, DC: Department of Defense, 2002), §56.

[26] International Institute for Strategic Studies, *The Military Balance 2003–2004* (Oxford: Oxford University Press, 2004), 233.

trying to manage change. Thus the QDR of 2001 stated that 'managing risks is a central element of the defense strategy'.[27]

The RMA provides a rationale for how the development of information technology is transforming one of the three elements of strategy: technology. As such, the RMA debate shows how strategy is being used to rationalise new means of using armed force, but the debate also shows that these means are not related to ends in the modern, Weberian understanding of the term. The belief in the RMA process makes thinking in terms of means and ends increasingly difficult. The focus on the RMA turns technological means into ends in themselves. Thus the US is ending up in an arms race with itself. In this way, the RMA has provided the conceptual background for how to deal with the risks of introducing new military technology.

In this section I have described how the RMA is managed in terms of political and military planning, but how are the new RMA weapons and strategies to be used, and how is this influencing the rational conception of strategy? This is the subject of the next section.

Strategic management

'Everything in war is very simple,' Carl von Clausewitz noted, 'but the simplest thing is difficult.'[28] In one of the greatest passages in *On War*, Clausewitz takes his reader on a trip from the edge of the battlefield to its centre to show how the reality of warfare distorts reason. As you move closer to the centre of the battle, Clausewitz explains, the volume of bullets and cannon-fire increases until 'the air is filled with bullets that sound like a sharp crack if they pass close to one's head'.[29] It becomes more and more difficult to move and keep a rational mind clear of fear and anxiety. The situation takes over the war plan. The soldier is no longer a means implementing a political end, but a frightened human being who is struggling to maintain his ability to act rather than to follow his instincts and hide the best he can. Thus, as Clausewitz describes it, the essence of battle is not about fighting, but about maintaining your ability to fight.

For most of the twentieth century, military training evolved around the question of how to turn recruits into people who could kill. Many people simply cannot operate in stressful combat operations. During the Second World War, a survey of American soldiers in the Pacific concluded that, when they were engaging the enemy, no more than

---

[27] *QDR* 2001, 57.   [28] Clausewitz, *On War*, 119.   [29] Ibid., 113.

25 per cent of soldiers actually fired their weapons, and those who did were often operating larger weapons at some distance from the enemy.[30] Clausewitz knew that 'it is an exceptional man who keeps his powers of quick decision intact if he has never been through this experience before'.[31] From his perspective, soldiering was the ultimate test of Prussian discipline and Protestant ethics. The soldier proves his worth by remaining rational, by not giving in to emotion but maintaining his means-end rational focus on the objective.[32] Still, bullets are only one of the many factors that make a battle a situation in which, in Clausewitz' words, 'the light of reason is refracted in a manner quite different from that which is normal in academic speculation'.[33] Terrain, weather, logistics and other factors add to the 'fog of war' that holds back the 'the light of reason'. Clausewitz termed it 'friction', and he argued that friction makes warfare like walking in water: the simple tasks of battle are extremely difficult to execute.[34] Napoleon described such friction in his *Military Maxims*:

A general never knows anything with certainty, never sees his enemy clearly and never knows positively where he is. When armies meet, the least accident of terrain, the smallest wood, hides a portion of the army. The most experienced eye cannot state whether he sees the entire army or only three quarters of it . . . The general never knows the field of battle on which he may operate. His understanding is that of inspiration; he has no positive information; data to reach a knowledge of localities are so contingent on events that almost nothing is learned by experience.[35]

What if one could lift this 'fog of war'? Then one could precisely identify and destroy the enemy's centre of gravity. One could make war simple for oneself and extremely difficult for the enemy. But first and foremost one could overcome the factors that make war irrational. Lifting the fog of war would enable the 'light of reason' to shine on war, making it possible to implement a plan and thus make war a true instrument of politics.

This is the strategic ambition of the RMA. By 'vastly reducing the fog of war',[36] the then Secretary of Defense William Cohen argued in

---

[30] The survey's findings have been the subject of some controversy: see Joanna Bourke, *An Intimate History of Killing: Face-to-Face Killing in Twentieth-Century Warfare* (London: Granta Publications, 1999), 75–6.
[31] Clausewitz, *On War*, 113.
[32] Ibid., 113–14.
[33] Ibid., 113.
[34] Ibid., 120.
[35] Quoted in Owens, *Lifting the Fog of War*, 11.
[36] William S. Cohen, *Remarks as Prepared for Delivery Secretary of Defense William S. Cohen National Defense University Joint Operations Symposium QDR Conference*, Fort McNair, Washington, DC, 23 June 1997 (Washington, DC: Office of Assistant Secretary of Defense (Public Affairs), 1997), www.defenselink.mil/cgi-bin/dlprint (21 July 2000), §4.

1997, information technology will enable the US armed forces 'to collect and distribute a steady flow of information to US forces throughout the battlespace, while denying the enemy the ability to do the same'.[37] Information and communication technologies enable the US military to know much more about what is going on on the battlefield than Napoleon could possibly have known. From their vantage point on some hill behind the front, even a military genius like Napoleon had to rely on his pre-made war plans and his commanders' ability to improvise. The Prussian military academy tried to convey this reality of battle to its students by making them play chess blindfold. Knowing the layout of the chessboard and the initial deployment of the pieces, the blindfolded cadets had to rely on their memory and their deductions of how the opponent was moving in order to know what was happening on the board. Only when they captured one of the other cadet's pieces or he captured one of theirs did they know where the opponent was and with what forces. The only way to play chess blindfold is to be very careful and apply your strongest pieces whenever possible, because you never know what the opposition will be.[38] For this reason, Clausewitz argued for the use of overwhelming force at a decisive point. Not knowing what lay ahead, and with less than perfect control of forces in the heat of battle, Western militaries have traditionally massed forces to overwhelm any obstacle ahead.[39]

The US military hopes that information technology can remove the blindfold from the chess-player, thus giving the player 'full-spectrum dominance'.[40] The military aims at dominating the electromagnetic spectrum as well as all the other elements of the theatre of operations. This is the guiding principle of the Joint Chiefs of Staff's *Joint Vision 2010*, which in effect states that the aim of US military operations should be to play the game of war without a blindfold while ensuring that the enemy remains blindfolded. By linking US military platforms (i.e. tanks or aircraft carriers) into 'the system of systems',[41] American forces are able to integrate existing military systems into a single information system, which will allow them 'dominant battlespace awareness'.[42] In

[37] Ibid., §11.
[38] Oliver Morton, 'The Softwar Revolution: A Survey of Defence Technology', *Economist*, 10 June 1995.
[39] Hanson, *Why the West Has Won*, 1–24.
[40] Joint Chiefs of Staff, *Joint Vision 2010* (Washington, DC: Chairman of the Joint Chiefs of Staff, 1997), 25–7.
[41] Admiral Owens developed the concept of 'the system of systems' and was instrumental in making it the guiding concept of what he terms 'the American Revolution in Military Affairs'; see Owens, *Lifting the Fog of War*.
[42] Cohen, *Remarks at National Defense University*, §10.

the Iraq war of 2003, the US forces used more than 100,000 Global Positioning System units to pinpoint the position of individual units.[43] Probably for the first time in military history, the majority of the troops actually knew where they were. This enabled them to call in precision air strikes and artillery support, thus vastly increasing the firepower of the individual unit. The widespread use of GPS also meant that the commanders knew where their forces were, which enabled them to position forces where they were actually needed. Information technology thus means that the use of force and the distribution of forces become much more precise, which in its turn means that forces deployed can be much more agile. 'Instead of relying on massed forces and sequential operations,' *Joint Vision 2010* states, 'we will achieve massed effects in other ways.'[44] By removing friction, it becomes possible to apply the right force at the right place and at the right time. It becomes possible for US forces, Cohen argued, 'to manoeuvre and engage the enemy at the times and places of our choosing throughout the entire battlespace'.[45]

For its proponents, the RMA is a way to let 'the light of reason' shine on the battlefield. By providing near-perfect information on the battlefield, information and communication technology can remove the 'irrationalities' of terrain, weather and human horror, and actually make it possible to realise the war plan. 'While friction and the fog of war can never be eliminated,' the Joint Chiefs write in *Joint Vision 2010*, 'new technology promises to mitigate their impact.'[46] To Clausewitz, means-end rationality was a guiding principle for thinking about war, not a description of actual war. The RMA can make reality as perfect as the plan. From this perspective, war is all about 'bandwidth' – how much information are you able to get from the front line, and how quickly can you communicate with your troops? General Robert Crone, who was in charge of the Pentagon's 'lessons learned' exercise following the Iraq war, argued at a news conference that bandwidth had been one of the most important factors for the effectiveness of US command and control capabilities during the Iraq war of 2003:

We had about 42 times the bandwidth in this conflict than we did in the first war [Gulf war, 1990–1]. And I say that, and a lot of guys are very impressed with what they see in these headquarters. The first thing commanders would tell you

---

[43] Seth Schiesel, 'On the Ground in Iraq, the Best Compass is in the Sky', *New York Times*, 17 April 2003.
[44] *Joint Vision 2010*, 17.
[45] Cohen, *Remarks at the National Defense University*, §10.
[46] *Joint Vision 2010*, 16.

is it's not enough. You know, 4.2 gigabytes, or whatever, is a lot. But the fact of the matter is . . . that the last tactical mile, I think people have seen the capabilities of what might be, if they had information. And we've still got problems getting down to the tip of the spear here in terms of getting information there.[47]

General Crone's remarks are yet another example of how the RMA is regarded as an end in itself. Better information points to the possibility of even better information and thus even better command and control. But at present, information is still not perfect. The units in front ('the tip of the spear') are limited in their communications by the friction of combat but, as General Crone tells the story, improving communication is only a matter of means. More bandwidth, more GPS units, better communication facilities and so on in front-line units can solve the problem and then realise the true capabilities of what Al Gore called an 'Information Age force'.

It is becoming increasingly clear in the US strategic debate, however, that while realising the full potential of the information age may make it possible to make the perfect Clausewitzian plan, a Clausewitzian plan may not be perfect for an information-rich environment. This is because, with near-perfect information, it becomes possible to fight war in a different way from that envisioned by Clausewitz. The US Marine Corps Warfighting Laboratory is following this line of thinking when it argues that 'for the last three centuries, we have approached war as a Newtonian system. That is mechanical and ordered. In fact, it is probably not. The more likely model is a complex system that is open-ended, parallel, and very sensitive to initial conditions and continued "inputs".'[48]

Clausewitz thought of war in terms of the mechanics of cause and effect; as such, the campaigns he envisioned were linear. His description of the battlefield in *On War* shows that he envisioned war in a way which could be drawn as a straight line, or a number of straight lines, on a map, showing how troops move from a jumping-off point on the periphery of the theatre to a 'centre of gravity' where a final battle settles the outcome of the war. Present-day Clausewitzians regard 'full-spectrum dominance' as a way to create the optimal environment for conducting linear operations, but, as the Marine Corps document points out, 'full-spectrum dominance' allows the US armed forces to think of the

---

[47] US Department of Defense, *News Briefing, Army Brig. General Robert W. Crone*, Washington, DC, 2 October 2003, http://defenselink.mil (2 October 2003), §28.

[48] Quoted in Steven Metz, *Armed Conflict in the 21st Century: The Information Revolution and Post-Modern Warfare* (Carlisle, PA: Strategic Studies Institute, US Army War College, 2000), 34.

battlefield as a four-dimensional 'box'. Within such a box, the general's battle plan can no longer be drawn as a straight line. In other words, wars are no longer directed by a number of officers crouched around a map. The American headquarters' operations room during the Iraq war of 2003 was dominated by a wall of screens which served to make it easier for staff officers to comprehend the data from many different dimensions of the battle at the same time. This illustrates how the RMA is forcing strategists to leave linear thinking in favour of thinking of the battlefield as a box. A linear plan enables you to operate only in one dimension, taking one decision at a time as your advancing forces encounter one problem at a time. In the box of battle, commanders experience events simultaneously in real time. They also experience what is happening behind the enemy's position at places where their units are not yet engaged in combat. In such a situation, strategy is no longer about taking the facts of the battlefield into consideration and then coming up with a plan. With near-perfect information, you do not think in such linear ways but perceive the totality of the battlespace, and it is this totality, the system of battle, which becomes the focus of strategy. This was the point of departure for Colonel John Warden when he used his plan for the Gulf war air operations as the template for how to fight future RMA wars. Warden argued that military strategy should not focus on engaging the enemy's forces but on 'paralysing' the enemy.

> The idea of paralysis is quite simple. If the enemy is seen as a system, we need to identify those parts of the system which we can affect in such a way as to prevent the system from doing something we don't want it to do. The best place to start is normally at the center for if we can prevent the system's leadership from gathering, processing, and using information we don't want him to have, we have effectively paralyzed the system at a strategic level.[49]

The idea of 'paralysis' as the guiding strategic principle shows how war, in Warden's terms, is about management. Warden does not want to achieve victory by annihilating the enemy; rather, the enemy's ability to command and control are to be destroyed by achieving 'full-spectrum dominance', resulting in the enemy's system of governance being in effect taken over until he has no choice but to comply. In order to achieve this, Warden argues that operations should be parallel rather than linear.

From the Air Force colonel's point of view this is the ultimate argument for strategic bombing, and to the politicians it seemed like a recipe

---

[49] John Warden, 'Air Theory for the Twenty-first Century', in Barry R. Schneider and Lawrence E. Grinter (eds.), *Battlefield of the Future: 21st Century Warfare Issues*, The Air War College Studies in National Security (Maxwell Air Force Base, AL: Air War College, 1995).

for cheap victories using air power alone. The NATO air campaign against Serbia in 1999 may be regarded as a partially successful attempt to implement such a strategy. President Clinton explained to the American people on 24 March 1999, when the bombing of Serbian targets began, that the purpose was to paralyse the Serbs' ability to pursue their current genocidal policies in Kosovo and leave them no other option but to accept NATO's demands. 'In short,' the President concluded, 'if President Milosevic will not make peace, we will limit his ability to make war.'[50] Paralysing the Serbian leadership proved difficult, however. What made NATO prevail in the end was the warning of a full-scale ground invasion and, perhaps more importantly, diplomatic pressure on Russia to lean on its friends in Belgrade, as well as the fact that NATO's full-spectrum dominance enabled the Kosovo Albanian insurgents to operate much more effectively against Serb forces. Using full-spectrum dominance to degrade the enemy while strengthening the hand of the local opposition was a method employed much more systematically in Afghanistan. In Kosovo, by contrast, NATO was reluctant to become the 'air force of the Kosovo Liberation Army'.[51] In Afghanistan, American commanders soon realised that they had to become the air force of the Northern Alliance if air power and the strategic dominance it gave the US were to have any effect on the ground.[52] Thus the US introduced a new component into the Kosovo model: special forces working closely with Afghan warlords as forward air-controllers and as a boost to their fighting power.[53]

However, Colonel Warden's general point is about much more than the use of air power. What made him the guru of cadets at military academies worldwide when he left the Air Force in favour of a career as a consultant and lecturer was the way in which his approach to battle as a system suggested a method of managing battle that permitted

---

[50] William Jefferson Clinton, *Statement by the President to the Nation*, 24 March 1999 (Washington, DC: The White House, Office of the Press Secretary, 1999), §14. See also, Wesley K. Clark, *Waging Modern War: Bosnia, Kosovo and the Future of Conflict* (New York: Public Affairs, 2001).

[51] For a description of how the alliance began the campaign by relying on air power alone, but increasingly came to appreciate the value of the Kosovo insurgents, see Dana Priest, 'A Decisive Battle That Never Was', *Washington Post*, Sunday 19 September (1999), A01.

[52] For an analysis of the US campaign in Afghanistan, see Anthony H. Cordesman, *The Ongoing Lessons of Afghanistan: Warfighting, Intelligence, Force Transformation, and Nation-building* (Washington, DC: Center for Strategic and International Studies, 2004).

[53] This is not to say that special forces were not used in Kosovo, but in Afghanistan such forces were used in larger numbers and in combat roles together with Afghan fighters, rather than exclusively as forward air-controllers.

the integration of political and military considerations. A linear, Clause-witzian approach would distinguish sharply between military means and political ends. The RMA makes this distinction increasingly impossible because the best strategy has become one of changing the conditions for conducting military operations, rather than attack-ing the operations actually being carried out by the enemy. The US Defense Review of 2001 reflects this consideration in stating that 'US defense strategy and doctrine are increasingly dependent upon information and decision superiority.'[54] The winner of a campaign is the side that can increase its options for political and military operations, while the loser is the side for which options decrease in the course of the campaign. Warden puts it this way: 'Contrary to Clausewitz, destruction of the enemy is not the essence of war; the essence of war is convincing the enemy to accept your position, and fighting his military forces is at best a means to an end and at worst a total waste of time and energy.'[55]

RMA technology makes combat itself almost banal from a strategic perspective. As Robert Leonhard puts it: 'the actual destruction of detected targets becomes a fait accompli'.[56] What matters are the avail-ability of targets and the consequences of hitting them. In a battle between 'RMA combatants', the real fight will be for the control of information systems, such as GPS, as the forces will position themselves for a battle that will be over moments after the opposing platforms identify one another. For this reason, Martin Libicki argues that the only way to fight a symmetrical RMA battle is to engage in 'pop-up warfare', where forces operate like minefields, hiding until the moment when they can be used. However, at that moment they make themselves known and will therefore surely be taken out shortly afterwards.[57] The high kill rate will be a strong argument for taking as many soldiers as far away from the front line as possible, leaving the actual fighting to remote-controlled platforms. Such autonomous weapons platforms, capable of making tactical decisions, will probably be technologically feasible by the 2030s.[58] They will also be cheaper and much more expendable than soldiers and their traditional fighting platforms like tanks. Thus RMA attrition will not be about 'bleeding the enemy white', but rather about destroying the enemy's system of systems. Because

---

[54] QDR 2001, 37.
[55] Warden, 'Air Theory for the Twenty-first Century'.
[56] Robert R. Leonhard, The Principles of War in the Information Age (Novato, CA: Presido Press, 1998), 20.
[57] Martin Libicki, The Mesh and the Net: Speculations on Armed Conflict in an Age of Free Silicon, McNair Paper 28 (Washington, DC: National Defense University, 1994), 12.
[58] JDCC, Strategic Trends, 4:11.

networked systems can reconstitute themselves in countless numbers of ways, the only available way to conduct operations will be to eliminate as many of the enemy's platforms as possible, thus gradually reducing the information input and decision output of his system.

Thus the RMA will eventually reintroduce attrition as a central element in Western warfare. This may seem paradoxical, given the many people who have argued that the RMA has actually saved the West's ability to fight wars because technology is allowing the United States and others to achieve military victory without paying a price in blood that they were no longer prepared to pay.[59] When considering the operations of the American 'RMA forces', this may seem even more paradoxical. The American advance on Baghdad in the spring of 2003 was much faster than the German advance on Moscow in 1941 or the Allied liberation of northern France and Belgium in 1944.[60] Certainly US forces moved about a lot, but they did not manoeuvre in relation to another armed formation. In 2003 as in 1991, the Iraqi forces remained passive, so from the Iraqi point of view the wars of 2003 and 1991 were wars of attrition, not wars of manoeuvre. In this sense, RMA technology seems to offer the same initial results that improved logistics and firepower gave the European powers before the First World War. When used in Africa and Asia, the machine gun and the railway gave European armies a decisive advantage exactly because they had more firepower and mobility than their opponents, but when the European powers turned the new military technology against each other, the result was not wars of manoeuvre, as the generals' colonial experience had taught them, but a war of attrition.[61]

During the First World War, technology did not allow attrition to take place without large-scale slaughter: 300,000 French soldiers died in the battle of Verdun, this being the price that France had to pay to show Germany that it was not possible for her to mount an offensive that could end the war on terms favourable to her. But in the long run the French forces could not stomach the high casualty-rates, and in May 1917, 54 of the 110 French divisions on the Western Front refused to obey orders. As John Keegan explains, discussing the mutiny, the French soldiers were no longer prepared to go over the top when their odds of returning alive were less than 50 per cent.[62]

---

[59] For example, Jeremy Black, *War in the New Century* (London: Continuum, 2001), 97.

[60] John Keegan, *The Iraq War* (London: Hutchinson, 2004), 186.

[61] Coker, *War and the 20th Century*, 5–6. See also Brian Bond, *War and Society in Europe 1870–1970* (London: Fontana, 1998), 13–134.

[62] John Keegan, *The Face of Battle: A Study of Agincourt, Waterloo and the Somme* (London: Pimlico, 1991), 271.

This was also true on the German side. Only people like Ernest Jünger, who was fascinated by the dangers of war, were prepared to risk going to the enemy's trenches with little prospect of returning.[63] Thus the First World War gave birth to some of the first special forces, when the Germans organised stormtroopers from the very few men in the ranks who were actually able to operate in the geography of attrition marked out by the trenches. People like Jünger will remain on the battlefield. In future RMA wars, however, special forces will be special not because they fight in special ways, as is now the case, but because they will be the only ones actually fighting as traditional infantry, since they will be needed for raiding nodes in the enemy's network and directing precision munitions. But the rest of the army will be far behind the lines because, on an RMA battlefield, the chances of survival will be far less than 50 per cent. As already mentioned, this will make it necessary to remove most human beings from the battlefield in favour of remote-controlled, or perhaps even automatic, platforms.

Pop-up warfare may suggest that, while actual battles between RMA combatants may be short, the future campaigns will not be short. In order not to risk the destruction of one's forces all at once, 'pop-up warfare' will be a game of hide and seek, for which reason it will probably take much longer than one expects from the speed at which the computer-guided platforms operate. Paul Virilio argues that, 'in the modern arsenal, everything moves faster and faster'.[64] While it is true that military technology makes it possible to strike incredibly fast, it is also true that, when it becomes possible for both sides in an engagement to move fast, then speed loses its inherent value. In fact it is probably true that, during the twentieth century, speed was the key to victory: to be first at a decisive point or be the first to be able to mobilise. In the twenty-first century, victory is more likely to fall to the side that can wait patiently when the other side rushes to battle. The key to victory in 'pop-up warfare' is to manage one's forces in a way that makes it possible to paralyse one's enemy at the right time.

If campaigns are to consist of sudden moments of fast and furious combat in between long waiting games, the political elements of warfare will become an even more integrated part of how combatants are seeking to manage the war. To influence the enemy and his population's

---

[63] Thomas Nevin, 'Ernest Jünger: German Stormtrooper Chronicler', in Hugh Cecil and Peter H. Liddle (eds.), *Facing Armageddon: The First World War Experienced* (London: Leo Cooper, 1996), 269–77.
[64] Paul Virilio, 'Military Space', James Der Derian (ed.), *The Virilio Reader* (Malden, MA: Blackwell, 1998), 23.

perception of what is actually happening on the battlefield will be of crucial importance. Once most of the soldiers are withdrawn from the battlefield, most of the reporters will remain far behind the lines, and the armed forces will be even better able to guide the news stream than is the case today. We will probably be fed more live combat scenes, but the narrative in which that information is placed will be more carefully managed, because much of the political dimension of the battle will be to persuade the enemy, as well as your own people, that the battle is being managed successfully.

While pop-up warfare is the logical consequence of the current strategies and technologies of the RMA, American forces are not yet faced with an RMA-equipped enemy. Today the US easily achieves what will be the most contested area of a RMA battlefield: full-spectrum dominance. In so-called asymmetrical encounters with non-RMA enemies the focus is on the actual engagements, which will be treated almost as an afterthought in a pure RMA battle. And as this will be the case in future battles, the ability to ensure full-spectrum dominance by the US armed forces makes the outcome of the campaign itself a foregone conclusion. For this reason, the political elements of the parallel strategy described by Warden are the most important at present. A failure to realise this made the Bush administration embark on war against Iraq in 2003 without the political support of the UN, many of its key European allies and the Arab world. While such political support was unnecessary for the US to prevail against the Iraqi army, it soon became clear after the fighting stopped that the inability to secure key international support meant that the Americans and their British allies had very few options for how to proceed with the post-war reconstruction of Iraq. Furthermore, their political isolation made their rule in Iraq far more vulnerable than it would otherwise have been to attempts by Iraqi insurgents to undercut the occupying powers' authority. President Bush could thus triumphantly declare 'major combat operations' (that is, the invasion of Iraq) a success in May 2003,[65] only to realise later that a successful invasion had not given the US decision-superiority in Iraq. Instead it had increased the international pressure for an equally swift handover of power to an Iraqi government, which produced a timetable that insurgents could all too easily exploit.

[65] George W. Bush, *President Bush Announces Major Combat Operations in Iraq Have Ended*, Remarks by the President from the USS *Abraham Lincoln* At Sea Off the Coast of San Diego, California, 1 May 2003 (Washington, DC: The White House, Office of the Press Secretary, 2003).

To sum up, initially the RMA was seen as a way to, in Clausewitz' words, lift 'the fog of war' and let the 'light of reason' shine on to the battlefield. However, as Ulrich Beck points out, when a total means-end rational approach becomes possible, it breaks down and becomes a theme and a problem in itself. The perfect Clausewitzian plan is simply not perfect in the strategic environment created by the RMA. In this multidimensional strategic environment, the strict division of labour between political ends and military means that Clausewitz set up is replaced by a focus on creating contingencies that increase the scope of political and military action for oneself while decreasing the options for the enemy. John Warden thus writes of 'paralysis' as the aim of warfare rather than the destruction of the enemy's forces, which is what Clausewitz had in mind. The new generation of RMA strategists is not focusing on making war perfect, but on making a new kind of war.

A new kind of strategy

Will the RMA change warfare? Colin Gray is adamant that technology changes the form, not the substance, of war:

> The history of warfare is replete with examples of prophets who saw war chariots, the stirruped cavalryman, the crossbow, gunpowder firearms (personal) and field artillery, the machine gun, the airplane, the tank, the atomic bomb and the hydrogen bomb – to pick a few – as the absolute, decisive and final weapon (system).[66]

While Gray is right to castigate the 'Wired magazine version of the RMA', his argument makes one wonder whether asking if the RMA will change war is the wrong question to put. The question should be whether the concept of a revolution in the technologies of war has led Western armed forces to rethink strategy.

Following the war in Afghanistan, Defense Secretary Donald Rumsfeld became very fond of referring to the battle of Mazar-e-Sharif on 9 November 2001. The battle involved American aircraft bombing Taliban positions in the town of Mazar-e-Sharif with advanced munitions guided to their target by special forces on the ground. The special forces were guiding the most sophisticated ordnance, while the American soldiers were fighting on horseback with their Afghan allies in what Secretary Rumsfeld likes to refer to as 'the first cavalry attack of the 21st century'.[67] As such, Secretary Rumsfeld believes the battle of Mazar-e-Sharif to be

---

[66] Colin S. Gray, *Explorations in Strategy* (Westport, CT: Greenwood, 1996), 240.
[67] Rumsfeld, *21st Century Transformation*, §11.

a 'transformational battle'.[68] This term is a very important part of the RMA literature, in which battles serve to date and illustrate the decisive advantages of new technologies or doctrines.[69] In the paper that inaugurated the discourse on RMA, Andrew Marshall compared the Gulf war to the first use of tanks in the battle of Cambrai during the First World War.[70] To Rumsfeld, the battle of Mazar-e-Sharif taught a similar lesson in military transformation: 'It showed that a revolution in military affairs is about more than building high tech weapons, though that is certainly part of it. It's also about ways of thinking, and new ways of fighting.'[71]

At Mazar-e-Sharif, US forces did in fact use stirruped cavalry as well as precision-guided munitions. Thus it was not the case that technology delivered a super weapon firing silver bullets, of the sort that Gray mentions; rather, information and communication technologies enabled US forces to combine different ways of fighting in a new strategy. General Richard Myers, Chairman of the Joint Chiefs of Staff, made a similar point following the Iraq war: 'the equipment is the equipment we have had for years. But the difference is how well integrated all the capabilities of the services are in this case.'[72]

Strategy is a way to rationalise the application of modern technology to warfare. It is with this tradition in mind that Gray castigates the belief in information and communication technologies revolutionising warfare, and he and other critics are right that most people started out regarding the RMA, as many still do, as a way to produce the perfect means-end rational war. From this perspective, the RMA is a case of what Jeremy Black calls 'machinism'.[73] But rationalisation is a process in which technological development and the strategic understanding of the application of that technology to warfare continuously interact. This chapter has described this process and thus shown how the RMA does not produce the perfect Clausewitzian war because information technology creates a systemic view of warfare that does not support means-end rationality. The process of rationalisation simply leads to a new rationality of war. Strategy becomes focused on managing the

---

[68] Ibid., §18.
[69] Richard O. Hundley, *Past Revolutions, Future Transformations: What Can the History of Revolutions in Military Affairs Tell Us About Transforming the US Military?* (Santa Monica, CA: RAND, 1999); MacGregor Knox and Williamson Murray (eds.), *The Dynamics of Military Revolution, 1300-2050* (Cambridge: Cambridge University Press, 2001).
[70] Marshall, *Some Thoughts on Military Revolutions*, 3.
[71] Rumsfeld, *21st Century Transformation*, §15.
[72] Quoted in Anthony H. Cordesman, *The Iraq War: Strategy, Tactics, and Military Lessons* (Westport, CT: Praeger, 2003), 57.
[73] Black, *War in the New Century*, 97.

multiple risks of war instead of realising the plan for a strike at a single, decisive point. At this point the RMA is no longer a question of technology. Cavalry, tanks and stealth bombs are all understood within a new strategic framework, in which case it does not matter whether the technology is new, because every weapon system can be used in a new context.

Once RMA strategy opens new possibilities for the use of old as well as new weapons systems, a very important aspect of strategy becomes predicting what will be possible next. It is this problematic to which I turn now.

The presence of the future

Generals are traditionally blamed for fighting the last war; today they are fighting the next war before it has even happened. The constant development of new technologies and new strategies that constitute the RMA means that not even the US military can be sure what it takes to prevail in battle. Since the first Gulf war, the US armed forces have evaluated their performance not only to learn what they did right and what could be improved, but also to ascertain whether the deployment of new weapons or strategies has provided a glimpse of the wars of the future. The utility of a weapons system is thus evaluated not only, perhaps not even primarily, on its performance in the actual conflicts of the day; technology is also evaluated in terms of whether it fits the image of the wars of tomorrow. Even though field artillery actually played an important part in the US offensive in Iraq in 2004,[74] the Pentagon cancelled an order for a new artillery system because it did not fit the image of the 'pop-up wars' of the future.[75]

The risk literature points out that the way technological innovation makes the perceived demands of the future determine present action is by no means limited to the armed forces.

Below I deal first with how defence planning is being transformed to deal with 'an uncertain future'. Secondly I argue that, by making belief in the RMA the premise for defence planning, the US is focusing on the possibility that the RMA might actually place US military superiority at risk because it might empower a 'peer competitor'. While the US is trying to defeat such a peer before it ever materialises, the US focus

---

[74] Williamson Murray and Robert H. Scales Jr, *The Iraq War* (Cambridge, MA: The Belknap Press, 2003), 263–5; Cordesman, *The Iraq War*, 358–62.
[75] Tim Weiner, 'Drive to Build High-Tech Army Hits Cost Snags', *New York Times*, 28 March 2005.

on realising the military of tomorrow is making current military cooperation in NATO increasingly difficult, because the military technology of the Europeans is becoming increasingly old-fashioned compared to that of the United States.

It's about the future: capability-based defence planning

'These capabilities are not drawn from the "X-files" or Starship Enterprise,' Defense Secretary Cohen said in 1997, when describing what the RMA could do for the US armed forces.[76] Science fiction is a recurrent theme in the debate about the RMA. This is not only because the RMA is realising technologies hitherto seen only in movies or described on the pages of sci-fi novels. The most important reason for invoking science fiction is not the science component of the genre, but the fiction itself. Anthony Giddens argues that 'a risk society is a society where we increasingly live on a high technological frontier which absolutely no one completely understands and which generates a diversity of possible futures'.[77] Science fiction is about gazing beyond the technological frontier and describes a possible future that will come into being if one or more technological innovations are made. It is this ability to imagine what the future might bring which becomes an essential part of strategy at the moment one accepts that technology is going to change war-making capabilities. Only by imagining what the future of battle might be is it possible to implement an RMA; therefore a RAND report argues that 'military institutions must be willing to develop a *vision* of how war may change in the future, or they are incapable of developing RMAs'.[78]

The need to imagine what might happen is even more pivotal when it comes to assessing what one's enemies might be up to. Following a Japanese cult's attack on passengers in the Tokyo subway with chemical weapons in 1995, President Clinton turned to the fiction of Tom Clancy and other popular novelists in order to think through what might happen if the United States was subjected to a similar attack, and he sent the books to his anti-terrorist team for comments.[79] No doubt a lot of people with PhDs in international security or strategy will look down their noses when people in high office use popular fiction

---

[76] Cohen, *Remarks at National Defense University*, §17.
[77] Anthony Giddens, 'Risk Society: The Context of British Politics', in Jane Franklin (ed.), *The Politics of Risk Society* (Cambridge: Polity Press, 1998), 25.
[78] Hundley, *Past Revolutions, Future Transformations*, 33.
[79] Richard A. Clarke, *Against All Enemies: Inside America's War on Terror* (New York: The Free Press, 2004), 162–3.

as the basis for policy, but in the context of 'risk society' it actually makes a lot of sense. In a series of bestselling novels, Tom Clancy has made standard national security scenarios come to life by placing them in a narrative form. A Clancy novel is basically a RAND report written in the style of a thriller. Though his work is not science fiction in the strict sense, Clancy has used Stealth bombers, Predator drones and other new military technologies in his books before they became fully operational or widely known to the public. Thus the narrative of the novel provides a possibility to see how the use of RMA technology will play out, just as Clancy's scenarios for a terrorist attack on the US with nuclear or chemical weapons served as a way to show President Clinton what could happen.[80] Clancy's novels are what Giddens describes as 'risk-profiling', which is what insurance companies undertake to calculate the odds on a house burning down as a basis for pricing an insurance policy. Luckily chemical attacks on civilians are a lot less common than houses burning down, but for this very reason the risk-profiling of such events is all the harder. Fiction is one way of making up for the lack of data.

Fiction makes possible futures real in a way the more dry narratives of intelligence services and military planners cannot. But the political skill needed to operate on the basis of such scenarios is akin to the skills of science-fiction authors: you must be able to imagine a future reality as if it were already real. In Ulrich Beck's words, the future becomes a 'real virtuality'.[81] From that point of view, defence planning in the United States, and increasingly in other NATO countries as well, is now science fiction. Of course, military planners do not call their work science fiction, but 'capability-based defence planning'. This approach focuses on *how* an adversary might fight rather than who that adversary might be or where he might want to engage in battle.[82] The 2001 QDR argued that a capability-based approach to defence planning would involve the United States in 'identifying capabilities that US military forces will need to deter and defeat adversaries who will rely on surprise, deception and asymmetric warfare to achieve their objectives'.[83] While US military power is very real, to those thinking in terms of RMA, the prospect of the enemies of the US developing new capabilities to attack the US is equally real. From this point of view, the US Defense Department argued, one cannot base military planning on the capabilities

[80] Tom Clancy describes a biological attack on the United States as part of an attempt to challenge US power in his *Executive Orders* (London: HarperCollins, 1996).
[81] Beck, *World Risk Society*, 136.   [82] *QDR* 2001, 13.   [83] Ibid., 14.

actually available to a specific adversary at present; one must shift focus to the future:

The shift is intended to refocus planners on the growing range of capabilities that adversaries might possess or could develop. It will require planners to define the military objectives associated with defeating aggression or coercion in a variety of potential scenarios in addition to conventional cross-border invasions.[84]

The Defense Department argues that scenarios are to 'bridge' the present and the future.[85] Basing scenarios on capabilities rather than intentions means that most of the 'bridges' lead to futures of danger. First of all, RMA technologies are based on developments in the civilian sector. It is Microsoft rather than some secret government laboratory that is developing the new information and communication technologies being used in the RMA. This means that in principle any society in the front line of industrialisation can also use RMA technology at the front line in warfare. Thus Indian or Chinese industrialisation, or the industrialisation of any other potential great power, turns out to be a cause of concern when one bases one's defence planning on scenarios and scenarios on capabilities. But it is not only new RMA capabilities that produce scenarios of danger. Jeremy Black is probably right that, at least at present, the spread of 'established technologies' is more important for future security than new RMA technologies.[86] The main reason for this is that the technology needed to develop chemical weapons and even nuclear bombs is becoming increasingly easier for nations in the second or third divisions of industrialisation to handle.

By focusing on capabilities, defence planners may therefore fall into a 'pre-emptive trap'. Any technological development may come to constitute a potential danger. This will make it almost impossible to control military spending because any potential capability which one's enemies might acquire needs to be countered by procuring a new capability for one's own forces. Furthermore, the focus on capabilities may make adversaries look more hostile than they would otherwise appear. This diverts attention away from the question of whether a government will in fact use its capabilities. If it is assumed that any capability will eventually be used, then attention inevitably turns to military options for destroying this capability rather than the political and diplomatic conditions under which use would cease to be necessary. Military planners and their political masters know very well that these dangers exist, but they feel they need to risk them in order to be able to keep pace with the revolution in military affairs.

---

[84] Ibid., 17.   [85] Ibid., 18.   [86] Black, *War in the New Century*, 64.

Peers?

When Andrew Marshall wrote his paper on the RMA, it was not only to award laurels to US technological superiority. On the contrary, the main message Marshall wanted to convey was that the US had opened up a Pandora's box by beginning on the RMA. 'A lesson for us', Marshall wrote, 'is that early leaders can easily lose out.'[87] The British had pioneered tank warfare but failed to follow on their invention with the development of new technologies and doctrines, leaving it to the Germans to come up with *Blitzkrieg*. This concern for what the RMA holds in store for the future of US military dominance is clear in the RAND definition of it, which has become the standard definition used directly or indirectly in most US government publications on the subject: 'An RMA involves a paradigm shift in the nature and conduct of military operations which either renders obsolete or irrelevant one or more core competencies of a dominant player or creates one or more new core competencies or both.'[88]

In American think tanks and government departments, people fear that the RMA will lead them into what the risk literature would identify as a 'risk trap'. Like the British in the interwar years, the United States will invent technologies that will be turned against them. One example of this is the GPS system that gives the US armed forces the ability to operate so effectively on the battlefield. However, the GPS system is also a global public good, and the civilian version of GPS has made it possible for China to make the guidance systems on their nuclear missiles 20–25 per cent more accurate. It is expected that new guidance systems based on GPS will make future Chinese missiles up to 70 per cent more accurate than the pre-GPS missiles.[89] By inventing GPS, the United States has made itself much more vulnerable to Chinese nuclear missiles, this being a consequence of the decision to pursue the RMA. The US Defense Department thus identifies the very technologies the department wants the US military to develop as a potential danger: 'Technologies for sensors, information processing, precision guidance, and many other areas are rapidly advancing. This poses the danger that states hostile to the US could significantly enhance their capabilities by integrating widely available off-the-shelf technologies into their weapons systems and armed forces.'[90]

---

[87] Marshall, *Some Thoughts on Military Revolutions*, 5.
[88] Hundley, *Past Revolutions, Future Transformations*, xiii.
[89] Zalmay Khalilzad et al., *The United States and a Rising China* (Santa Monica, CA: RAND, 1999), 44.
[90] *QDR 2001*, 6.

What at present is a US advantage may thus turn into a future challenge to US power. Thus RMA becomes a competition which the US must win – not because anyone can challenge the US at present, but because the scenario that China or some other emerging power might be able to challenge the US becomes a 'real virtuality'. In 2002, the Bush administration thus made it a national security priority to 'build and maintain our defenses beyond challenge'.[91]

Of course, US military planners would rather avoid other armed forces having the RMA capabilities that the US has. This would lead to symmetrical battles, which probably would make the costs of war much higher to the United States than is the case today. The US has reason to be confident, however, that it would be able to stay ahead in technological innovation and develop superior strategies for any 'RMA battle' it will have to fight. What really scares US military planners is the prospect that another power may revolutionise warfare in ways that the United States has not thought of, thus rendering US military power obsolete. The Joint Chiefs of Staff write: 'Our most vexing future adversary may be one who can use technology to make rapid improvements in its military capabilities that provide asymmetrical counters to US military strengths, including information technologies.'[92] In risk terms, the United States fears that another power would reject competition with the US altogether and opt for a scenario of its own imagination.

Since the RMA is driven by civilian technological innovation, the US fears that high-growth economies like China might make a breakthrough in, for example, nanotechnology that will constitute a completely new RMA. If the Chinese economy grows at its present rate, Chinese defence spending is expected to reach US$100 billion in 2030. This will still be only a third of what the United States expects to spend, but it will be twice what Britain and France are likely to spend.[93] This places China on the top of the US's list of possible 'peer competitors', but how does the US best deal with the risk of China challenging the US lead in the RMA? One way could be to do to China what Britain did to Germany in the early twentieth century when Germany challenged British naval superiority: introduce a new class of weapons, in the British case Dreadnoughts,[94] thus preventing one's rival from just copying well-known

[91] *The National Security Strategy of the United States of America*, 17 September 2002 (Washington, DC: The White House, 2002), 29.

[92] *JV 2010*, 10–11.   [93] JDCC, *Strategic Trends*, 8:4.

[94] Holger H. Herwig, 'The Battlefleet Revolution, 1885–1914', in Knox and Murray (eds.), *The Dynamics of Military Revolution*, 114–31.

weapons designs for which one has paid the development costs, and thus making the entry costs for joining the arms race much higher. By increasing its defence spending, the United States might be said to have opted for this course. A clean slate also carries a risk to the United States, however: if it does not need to start building the weapons the US already has, China will be able to start afresh on developing RMA technology; also, because it does not have to match US systems, it will actually be able to create its own unique RMA. However, a more fundamental risk in identifying China as a peer competitor is that it may lead to a pre-emption trap. What if the increase in US armaments actually provokes a 'security dilemma', making China increase its defence spending because it fears what the US might do?[95]

The US faces great risks in managing the RMA process in relation to potential adversaries, but it also risks its relationship with its closest allies in NATO. Robbin Laird and Holger May conclude that there is a 'core tension between the strategic redesign of the US military and the requirement of reaching outward to work with allies'.[96] As noted previously, the RMA is about integrating forces in ways previously unheard of. When the US integrates its own armed forces this way, it is at the same time running the risk of disintegrating its forces from NATO, thus robbing the US of its closest allies.

For Europeans, the RMA places their ability to conduct strategy at risk because they do not have the military means to translate their policy into military action. In 1999, the Kosovo war made the Europeans realise that their strategic goals did not match their military technology. The Europeans wanted a precision air campaign and worried about the collateral damage that might be caused, but, with the exception of the British and the French, the Europeans had neither the planes nor the precision-guided munitions to carry out the campaign. Accordingly it was the US Air Force that accounted for more than 80 per cent of the sorties.[97] To many Europeans, this showed the inability of European governments to fight the wars of the twenty-first century. Following the war, France and Britain concluded that 'the crisis reinforced our conviction that

---

[95] On the 'security dilemma', see Robert Jervis, *Perception and Misperception in International Politics* (Princeton, NJ: Princeton University Press, 1976); Herbert Butterfield, *History and Human Relations* (London: Collins, 1951); John Herz, *Political Realism and Political Idealism* (Chicago, IL: Chicago University Press, 1951).

[96] Robbin F. Laird and Holger H. May, *The Revolution in Military Affairs: Allied Perspectives*, McNair Paper 60 (Washington, DC: National Defense University, 1999), 97.

[97] Anthony H. Cordesman, *Lessons and Non-Lessons of the Air and Missile Campaign in Kosovo* (Washington, DC: Center for Strategic and International Studies, 2004), 109.

the European nations need to increase their defence capabilities'.[98] Thus one crucial factor in the future of the Atlantic alliance is whether the RMA will bring the allies together or pull them apart.

Fighting the future

In 1962, President Kennedy read Barbara Tuchman's *The Guns of August*, which described how in 1914 European governments were driven to a war that none of them wanted.[99] The book taught the President a lesson that he applied during the Cuban Missile Crisis – if one tries to control events, one might just avoid war.[100] In 1995, President Clinton did not turn to history books in order to learn how to conduct his security policy. Instead, he read the fictional scenarios of future conflicts, in which new weapons are used for the first time. Cynics may say that this reflects the falling intellectual standards of presidents of the United States. Be that as it may, the preferred reading of these two Presidents suggests a shift from basing policy on the lessons of history to basing it on the lessons of the future. Of course the future cannot teach us anything because it has not yet occurred. However, our expectations of the future can be so real that they shape our actions as if future events had already occurred and left their mark on us. Furthermore, the belief that the future holds such stark dangers that they must be prevented at all costs makes it more plausible to seek to learn lessons from scenarios for the future. For better or worse, the focus on the future is probably a characteristic of a time of change in which the lessons of the past seem to have less and less to teach us.

Believing that the RMA will change the parameters of conflict in the future, US defence planners, along with those in other NATO countries, are turning to a 'capability-based approach' to defence planning. This focus on future capabilities is also leading to a focus on those powers that want to make an RMA of their own, thus challenging American military dominance. This focus on the future means that the RMA is becoming a risk in itself. The proliferation of new RMA technologies and older technologies, like those used to make weapons of mass destruction, seems to promise a more dangerous future for Western powers. The possibility that a 'peer competitor' like China may make

---

[98] *Joint Declaration by the British and French Governments on European Defence*, Anglo-French Summit, London, Thursday 25 November 1999.
[99] Barbara W. Tuchman, *The Guns of August* (New York: Macmillan, 1962).
[100] Graham T. Allison, *Essence of Decision: Explaining the Cuban Missile Crisis* (Boston: Little, Brown and Company, 1971), 217–18.

its very own RMA threatens an erosion of the entire basis of US military power. 'Periods of revolution are inherently unstable,' Defense Secretary Cohen observed in 1997; 'we must not, in our hubris, assume that we will be the sole vanguards of the new Revolution in Military Affairs'.[101] Being in the vanguard of the RMA might also be risky, however, because by revolutionising its armed forces, the US risks losing the ability to operate with its allies.

The RMA thus makes the future a risk, but it is a risk that cannot be avoided if one believes at the same time that the RMA is the key to military power in the future. These scenarios focus on the ability of other states to do their own RMA, but what if the most potent strategic answer to the RMA is not more RMA, but something completely different? This is the question I turn to next.

The boomerang effect

What makes the rationality of politics different in risk society is not that actions carry risk. The difference between risk society and modernity proper is the fact that in risk society the risks of action are inherent in decision-making. In other words, one acts knowing the risks of doing so: one cannot do much without risking more. This point is especially important in relation to the RMA because, seen from a means-end rational point of view, one should assume that the new weapons and strategies simply provide more capabilities for acting. These new capabilities carry their own risks, however. The risk literature terms the risks that arise from new or greater than average capabilities 'risk compensation'. An example of risk compensation is how using seat belts apparently makes driving more risky. When drivers are confident that they will be safe in an accident because of the seat belt, they tend to drive in a riskier manner. In effect, the RMA has given the West in general and the United States in particular a strategic seat belt and, as the risk literature would lead one to expect, they have used military force more often in the past fifteen years. If the United States is able to fight more wars because the risks are lower, then the best way to counter US armed force must be to take risks. The risk literature will identify this kind of behaviour as 'risk-taking', and risk-taking is in fact well known within the strategic literature as well. This part of the chapter on RMA will deal with risk compensation and risk-taking in order to show what happens when RMA is introduced into the strategic equation. We turn to risk compensation first.

---

[101] Cohen, *Remarks at National Defense University*, §36.

The RMA calculus of war

From the First World War to Vietnam, one US soldier in every fifteen died or was wounded in action. If one translates these numbers to the Iraq war of 2003, the United States should have lost 16,000 troops.[102] By 12 April 2003, when the major population centres, including Baghdad, were under US control, the American armed forces had suffered 108 dead, 399 wounded and 14 captured. This meant that 1 per 480 soldiers involved in Operation Iraqi Freedom had died, and while every death is a tragedy beyond statistics, it meant that one day of combat in Iraq carried the price of 5 lives, while one day of combat during the Second World War carried the price of 211 persons, and one in Vietnam 18 lives. While it is no doubt true that any casualty weighs heavy on the minds of the leaders who commit soldiers to combat, the prospect that 1 in 15 will be killed or wounded each day that one wages war must weigh a lot heavier than the prospect that 1 in 480 will die. Carl Conetta calls this 'a new calculus of war'.[103]

The risk literature identifies such a calculus as a case of 'risk compensation'. The risk-compensation calculus says that if the level of acceptable risk is constant, then the reduction in the risk of doing something may lead to an increase in the particular activity. For example, do studies of racing drivers show that they have more road accidents than the average motorist? One would expect the opposite: since the racing drivers are so much better at driving cars, they should have far fewer accidents than the average driver. However, John Adams argues that precisely because racing drivers are better at driving than the average person they take more chances, drive more quickly etc. – and therefore end up in more accidents. In other words, racing drivers compensate for their ability to reduce risk by taking more risks.[104] The 'RMA calculus of war' is a similar case of risk compensation. The risks of waging war are falling, which leads to more wars.

President Bush was referring to this RMA calculus of war in April 2003 when he addressed workers at the Boeing plant in St Louis, where F-18s are made: 'More than ever before, the precision of our technology is protecting the lives of our soldiers, and the lives of innocent civilians. The overwhelming majority of the munitions dropped in

---

[102] Cordesman, *The Iraq War*, 238–9. The number is based on the assumption that c. 250,000 troops were involved. See also http://icasualties.org/oif/ (13 April 2005).

[103] Carl Conetta, *The 'New Warfare' and the New American Calculus of War*, Project on Defense Alternatives, Briefing Memo No. 26, 30 September 2002, www.comw.org/ (13 May 2004).

[104] Adams, *Risk*, 54–5.

the Iraqi campaign were precision-guided. In this new era of warfare, we can target a regime, not a nation.'[105] The President was describing how civilians are protected by the precision of RMA weapons and how US troops using these weapons are even less at risk. He does not mention the enemy army, in this case the Iraqi army, and with good reason. The Iraqi army has been so unfortunate as to be subject to attack from far more advanced US forces twice in twelve years. On both occasions the Iraqi army tried to engage US forces in open battle, and on both occasions it suffered heavy losses. Carl Conetta estimates that 9,200 Iraqi combatants were killed during the war of 2003. It is difficult to say whether this number is correct, but if it is, this would mean that 85 Iraqi soldiers were killed for each American killed.[106] This emphasises the previous point about the attrition character of RMA warfare. While the Iraqi wars were perceived as wars of manoeuvre with swift results and low casualties from a US point of view, the Iraqi side had every reason to perceive them as wars of attrition in which the Iraqi army had 383 deaths per day, that is, 172 more people dead per day than the 211 deaths per day the United States suffered during the Second World War.

Martin Shaw describes this discrepancy in the new calculus of war as 'risk-transfer militarism'.[107] Now, one could argue that transferring risk to the enemy is what successful military strategy has always been about, but Shaw's point is that the United States and its allies present the new wars as risk-free when in fact the risks for Western soldiers are reduced at the expense of the soldiers and civilians of the countries being attacked. The US President does not give Iraqi military casualties, and US military briefers prefer to refer to civilians accidentally killed by American forces as 'collateral damage'. Furthermore, the US armed forces do not produce statistics on the extent of this 'collateral damage'. This leads Carl Conetta to write about the 'disappearing dead' which he estimates to be the 9,200 Iraqi combatants mentioned above as well as 3,700 Iraqi civilians.[108]

---

[105] George W. Bush, *President Bush Outlines Progress in Operation Iraqi Freedom*, Boeing Integrated Defense Systems' Headquarters, St Louis Missouri, 16 April 2003, http://whitehouse.gov (22 April 2004), §20.

[106] Carl Conetta, *The Wages of War: Iraqi Combatant and Noncombatant Fatalities in the 2003 Conflict* (Cambridge, MA: Commonwealth Institute, 2003). However, this number is far higher than Iraqi claims of 3 April 2003 cited by Cordesman as 1,252 killed and 5,103 injured; Cordesman, *The Iraq War*, 246–7.

[107] Martin Shaw, *Risk Transfer Militarism and Legitimacy of War after Iraq*, www.theglobalsite.ac.uk/press/402shaw.htm (31 October 2004). See also his *The New Western Way of War: Risk-Transfer War and Its Crisis in Iraq* (Cambridge: Polity Press, 2005).

[108] Conetta, *The Wages of War*.

Shaw and Conetta attack the view that the RMA can produce clean wars, but their argument actually shows that, far from making civilian deaths disappear, the RMA is placing civilian casualties at the centre of attention. As Anthony Cordesman argues, 'one irony behind the increased lethality of modern weapons and tactics, is that they can be used to defeat the enemy with far fewer secondary costs'. Because the USAF can pinpoint a target precisely with GPS, warplanes can drop a 500 lb bomb instead of a 2,000 lb bomb and still be certain of destroying the target.[109] This improved accuracy means that there is no longer any need to destroy a town in order to save it. At this point risk compensation sets in. Compared with the total wars of the twentieth century, and even compared with guerrilla wars like Vietnam or Afghanistan, it is almost improbably safe for civilians in the new RMA wars: civilians may be neither targeted nor regarded as regrettable but necessary 'secondary' targets, but they are still at risk. A racing driver driving fast through a village may not hit anyone, but the fact that he is driving fast still makes it dangerous for children to play by the road. The fact that the RMA allows more wars to be fought puts more civilians at risk, and inevitably these risks are realised in the killing of innocent civilians. Furthermore, the firepower of new weapons means that, when civilians are hit, they are hit very badly.

Because hitting civilians is a risk rather than a deliberate act, each case in which civilians are hit is a problem for the narrative that the United States and its allies want to produce about their wars. The irony is that the problem would not occur, or at least not occur in this way, if the United States and its allies targeted civilians deliberately as they did during the Second World War. Thus the fact that the RMA enables armed forces to avoid civilian casualties to a degree unheard of in historical terms has a 'boomerang effect' because it focuses attention on the civilians who are killed nonetheless.

In spite of the way in which civilian casualties highjack political agendas, war has become a true means of policy, as Clausewitz imagined it, to the United States because the RMA enables American armed forces to fight at very low risk to themselves, and with a very high probability of winning. Perhaps the greatest risk of war used to be that its outcome could not be predicted, and thus a government could not know whether the use of military force would blow up in its face. But in the case of the Iraq war, as Anthony Cordesman notes, 'the Coalition had so great a superiority in every area of space that Iraq's capabilities

---

[109] Cordesman, *The Iraq War*, 257.

were trivial in comparison'.[110] The United States could not fail to win. Another reason why the United States can go to war with few concerns for the outcome is the fact that the balance of power is so much in its favour that one military victory does not trigger another military challenge. By invading Iraq, the United States did not end up in the position of the Austro-Hungarian empire in 1914, which launched an operation against Serbia in which they were bound to prevail, but by doing so provoked a European war that the empire was bound to lose.

However, the RMA does not only make it easier for the United States to project military power – as RMA technology becomes more readily available and more countries invest in the logistical means to project military power, it has become easier for *anyone* to use such power. The British troops fighting alongside the Americans in Operation Iraqi Freedom had an even lower casualty rate than their American brothers-in-arms: 1 per 1,451 British soldier died in the war.[111] Such low levels of casualties make it easier for any British prime minister to commit his forces to battle, but in the particular case it also made it easier for Tony Blair to go against public opinion and many of his own backbenchers to take part in the war. However terrible the deaths of thirty-one British soldiers were, their impact was still smaller than it would have been if thousands of British troops had died.

The RMA is also making it easier for small countries to project military power. Previously, friction would have prevented small powers like Denmark and Norway from projecting military power halfway around the world. In 2003, Danish and Norwegian F-16s using precision munitions provided close air support for US special forces operating in Afghanistan. Thus a Danish white paper on defence published in August 2003 concluded that 'the rapid innovations in military technology are of crucial importance because they make it less costly and less risky to use military force'.[112]

Although it is less risky to use military force, this does not translate into a carefree attitude to casualties. As in the case of civilian casualties,

---

[110] Ibid., 196.

[111] For statistics on British and other allied casualties in Iraq, see http://icasualties.org/oif/ (13 April 2005). This figure is based on the assumption that 45,000 British troops took part in the combat phase of the Iraq war; see www.operations.mod.uk/telic/index.htm (14 May 2004). On the British war, see Keegan, *The Iraq War*, 165–82.

[112] Translated from the Danish by the author, *The Security Policy Conditions for Danish Defence*, August 2003, Royal Danish Ministry of Foreign Affairs, www.um.dk (30 September 2003), 37. The ability to project power to faraway lands emphasises the need to be able to operate with American forces. Thus the new capabilities provided by the RMA highlight the dilemmas of the smaller NATO countries when they try to keep up with US military transformations.

the technological ability to limit casualties highlights the deaths that actually do occur. The lower combat casualties mean that a much higher percentage of casualties than previously stem from mistakes made by the armed forces themselves. During the war against Iraq in 1991, 23 per cent of the US soldiers who died were killed by friendly fire.[113] Friendly fire and other causes of death that the armed forces bring on themselves are further boomerang effects of the RMA. The increased effectiveness and precision of RMA forces means that one of the greatest risks in combat is no longer the enemy but one's own comrades. Friendly fire is a particularly sensitive problem for the US's coalition partners as from time to time they find themselves at the wrong end of US guns. The integration of forces that is at the heart of the RMA is making it increasingly difficult to coordinate with allied forces but makes it increasingly easy to shoot them.

Friendly fire incidents show how the deaths of individual soldiers have become a story in their own right. When 221 soldiers die per day, the story of the individual death is lost in the crowd. The individual stories are told because they are believed to be emblematic of the fate of all. When so few soldiers die, the twenty-four-hour media has plenty of time to tell each individual story, in which case each individual death must have merit. If not, generals and politicians will be seen as having squandered the lives of their soldiers, in which case it does not matter whether it was only one solider who died and not 2,000. Thus the boomerang effects of a low casualty rate are a correspondingly increased focus on the casualties that wars still bring.

The RMA makes it easier to fight wars, but harder to justify the death and destruction that war still brings. Perhaps the greatest boomerang effect of the RMA is that it gives a false sense of security in the belief that wars are relatively cost-free. While it is undoubtedly much easier to start a war, it is still very difficult to end it. I began this section by describing how, during the invasion of Iraq in 2003, US forces lost only 108 soldiers. However, by 28 June 2004, when the US formally handed the authority of the Iraqi government over to the Iraqis, 715 more US soldiers and marines had died. From that date to 30 January 2005, when Iraqis voted in their first free election, 579 US servicemen and women died. By the end of 2005 almost 2,000 soldiers and marines had died since the end of the campaign in which the US conquered Iraq.[114] This still leaves the US with a casualty rate far below that it suffered in Vietnam, but it shows that Western forces are weakest when

---

[113] Cordesman, *The Iraq War*, 239.
[114] http://icasualties.org/oif/ (13 December 2005).

they are challenged in unconventional combat, where their technology does not give them a decisive advantage. Such counter-strategies are the next example of a RMA boomerang effect.

Risk strategies: who dares wins

War used to be risky business: a government never knew what it actually would achieve by fighting a war or what the costs of winning would add up to in the end. This was what playing chess blindfold was supposed to teach the cadets in the Prussian military academy. The strategic promise of the RMA is to reduce the risk of war and pre-empt or manage the risks that remain, thus making war a true continuation of policy. This rational calculus of strategy is based on the assumption that strategic actors seek to minimise risk. If the United States can lower its own risks when waging a campaign while increasing those of its opponents, then it has achieved an unrivalled strategic pre-eminence. However, research on both strategy and risk suggests that, while minimising risk is the strategy that most modern people regard as being most rational, taking risks may prove even more rewarding.

John Adams argues that 'excessive prudence is a problem rarely contemplated in the risk and safety literature'.[115] Adams points out that although reducing risks is, of course, a good idea, at some point new risk-reducing measures are actually just making it harder for people to do their job because the risk that the measures are trying to reduce are inherent in the job itself. Adams believes that the risk literature overlooks the fact that a lot of people like their jobs or enjoy their sports *because* they are risky.[116] The nuclear strategist Thomas Schelling pointed out that taking risks might be the most effective thing to do in a strategic environment dominated by agents who are focusing on minimising risks. In such a situation, the strategic actor prepared to maximise his risks will dramatically reduce the bargaining position of the one who is seeking to minimise risks.[117]

From the berserks to the brinkmanship of US Secretary of State John Foster Dulles, risk-taker strategies have been an important part of the strategic landscape, but they have more scope today because Western strategy in general and US strategy in particular is based on minimising risks. Thus risk-taker strategies are the antithesis of the perfect

---

[115] Adams, *Risk*, 55.   [116] Ibid., 65–6.
[117] T. C. Schelling, 'The Retarded Science of International Strategy', *Midwest Journal of Political Science* 4 (May 1960), 128–9.

Clausewitzian war, and as such central for an understanding of the strategic practice that the RMA will produce.

Few have described risk-taker strategies better than Colonels Qiao Liang and Wang Xiangsui of the Chinese People's Liberation Army. Their work entitled *Unrestricted Warfare* serves the same intellectual purpose as *On War* did for Clausewitz. From the point of view of the elites in the Third World, the United States' victory in the Gulf war of 1990–1 sent a message as clear as that which Napoleon sent the European *anciens régimes* at Jena: either you adapt to the new ways of politics and economics that gave us this victory, or you will be dominated in the new age at hand.[118] After Jena, Clausewitz set out to define the new maxims of war that Napoleon understood so well in order to be able to beat him. The Chinese colonels told the *International Herald Tribune* that they began their studies in order to overcome the sense of power-lessness and humiliation they felt when US carrier groups were able to face down the Chinese during their 1996 'military exercises' around Taiwan. After that experience the colonels realised that China had to rethink its strategy if the country was to be able to get its way in face of US military power.[119]

The Chinese colonels' main point is that the most powerful weapons in the US arsenal may not be the RMA platforms, but the framework within which the US is able to deploy the new weapons. As a status quo power, the United States is, for example, able to control the international economy via the International Monetary Fund or the rules of trade set by the World Trade Organization. Within these dimensions, the colonels argue, non-state actors work to increase the power of the West in ways that may follow the invisible hand of the markets but that give very visible advantages to the West. In their book, they thus return again and again to the case of the financier George Soros, whose ability to raid a nation's currency and thus undermine its financial standing the colonels, obviously schooled in materialism, see as an attack on society's basic structure. From a strategic point of view, they do not see any difference between George Soros and Osama bin Laden. The terrorist makes 'the Western world shake in its boots'[120] because al-Qaeda attacks Western societies in areas where their military superiority is to little avail, while the banker attacks the equally defenceless economies of the

---

[118] Qiao Liang and Wang Xiangsui, *Unrestricted Warfare* (Beijing: PLA Literature and Arts Publishing House, 1999). English translation by FBIS, www.c4i.org (12 June 2002), 4.
[119] John Promfret, 'China Looks Beyond Old Rules', *International Herald Tribune*, 9 August 1999.
[120] Liang and Xiangsui, *Unrestricted Warfare*, 47.

non-Western world. 'Who is to say that George Soros is not a financial terrorist?', ask the Chinese colonels.[121]

The colonels clearly identify the American concept of using full-spectrum dominance to manage the battlespace, but they want to offset the US superiority in battle by broadening the scope of the battlespace. What the Americans naturally regard as the underlying conditions for international order (e.g. global financial markets) thus become a battle-ground for the Chinese colonels: 'there is no domain which warfare cannot use, and there is almost no domain which does not have warfare's offensive pattern'.[122] They call this the 'grand warfare method', which is based on 'ten thousand methods combined as one'.[123] Where US strategic planners would regard the conflict of the market place as a civilian type of conflict in which people like Soros engage in healthy competition with no direct strategic implications, the Chinese colonels regard any conflict as something that can be harnessed as part of an overall strategy. There is almost no dimension of human intercourse that cannot be militarised. The 'combination warfare' that the colonels are proposing is thus based on the idea that China can add to its relatively weak military capabilities by moving the war into other spheres.

Moving the war into other social spheres was, of course, a defining characteristic of total war as we knew it in the twentieth century, but 'combination warfare' is not total in the sense that the whole of society is mobilised in an effort to generate the capabilities (military or otherwise) that the state needs in order to win the war. The colonels operate in a post-sovereign framework, where the economy is part of trans-national structures that make it both difficult and unnecessary for it to be mobilised in the way that the British and German economies were mobilised for national ends during the Second World War. The Chinese colonels believe that today it is a matter of influencing other societies by manipulating transnational structures. In their view, the demise of total war does not mean the end of large-scale conflict, but is rather the result of changing social circumstances that redefine the meaning of 'total'. 'Even in the so-called post-modern, post-industrial age, warfare will not be totally dismantled. It has only re-invaded human society in a more complex, more extensive, more concealed, and more subtle manner.'[124]

The Chinese colonels' 'subtle manner' of war is about turning the conditions for Western military action against the West. In other words, causes become effects and effects causes. The colonels want to devise

---

[121] Ibid., 48.   [122] Ibid., 189.   [123] Ibid., 117–19.   [124] Ibid., 6.

a strategy to ensure that US strategy does not create full-spectrum dominance but instead produces boomerang effects, which will adversely influence first the American military's dominating position and then its political will to fight a given conflict. Qiao Liang and Wang Xiangsui suggest three ways of doing this: turning the RMA calculus of war into a boomerang effect, targeting civilians and turning US international dominance into a weakness.

If the RMA calculus of war is the basis of US willingness to risk using military force in wars an American government would otherwise not have risked, then the US's adversaries should aim to increase the risks of the conflict. This strategy places the ordinary American soldier at the centre of attention, the Chinese colonels note:

> These common American soldiers who should be on the battlefield have now become the most costly security in war, like precious china bowls that people are afraid to break. All of the opponents who have engaged in battle with the American military have probably mastered the secret of success – if you have no way of defeating this force, you should kill its rank and file soldiers.[125]

What the colonels advocate is for opponents of the United States to take the risks of attrition. While they must accept that an RMA force can inflict enormous casualties on their side, at the same time they must realise that if they are prepared to risk the lives of thousands of troops while the United States is reluctant to risk the lives of even a few soldiers, then they are able to turn the odds to their advantage. This was what happened in 1993 in Somalia, where the local warlords were able to mobilise the people of Mogadishu to launch themselves against American forces. The American Rangers and Delta Force operatives were able to inflict terrible losses on these untrained fighters, but nonetheless eighteen Americans ended up dead and seventy were wounded.[126] Such casualties were not part of the calculus for an operation of little perceived strategic importance, and the US withdrew its troops. The US did not appreciate at the time that the attack was coordinated by al-Qaeda and thus formed an important part in a developing doctrine for how to increase the risks for US forces operating in the region. The fact that the US would accept only relatively low risks in Somalia thus sent an invitation to anyone who wanted the 'Yankees to go home'.[127] In January 2001, Osama bin Laden recited a poem on how an al-Qaeda suicide squad rammed the USS *Cole* with a dinghy filled with explosives, killing

---

[125] Ibid., 93.
[126] For the now famous description of the battle, see Mark Bowden, *Black Hawk Down: A Story of Modern War* (New York: Penguin Books, 1999).
[127] Clarke, *Against All Enemies*, 87–8.

seventeen US sailors. The poem shows not only the al-Qaeda leader's fascination with the technology of his opponent (a fascination he shares with the Chinese colonels), but also his belief in the hubristic nature of the power of the RMA:

> A destroyer, even the brave might fear,
> She inspires horror in the harbour and the open sea,
> She goes into the waves flanked by arrogance, haughtiness and false might,
> To her doom she progresses slowly, clothed in a huge illusion,
> Awaiting her is a dinghy, bobbing in the waves.[128]

Bin Laden's strategy is to prove that full-spectrum dominance is 'a huge illusion', a strategy that was also successfully employed by Iraqi insurgents following the war of 2003. They soon realised that the best targets for undermining the US project of creating a new Iraq after the fall of Saddam Hussein's regime was to target the most risk-averse elements of the reconstruction effort. Thus by bombing the UN headquarters and targeting aid workers and foreign civilian contractors, the insurgents were able to prevent the British and American occupation forces from creating a civilian infrastructure that could deliver the promise of a better life after Saddam. In the absence of a large civilian element to the occupation, the insurgents were able to force the occupation forces to be very much more at the forefront of affairs, and the continued terror bombings forced them to go on to the offensive as well. The result was a further alienation of the Iraqi people towards the British and American forces in the spring of 2004. At the same time, as the occupation grew more unpopular, the occupying powers were increasingly isolated because they were not able to internationalise Iraqi governance. The Americans and British had to run the risks of occupying Iraq mostly on their own, and the risks kept mounting.

What happened in Iraq shows how targeting civilians can have a boomerang effect on the political and military standing of the United States or other Western powers when they deploy forces overseas. Targeting civilians in acts of terrorism in Western countries themselves is another way of creating boomerang effects. Following the attacks on a suburban rail service in Madrid on 11 March 2004, the Spanish electorate kicked out the government that had led them to war against Iraq in the US coalition and had thus apparently put them at risk of al-Qaeda terrorism. The new government wasted no time in announcing

---

[128] Quoted in Rohan Gunaratna, *Inside Al Qaeda: Global Network of Terror* (New York: Columbia University Press, 2002), 49.

the withdrawal of the Spanish troops in Iraq. While different govern-ments and different electorates will act differently when faced with the effects of their actions, the Spanish example serves to show that creating costs back home for foreign military adventures can radically change the risk calculus of war. Where the RMA is making it easier to deploy military force, even for minor powers, it has also become more danger-ous to do so. The Chinese colonels conclude: 'Precisely in the same way that modern technology is changing weapons and the battlefield, it is also at the same time blurring the concept of who the war participants are. From now on, soldiers no longer have a monopoly of war.'[129]

According to the colonels, the third way for risk-takers to create a boomerang effect is to take war beyond the military sphere where the RMA will ensure US victory. Not only should strategists seek to combine different capabilities, Qiao Liang and Wang Xiangsui argue, but strat-egists should also seek to combine different types of international agents in networks that will give US military intervention boomerang effects in other areas. 'The national strategy for ensuring the realization of national strategy targets, what is generally called grand strategy,' the colonels argue, 'also necessitates carrying out adjustments which go beyond military strategies and even political strategies.'[130] The Chinese colonels thus point out that, by taking risks that the United States is not willing to take and which the RMA allows it not to take, it might be possible effectively to counter the power of the RMA. This realisation makes the Chinese colonels two of the first real theorists of the RMA because they are able to focus on the general strategic consequences of using RMA weapons and strategies, rather than just focusing on the possibilities that the RMA creates for the United States. Furthermore, their focus on 'combination' makes them able to link international order and military power in ways that most Western strategists cannot, because they all too often regard the international order as natural rather than as a strategic asset. However, Qiao Liang and Wang Xiangsui ultimately fail to become the Clausewitzs of the RMA because they do not take the American response to their counter-strategies into account.

The Chinese colonels' disdain for American culture means that they basically do not think that Americans are smart enough to realise the limits of their technological powers. This is clearly not the case. The Defense Review of 1997 notes that 'US dominance in the conventional military arena may encourage adversaries to use such asymmetric means to attack our forces and interests overseas and Americans at home.'[131]

---

[129] Liang and Xiangsui, *Unrestricted Warfare*, 48.
[130] Ibid., 118.   [131] *QDR* 1997, Section Two.

By studying the colonels' counter-strategies as boomerang effects, one is able to understand how American awareness of all the possibilities to counter its RMA power constitutes an integral part of the US understanding of the RMA. In other words, the boomerang effect is part of RMA rather than its negation.

The focus on 'cyber warfare' (the use of hackers and computer viruses to penetrate the control systems of critical infrastructures) reflects the fact that Western vulnerabilities are as much in focus as the new strategic opportunities. The US military construes strategic information warfare as a danger rather than a strategic opportunity.[132] The 2001 American Defense Review argues that 'the increasing dependence of societies and military forces on advanced information networks creates new vulnerabilities'.[133] Though one can hardly expect an official document to praise new opportunities for offensive strategic warfare, the focus on 'cyber war', which so inspires those believing in the '*Wired* magazine' version of the RMA, does not stem from a wish to wage 'cyber war', but from the realisation that it is advanced late modern societies like the United States that are more vulnerable to cyber warfare than most of its possible adversaries.[134] 'Cyber attacks', Steven Metz notes, 'might erode the traditional advantage large and rich states hold in armed conflict.'[135]

Although the Americans are painfully aware of the boomerang effects, they cannot act in ways that produce no boomerang effects at all. The boomerang effects become part of the RMA calculus of warfare, making it a very different calculus from the means-end rational way of thinking about war that we know from Clausewitz. For this reason it cannot simply be concluded that the RMA has made wars so easy for the West that it can simply transfer the risk of waging them on to others. Like most policies in risk society, war has become its own contradiction.[136] Yes, it is

---

[132] The United States is reported for the first time to be developing a paradigm for offensive information warfare in OPLAN 3600. As this contingency plan does not seem to involve the strategic use of information weapons nor to challenge the belief that the United States is more vulnerable to information warfare than most of its prospective enemies, the construal of information warfare as a danger rather than an opportunity remains. In fact, OPLAN 3600 seems to be a means to strike back following an information attack rather than a plan for the first strike of information warfare. See, 'United States: Vulnerable to Cyber Attack', *Stratfor*, 31 March 2001, www.stratfor. com/europe/commentary/0103302345 (1 April 2001).

[133] *QDR* 2001, 31.

[134] Freedman, *The Revolution in Strategic Affairs*, 57.

[135] Metz, *Armed Conflict in the 21st Century*, xviii.

[136] To many the idea that wars create more problems than they solve will come as no surprise. What is new is not only that these problems are being pointed out by 'peaceniks', but that they have become an integrated part of the political and military strategists' perception of military campaigns.

easier to wage it, but it is also a lot more risky to do so. And no, the increased risk of waging war does not mean that fewer wars are fought, because, given the way in which Western governments perceive the security environment, they do not dare to risk not intervening in failed or dangerous states or to wage war in other ways.

Conclusions

The concept of strategy is being used to rationalise new technologies in order to make the tools of war fit the idea of how to fight a war. Information technology leads military men and politicians to expect new things of military power, and both they and scholars within strategic studies are using the concept of the RMA to describe the new military possibilities. For this reason the point of the RMA is not whether all the gadgets described by the 'revolutionaries' have been deployed and are working as described by *Wired* magazine. In this case there would not be much of an RMA, and nobody is more aware of this than the US military. However, the point about the RMA is not the gadgets, but the fact that the use of communication and information technologies has led to a rethinking of strategy. This chapter has demonstrated this and suggested that, from the vanguard of the RMA, the point is not what can be achieved with new military technology today, but what can be expected of the future. The RMA defines expectations of military force in terms of what transformed armed forces will be able to do in the future rather than what they are able to do now. Thus in the final analysis the RMA is about possibilities: new possibilities of wars with low casualties, which makes war a more acceptable political means, the possibility of precision-strikes, the possibility of maintaining rather small armed forces while still achieving decisive military results and so on. However, for each thing that the RMA makes possible for Western armed forces in general and the US armed forces in particular to achieve, new risks appear.

The fact that strategy is used to rationalise the development of new military technologies is clear from the challenge the RMA poses to the Clausewitzian understanding of war, which has dominated the West's, and much of the rest of the world's, understanding of how wars are fought and won. Instead of seeking decisive battles by overwhelming force, strategists of the RMA are focusing on how to manage war by achieving full-spectrum dominance. Perhaps it should come as no surprise that two Chinese colonels are among the most informed observers of this transformation of strategy. Their thinking is clearly informed by classical Chinese thinking on war, as formulated by Sun Tzu in *The*

Art of War 2,500 years ago, a way of thinking that departs radically from the means-end rational strategy that Clausewitz thought in terms of:

Clausewitz' way of thought goes back at least to Aristotle and is based on the distinction between means and ends. By contrast, it is a fundamental characteristic of Chinese thought that such a distinction is absent – to Lao Tzu and his followers, admitting its existence would constitute a departure from *Tao*. Accordingly, the Chinese texts regard war not as an instrument for the attainment of this end or that but as the product of stern necessity, something which must be confronted and coped with and managed and brought to an end.[137]

Qiao Liang and Wang Xiangsui describe the 'Tao of Risk Society'. To the Chinese colonels, strategy is a way of reflecting on the necessities of war rather than a means-end schema which wars must be made to fit.[138] In other words, they find that 'measures are inseparable from objectives'.[139] From this point of view, war is a process that involves a number of different dimensions (political, social, economic and psychological as well as military), rather than a decisive battle. This was how Sun Tzu regarded war. Where Clausewitz uses water as a metaphor for what comes in the way of 'real' war, Sun Tzu uses water as a metaphor for war itself. 'An army may be likened to water,' *The Art of War* states, 'for just as flowing water avoids the heights and hastens to the lowlands, so an army avoids strength and strikes weakness.'[140] Sun Tzu rejects the direct approach (Cheng) in favour of the indirect approach (Ch'i).[141] Instead of offering battle, Sun Tzu argues that one should avoid battle unless one is absolutely certain of winning. Otherwise one should focus on depriving the enemy of any opportunity for carrying out its strategy.

One example of the way in which means and ends are compressed in the process of conflict is how civilian casualties have become a major focus in the Western public's perception of war. Casualties are no longer regarded as a necessary consequence of the employment of certain means in order to achieve certain ends. Before D-Day, Allied bombers targeted railway hubs in northern France in order to limit the Germans' ability to get reinforcements in place so as to turn back the Anglo-American invasion force. Unfortunately, most of the railway installations

[137] Martin van Creveld, *The Art of War: War and Military Thought* (London: Cassell, 2000), 118–19.

[138] Liang and Xiangsui, *Unrestricted Warfare*, 212.

[139] Ibid., 210.

[140] Sun Tzu, *The Art of War*, trans. and with an introduction by Samuel B. Griffith (Oxford: Oxford University Press, 1963), VI, 27.

[141] Ibid., V, 11. Liddell Hart thus believed Sun Tzu to be an early exponent of his own 'indirect approach': B. H. Liddell Hart, 'Foreword', Sun Tzu, *The Art of War*.

were situated in heavily populated areas, and thousands of French civilians were consequently killed in the air raids; these casualties, among the very people that the Allies wanted to liberate, being accepted as a means to a better end. Today such casualties would probably not be accepted because the process view makes the way war is fought inseparable from the reasons for fighting it. In order to shape the perception of this process, one of the most important strategic tasks is to frame the use of military force in a narrative that provides the war with a beginning and an end that justifies every element of the strategic process in between. Thus, despite fighting a campaign that sparkled in the annals of military history, British and American forces had constant difficulties in presenting the Iraq war of 2003 as a success because the story of the war began with a risk of weapons of mass destruction which no one was subsequently able to find, and ended, not with the liberation of the Iraqi people as scripted, but with looting and insurgency.[142]

How defining problems and the means to deal with them becomes the real political battleground is a cornerstone of the risk literature. In risk society the political process is about choosing which risk to act upon, which to ignore and how to deal with the new risks that arise as a consequence of your actions. The RMA has made these choices easy in the sense that the new technology has allowed for very low casualty rates among the high-tech forces. However, the low casualty levels have themselves highlighted the casualties that inevitably occur. Thus since the end of the Cold War the United States has fought a number of conflicts it would probably not have fought if the stakes had been higher. For that reason enemies who were prepared to take risks that the US would not take could, comparatively easily, increase the risks of an operation to the point where the United States no longer believed that it was worth the trouble. The engagement in Somalia is a case in point. This has led people to argue that the RMA is really making it too easy to commit troops and too difficult actually to use them.[143] After more than ten years of 'RMA operations', however, a boomerang effect in the form of low casualties is beginning to show. President Bush highlighted this in June 2004 as a reason for not withdrawing American troops from Iraq: 'The terrorist movement feeds on the appearance of inevitability,' the President argued. 'It claims to rise on the currents of history, using past America withdrawals from Somalia and Beirut to sustain this myth

---

[142] On the contrast between the dazzling effectiveness of the campaign and the media reaction to its end, see Keegan, *The Iraq War*, 204–19.
[143] Black, *War in the New Century*, 97; cf. Gray, *Explorations in Strategy*, 238–44.

and to gain new followers.'[144] In the President's analysis, the fact that the United States had not previously been ready to accept the risks of low-intensity conflict when the US had withdrawn after the bombing of the Marine barracks in Beirut and after the 'Black Hawk Down' episode in Mogadishu had weakened the ability of US military power to deter its enemies in Iraq and elsewhere. America's enemies were prepared to die and had little respect for the risk-aversion of the US armed forces. The boomerang effect of the ability to achieve low casualties might thus be the need to show a willingness to accept continuous casualties. In Iraq the United States reasserted its resolve to fight the war at the grim price of two dead soldiers a day.[145]

The Iraq casualty figures are historically low, as are the figures for civilians suffering the effects of war.[146] John Keegan even argues that the ability the RMA gave the American and British forces to focus directly on enemy combatants led non-combatants to expect that they could go about their daily business as if the war was not going on: 'one of the most bewildering characteristics of this strange war', Keegan notes, 'was the apparent refusal of civilians to accept that a war was indeed going on'. Keegan believes this to be the reason for many of the civilian casualties of the Iraq war. Civilians took the US President at his word when he said that the US was not targeting them and insisted on going about their daily business. For example, civilians drove their cars into the combat zone, not expecting to get hurt.[147] In future wars civilians might not have any such illusions. The technological abilities that allowed the US armed forces to target so precisely that some Iraqi civilians did not find the fighting around the corner to be any of their business also enables an RMA power to raze a city to the ground if that is what it wants to do. Paul Hirst characterised the conflicts of the 1990s as 'precision-guided vengeance',[148] that is, vengeance directed against the regimes of Slobodan Milosevic or Saddam Hussein. However, if vengeance had been directed against the Serbian or Iraqi people, then the precision-guided munitions could have devastated Belgrade or Baghdad in the same way that Tokyo or Dresden were devastated during the Second World War, though with much less effort.

---

[144] George W. Bush, *Remarks by the President at the United States Air Force Academy Graduation Ceremony*, Falcon Stadium, United States Air Force Academy, 2 June 2004 (Washington, DC: The White House, Office of the Press Secretary, 2004), §29.

[145] The precise average of fallen servicemen seems to be 2.34 (including allied casualties), as of 17 November 2005, http://icasualties.org/oif/.

[146] I am referring to the actual British–American invasion of Iraq in 2003, not the ensuing insurgency and civil war.

[147] Keegan, *The Iraq War*, 200.   [148] Hirst, *War and Power*, 98.

For the ultimate potential of the RMA is to make war more terrible than ever before. In fact, Marshal Ogarkov realised this when he first identified the American 'military technical revolution' in the 1980s. He argued that the effectiveness and precision of the new weapons would bring 'them closer, so to speak, to weapons of mass destruction in terms of effectiveness'. The possibility of the RMA making war more destructive becomes more ominous when compared to the fact that the RMA is also making it possible for many more nations to project power across the globe. If Denmark can project military power because of the RMA, so can China or any other society that is creating economic growth by means of the new information and communication technologies. These technologies can easily be harnessed for military purposes. A study by the British Ministry of Defence concludes that in the next thirty years more and more powers will acquire capabilities to project power beyond their own region.[149] This opens up the possibility that RMA forces will engage one another, probably leading, as argued, to battles of attrition. Such battles need not involve the civilian population. Actually, RMA technology may favour battle environments with as few 'disturbing factors' as possible. However, the increased capabilities of states to project their power suggests that their military forces will be fighting further and further away from home. Conflicts between different cultures quickly turn into total wars against the enemy's population as well as its government. In this case the terror bombing of population centres by means of the RMA is a real possibility. If such possibilities are realised, then debates over collateral damage and the possibility of 'clean' wars in the 1990s will seem slightly naive because they focused on the relatively benign use of force by the Western powers, but ignored the horrible possibilities that the RMA has brought with it. From this future point of view, the wars in Iraq and in the Balkans will seem like 'experimental horrors', in the way that the Luftwaffe's bombing of Spanish cities during the civil war in the 1930s seemed to Winston Churchill when he wrote about them after the Second World War.[150]

The RMA creates more powerful military means and the risk of them being used to devastating effect in a great-power confrontation, but under which doctrines are these military means being deployed? This is the subject of the next chapter.

[149] JDCC, *Strategic Trends*, 8:5.
[150] Winston S. Churchill, *The Gathering Storm*, vol. 1 of his *The Second World War* (London: Cassell, 1948), 168.

4   Doctrines: precautionary principles and anticipatory defence

In June 1994 President Clinton was briefed by General John Shalikashvili, Chairman of the Joint Chiefs of Staff, and Secretary of Defense William Perry on the situation in Korea. The US had grown increasingly concerned with North Korea's nuclear weapons programme, and the administration had come to believe 'that such a development would create intolerable risks'.[1] The Chairman and the Secretary presented Clinton with options for how to reinforce US troops in South Korea in order to repulse an attack from the North if the US bombed nuclear facilities in North Korea. The President was about to make his choices and issue the relevant orders when the meeting was interrupted by a message from former President Jimmy Carter that he had been able to broker a deal with the North Korean leadership. North Korea would stop its nuclear weapons programme in exchange for aid and negotiations with the United States.[2]

Had Clinton authorised the use of armed force against North Korea, then doctrines of preventive or pre-emptive defence would probably have dominated the strategic debate from 1994 onwards. The regular bombing of Iraq and what were believed to be al-Qaeda facilities in Sudan and Afghanistan in 1998, as well as the 1999 air campaign against Serbia, would have been seen as examples of a new pre-emptive defence doctrine, and we would have been debating whether such a doctrine was the appropriate answer to the threats of a globalising world. Secretary of Defense Perry believed that it should have been this way. In entitling his political testament *Preventive Defense*, Perry argued that in the post-Cold War period the main purpose of security policy was to implement strategies to prolong the peace for as long as possible. Perry preferred to use civilian preventive measures such as building international institutions and supporting domestic reform movements, but, as in the case of North

---

[1] William Perry and Ashton Carter, *Preventive Defense: A New Security Strategy for America* (Washington, DC: The Brookings Institution, 1999), 126. See also Robert S. Litwak, 'The New Calculus of Pre-emption', *Survival* 44 (Winter 2002–3), 64–5.
[2] Perry and Carter, *Preventive Defense*, 130–3.

Korea, he was also prepared to use military force. Because Clinton chose the diplomatic rather than the military approach in dealing with North Korea, it fell to his successor as president, George W. Bush, to make a doctrine of military pre-emption a central element of US strategy.

The Bush administration's doctrine of pre-emption caused an uproar because it was seen as the intellectual foundation for the 2003 Iraq war, which in turn was widely regarded as an especially malign case of imperial hubris. However, the pre-emptive doctrine is neither as innovative as the administration argues nor as deviant from the norms of politics in the twenty-first century as the administration's critics suggest. Bush continued Clinton's policies in much the same way as Eisenhower continued Truman's at the beginning of the Cold War. The Eisenhower administration came into office with the belief that their predecessors had been too soft and had focused too little on the really relevant security issues, but it ended up pursuing much the same doctrine of containment which had been established during Truman's reign.[3] During the 2000 US presidential campaign, George W. Bush made much of the allegation that the Clinton administration had been squandering the military resources of the United States by committing military forces to peace-keeping as well as peace-enforcement operations from Haiti to Kosovo. It was time, Bush argued, for the armed forces to concentrate on what he perceived to be their core function: to 'fight and win wars'.[4] As president, George Bush soon found that fighting and winning wars in the twenty-first century is about nation-building and the management of risk. Thus in Afghanistan and Iraq his administration engaged in nation-building efforts far more ambitious than anything the Clinton team had dared to contemplate.

The Bush administration did add military pre-emption to the strategic 'to do' list, but there is reason to believe that this reflected the different problems facing the Clinton and Bush administrations rather than any profound philosophical differences. If Clinton had been president from 2001 to 2008 and Bush from 1994 to 2000, their roles would probably have been reversed. For this reason, Lawrence Freedman argues that there is 'less to the new doctrine than met the eye'.[5] Actually, however, there is more. One can argue with some plausibility that both Bush and Clinton would have followed pre-emptive doctrines for the use

[3] Andrew J. Bacevich, *American Empire: The Realities and Consequences of US Diplomacy* (Cambridge, MA: Harvard University Press, 2002), 198–9.
[4] George W. Bush, *Governor Bush Addresses American Legion*, Milwaukee, Wisconsin, Wednesday 6 September 2000.
[5] Lawrence Freedman, *Deterrence* (Cambridge: Polity Press, 2004), 105.

of military force after 9/11 – though not necessarily for the same objectives – because both pre-emptive doctrines reflected a general policy
shift in the Western world. It is globalisation that provides the context
which gives the classic debate about pre-emption a new dimension.
During the Cold War, while a pre-emptive first strike was to be prevented
by deterrence, pre-emptive self-defence was a doctrine utilised in a
number of minor conflicts, such as the Israeli attack on Egyptian
and Syrian targets in the run-up to the Six Day war. In the case of both
nuclear strategy and conventional war, the point about pre-emption was
that it was directed against a specific threat that was closing in on you.
The dangers that risk society identifies are much more abstract and far
away in time as well as in space. Again, the theories of risk society enable
one to situate strategy in its proper context. The doctrines of 'preventive
defence', in Perry's words, or 'anticipatory defence', as Bush's first
National Security Advisor, Condoleezza Rice, called it, closely mirrors
the 'precautionary principle' applied in environmental policy. When
viewed in such abstract terms, the debate over the precautionary principle
is remarkably similar to the debate over the need to invade Iraq in 2002
and 2003. These and other similarities demonstrate that in risk society
strategy has become normal policy. The doctrines for environmental
protection and crime prevention are very similar to the doctrines for the
use of military force.

NATO defines doctrine as the 'fundamental principles by which the
military forces guide their actions in support of objectives. It is authoritative but requires judgment in application.'[6] These 'fundamental principles' are, of course, meant to be operational and immediately useful
for field commanders. Officers are taught doctrine in order that they
can absorb the collective memory and experience of the armed forces.
The definition of doctrine as the principles that are taught to practical
men reflects the origins of the term in religious doctrine, where it refers
to the dogmas taught to priests so that they can lead and educate their
congregations. This meaning of the word implies that military doctrine
is not necessarily as practical and empirical as military academies like to
present it. As with any other kind of knowledge, military doctrine is
based on particular ontological and epistemological foundations. What
commanders are believed to be able to do depends on the legitimate
aims of armed force and the principles according to which it can and
should be used. From this perspective, the NATO definition of doctrine
not only points forward to the practical application of military force, it

---

[6] Defense Technical Information Center, *DOD Dictionary of Military and Associated Terms*,
www.dtic.mil/doctrine/jel/doddict/natoterm/d/00401.html (2 December 2004).

also points back to the idea of the security environment and the strategic requirement and potential for influencing it. It is these 'fundamental principles' that this chapter will focus on.

The concept of pre-emption is such a fundamental principle because it dictates certain military and diplomatic action based on a perception of risk in a globalising world. Much has been made about the distinction between prevention and pre-emption. As the Bush administration made pre-emption a core concept in US grand strategy, opponents of American policy naturally started to argue for the merits of prevention. In this case, whereas prevention is often presented as a non-military approach to security issues that concentrates on root causes, pre-emption is regarded as a blunt instrument of military force to be deployed against an immediate threat.[7] International law makes a similar distinction between pre-emptive actions which are merely the first strike of a war and as such constitute legitimate self-defence under the terms of the UN Charter, and military prevention as the legally more dubious use of armed force against a threat which has yet to materialise.[8] However, the logic of the distinction between pre-emption and prevention breaks down when the distinction is transplanted from theory or law into strategic practice. How acute should a threat be before it is imminent enough for action against it to constitute pre-emption rather than prevention? No use of military force comes out of the blue, but how is one to distinguish the diplomatic quarrels that lead up to a military action from the military action itself? Are civilian means of strategy preventive and military means pre-emptive? A legal or theoretical answer to these questions is no doubt possible, but the question is whether they will help us untangle the concepts or just entangle us even more in the political implications of using the terms. This suggests that John Lewis Gaddis is right when he argues that 'the old distinction between pre-emption and prevention . . . was one of the many casualties of September 11'.[9] In this chapter I shall refer to 'pre-emption' because this is the concept that lies at the centre of the policy debate. However, in other policy areas referred to in the chapter ('crime prevention' being foremost among them), prevention is used in ways similar to how pre-emption is used in the post-9/11 strategic discourse.

[7] François Heisbourg, 'A Work in Progress: The Bush Doctrine and Its Consequences', *Washington Quarterly* 26 (Spring 2003), 77–80.
[8] Anthony Clark Arend, 'International Law and the Preemptive Use of Military Force', *Washington Quarterly* 26 (Spring 2003), 89–103.
[9] John Lewis Gaddis, 'Grand Strategy in the Second Term', *Foreign Affairs* 84 (January/February 2005), 5.

The chapter is structured around the core risk concepts of 'management', the 'presence of the future' and the 'boomerang effect', in that order. I start by showing how strategic doctrines have moved from principles of deterrence to management. Lawrence Freedman defines deterrence as 'the potential or actual application of force to influence the action of a voluntary agent'.[10] Deterrence used to guide many government policies. Crime prevention is a prime example, but in crime prevention deterrence has been abandoned in favour of managing the risks of crime. Because of the Cold War, deterrence ruled strategy much longer than crime prevention, but when Western societies began to define themselves in terms of globalisation following the end of the Cold War, they found themselves faced with the same unpredictable and essentially uncontrollable environment that those fighting crime had faced since the 1970s. The first part of the chapter thus uses the development of crime prevention to track that of security doctrines.

Secondly, the chapter turns to the presence of the future in order to describe how doctrine in risk society identifies threats and provides suggestions for acting upon them. The central feature here is how acting on scenarios for risks that will never materialise if the strategy is successful places policy-makers' judgement at the centre of attention, as well as setting new standards for judging judgements. These new dilemmas are illustrated in a review of the debate about whether or not to invade Iraq in 2002–3. In this part of the chapter, the parallel development in environmental debates with regard to the so-called precautionary principle is used to demonstrate that the strategic agenda was becoming much more 'normal' in risk society. Thirdly, the chapter turns to the 'boomerang effect', in investigating which different 'risk cultures' are a prime concern. It is argued that many of the transatlantic differences on how to approach the 'Iraq problem' and security issues like it stem from different interpretations of how to 'live with terrorism'. In addition, the chapter shows how pre-emptive military action can produce many more risks than those it is supposed to avert. Again the Iraq war is a good example.

Management

Globalisation means that Western strategy is increasingly focused on managing risks rather than creating enduring security. Following the Cold War, this has meant a gradual recalibrating of doctrines from a

---

[10] Freedman, *Deterrence*, 26.

logic of deterrence to a management logic. The process was accelerated when American strategists had to come up with a response to 9/11. Because of this suddenly accelerated pace, the shift from deterrence to management may seem revolutionary and perhaps even arbitrary, but in fact it is strategy which has been rather slow in embracing a general move from deterrence to management. This move is perhaps most clear and most easily comparable with strategy in crime prevention, but it has taken place in relation to many governmental strategies. The move to management is a reflection of the advent of risk society. Where modern politics was about creating final solutions, the politics of risk society is about managing imperfection.

First, I deal with how the post-Cold War security environment is actually a lot like the security environment at the beginning of the Cold War, in the sense that what constitutes a viable doctrine is still being debated. While the plasticity of the security environment is the same, the role of the strategist is very different because of the unpredictability of the threats. Secondly, I turn to the phenomenon which is believed to be creating these new threats, namely globalisation, which defines Western expectations of the future and defines them in terms of risk. In the context of globalisation terrorism, the proliferation of weapons of mass destruction and other 'new security challenges and risks' cannot be determined – they are risks that will have to be managed. But how are they to be managed? Since the management paradigm is not yet fully developed within the strategy, I turn to crime prevention in order to show the similarities between developments in this field and in strategy, as well as to show where strategy is going if it is to follow the path of crime prevention away from deterrence and towards the management of risks.

From predictability to unpredictability

Today, strategists are in much the same intellectual confusion as they were in the late 1940s (see Chapter 2). Just as George Kennan and his contemporaries argued about how to deal with the Soviet Union as a new, powerful agent in world affairs, so the strategists of the early twenty-first century are arguing about the significance of the rise of terrorists as 'security agents', that is, agents able to conduct warfare or operations approaching warfare at least in their political signifiance. And just as people of Kennan's generation were debating the true motives of the Kremlin and whether the Bolshevists living there were still bent on world revolution, the strategists of the early twenty-first century are arguing what to make of militant Islamists. Finally, just as Kennan and his contemporaries discussed how to build a new world order after the end of a world conflict, so today's strategists are trying to develop doctrines for managing the post-Cold War world. While the questions being raised in the two cases may be the same, the solutions offered by the two generations of strategists are radically different.

Western strategists followed the political rationale of the welfare state in developing strategies of containment. On the national level, governments built government institutions to deal with social security, health and the numerous other welfare issues for which post-World War II governments took over responsibility. This belief in the power of institutions was translated into the international realm, where, for example, NATO represented an attempt to create an institutional solution to the problem of transatlantic security. On the national as well as international levels, this belief in institutions rested on a firm belief in the ability of governments to calculate the right response to social problems.[11] From this point of view, international security was predictable and calculable. On the basis of game theory, the strategists at RAND were able to learn not from history, as Kennan advocated, but from a virtual Cold War fought out in their equations for how to apply strategies of deterrence.[12] I have already quoted Lawrence Freedman's definition of deterrence as 'the potential or actual application of force to influence the action of a voluntary agent'.[13] The point of deterrence, as the doctrine was applied during the Cold War, was to create predictability. The theory held that, once they knew when and how the United States would respond to Soviet aggression, the leadership in the Kremlin would step back from the nuclear brink.

When Clinton's Secretary of Defense from 1994 to 1997, William Perry, talked about Russia, he did so in terms very different from Kennan. Where Kennan had argued that the Russian mind simply would not accept the liberal rules by which the US wanted to define the international order, Perry argued: 'A central challenge for Preventive Defense is to assist Russian foreign leaders to conceive a post-Soviet security concept that matches Russia's national interests to the interests of international stability.'[14] Russia's interests were not regarded as given, but as something which could be shaped. This view reflected the power of the United States to shape its own security environment, but this

---

[11] For more on this argument, see Latham, *The Liberal Moment*, Rasmussen, *The West, Civil Society and the Construction of Peace*, 112–26.
[12] Kaplan, *Wizards of Armageddon*; see also Freedman, 'The First Two Generations of Nuclear Strategists', 735–78.
[13] Freedman, *Deterrence*, 26.   [14] Perry and Carter, *Preventive Defense*, 52.

power also carried an immense responsibility for a lot of factors determining the security environment, which had hitherto been regarded as beyond the control of the United States or any other great power. When the strategic environment was analysed on the basis of interests rooted in history and in terms of the games of rational actors, the question a president or a prime minister had to ask himself was how to respond. In a more plastic security environment, where threats assume new shapes, the question is how to prevent new threats from accumulating.

In a plastic security environment, the strategist is no longer the one to teach statesmen the lessons of history (be it actual history or the virtual history of game theory) – now the strategist has to predict the future in order to identify emerging threats. From this point of view, Jean-Marie Guehenno argues that 'the strategist of tomorrow may well look more like a meteorologist'.[15]

Where George Kennan actually contrived a strategy for how to bring down the Soviet Union, a meteorologist does not strive to draw up a strategy for achieving sunshine by enduring a certain number of rainy days. Meteorologists do not have a particular end-state in mind, but try and predict what is going to happen in order to give people a chance to take the weather into account in making their plans. People take an umbrella with them on their way to work in the morning, in spite of the fact that it is a beautiful sunny morning, because the weather forecast gives them reason to believe that it will start raining in the evening. The sun may still be shining in the evening when they return home with their dry umbrella, but that does not make people stop listening to the weather forecast on television in the morning. People know that the weather is basically unpredictable. Meteorology is a method for making the unpredictable predictable by creating a scenario for what will happen and giving people the opportunity to act accordingly. Based on a reading of processes, these scenarios constitute a different kind of prediction than the scenario generated from the hypotheses of game theory and other means-end rational approaches to politics and strategy. The meteorological scenarios are based on the premise that most things change; game theory is based on the enduring characteristics of key agents.

If the strategist is becoming less like a natural scientist or a history professor and more like the weatherman showing computer-generated scenarios of the development of a storm system to viewers of a morning news show, this will produce a new role for strategy as a 'guide to the prince'. During the Cold War, the strategist's role was to explain the

---

[15] J.-M. Guehenno, 'The Impact of Globalisation on Strategy', *Survival* 40 (Winter 1998–9), 14.

logic and rules of the security environment to presidents and prime ministers, who then had to decide how to turn the nuts and bolts of the deterrence machine. In assuming a role like that of meteorologists, strategists will have to predict future strategic environments and ask presidents and prime ministers to act upon them, in spite of the fact that the threats they have to counter have not yet materialised. This changes the politics in strategy. If one examines the Cuban Missile Crisis, one finds that President Kennedy and his advisors debated what would be the proper response to the Soviet deployment of missiles to Cuba in the context of deterrence;[16] if one examines the debate in the Bush administration about whether to go to war against Iraq or not, one finds different contexts being presented for the same action. Viewing the problem of Iraq in terms of 'the war on terror', an invasion made sense to some, while others feared it because they saw Iraq in terms of Middle East resentment towards the United States, something an invasion would only make worse. The Pentagon created its own team of 'meteorologists' to search out intelligence that fitted its scenario, while other parts of the administration, not to mention the opposition, highlighted other snippets of intelligence that supported other scenarios.[17] As the risk literature would lead one to expect, the debate about risks leads to endless reflection about the 'scale, degrees and urgency of risks'.[18] Intelligence becomes more political because more is at stake when one decides doctrine on the basis of scenarios that describe a process rather than a condition. The processes that are believed to be dictating strategy are best described with reference to the concept of globalisation; and it is the perceptions of how one should manage the dangers and opportunities of the globalisation process which we turn to next.

The risks of globalisation

Most people in Western societies find that globalisation is like the weather. A simple definition of globalisation is the social, economic and political results of cumulative lower global transaction costs. Revolutions in information and transportation technologies have reduced the transaction costs of global interaction to ever lower levels since the mid-1980s. As it became easier to talk and trade, production and finance

---

[16] Jutta Weldes, *Constructing National Interests: The United States and the Cuban Missile Crisis* (Minneapolis, MN: University of Minnesota Press, 1999).
[17] Seymour M. Hersh, *Chain of Command: The Road from 9/11 to Abu Ghraib* (London: Allen Lane, 2004), 203–47.
[18] Beck, *Risk Society*, 46.

became increasingly global. By the 1990s it became a main point among sociologists that globalisation was not only about the internationalisation of the production base of Western societies – increasingly other social spheres attained some degree of international dynamics.[19] In other words, globalisation ceased to be a description of economics and became a way to construct identity and social institutions. Globalisation became the watchword for societal change, and as such it was perceived as much as a cause as a remedy for social change. Ulrich Beck thus distinguishes between the analysis of a societal 'globality' and the political advocacy of globalisation (globalism).[20] Irrespective of whether globalisation is seen as a cause or a policy, in Jens Bartelson's words it structures 'a horizon of political imagination structured around expectations of transcendence'.[21] Believing that society is redefined by the changes brought about by globalisation, and further believing that these changes can be harnessed only by a political commitment to globalisation, the management of change has become the cornerstone of Western political discourse. It is in this sense that globalisation is perceived in the same terms as the weather.

Like the weather, globalisation is a fact of life, which most people and most politicians believe is uncontrollable. One adjusts to globalisation as one adjusts to the weather. When you have reason to believe it is going to rain, then you have the chance to make a choice about how to react to future events: will you take your umbrella with you or not? Globalisation defines the political and social environment in similar ways, in that it requires a form of 'social imagination' different from the one you need to operate in a more static society. Whereas the hallmark of modernity was to understand structures, the hallmark of late-modernity is the reflexive imagination that enables you to identify trends in current social processes that provide a guide to what the future will bring. As Zygmunt Bauman puts it, 'all of us are, willy-nilly, by design or by default, on the move'.[22] But where are we going, and where would we like to go? Asking such questions is central to what the risk literature describes as the reflexive rationality that defines late modern society.

---

[19] For a seminal presentation of this argument, see Anthony Giddens, *Runaway World: How Globalisation is Reshaping Our Lives* (London: Profile, 1999). As Justin Rosenberg puts it in a critical review of the globalisation literature, 'it is globalisation which now explains the changing character of the modern world': Justin Rosenberg, *The Follies of Globalisation Theory* (London: Verso, 2000), 3.

[20] Beck, *What Is Globalization?*, 9–12.

[21] Jens Bartelson, 'Three Concepts of Globalization', *International Sociology* 15 (2000), 192.

[22] Zygmunt Bauman, *Globalization: The Human Consequences* (Cambridge: Polity Press, 1998), 2. Cf. Manuel Castells, *The Rise of the Network Society* (Oxford: Blackwell, 1996), 376–428.

When faced with the question of how to manage the post-Cold War peace in ways that would make it last as long as possible, this 'globalist imagination' becomes the key. If globalisation defines the post-Cold War world, then it also places new requirements on security policy. On 23 April 1999, during the NATO air campaign to stop genocide in Kosovo, UK Prime Minister Tony Blair told the Economy Club of Chicago:

Twenty years ago we would not have been fighting in Kosovo. We would have turned our backs on it. The fact that we are engaged is the result of a wide range of changes – the end of the Cold War; changing technology; the spread of democracy. But it is bigger than that. I believe the world has changed in a more fundamental way. Globalisation has transformed our economies and our working practices. But globalisation is not just economic. It is also a political and security phenomenon. We live in a world where isolationism has ceased to have a reason to exist.[23]

Blair wanted to ensure US commitment to fighting the war in Kosovo and he did so by making a 'weatherman argument'. One could not stand back and let conflicts run their course, he argued, because they were no longer fought in isolation. One could no longer regard the reason for a conflict in terms of local causes and effects. Now, the world was interdependent in ways that made regional conflict and chaos a global concern.

Globalisation became an argument for strategic activism because Blair and others argued that one had to intervene early in order to not become the victim of the effects of conflicts around the world. During the 1990s, the 'weatherman argument' also came to focus on the activism that globalisation might enable the enemies of the West to engage in. Actually, one of the less noticed reasons that President Clinton gave for going to war on the issue of the treatment of Albanians in Kosovo reflected a growing concern about the new threats that unstable countries prone to Islamic fundamentalism might produce:

Bringing the Kosovars home is a moral issue, but it is a very practical, strategic issue. In a world where the future will be threatened by the growth of terrorist groups; the easy spread of weapons of mass destruction; the use of technology including the Internet, for people to learn how to make bombs, and wreck countries, this is also a significant security issue.[24]

In the President's words, it was not Europe or the United States or even the nations in the Balkans that were threatened – the strategic concerns

[23] Tony Blair, *Prime Minister's Speech to Economic Club of Chicago*, Chicago, 23 April 1999 (London: Prime Minister's Office, 1999), §§19–21.
[24] William Jefferson Clinton, *Remarks by President William Clinton to the Veterans of Foreign Wars on Kosovo*, Eisenhower Hall, Fort McNair, 13 May 1999 (Washington, DC: The White House, Office of the Press Secretary, 1999), §35.

that Clinton spoke about did not have a nation as their subject, but were directed at 'the future'. This shows how perceiving the world in terms of globalisation has made presidents and prime ministers view strategic issues in terms of their consequences for the future, rather than on their effects on the specifics of the present. Clinton's belief that the globalisation process has produced new risks reflected a widespread belief in the strategic community on both sides of the Atlantic. Javier Solana, the EU foreign policy chief, argued in 1999 that 'globalisation has brought with it a wide range of transnational challenges, many of which were unheard of a generation ago'.[25] Globalisation has reduced the transaction costs not only for people wanting to spread democracy and trade or learn about the qualities of different cultures, but also for refugees, criminals and terrorists. The belief in globalisation is the belief in the realisation of potentials – if people are able to trade, they will; if terrorists are able to bomb the US, they will. Following this line of reasoning, a bipartisan US report on national security in the twenty-first century concluded in 1999: 'States, terrorists, and other disaffected groups, will acquire weapons of mass destruction and disruption, and some will use them. Americans will likely die on American soil, possibly in large numbers.'[26]

Expecting terrorists to realise their potential, the strategic debate in the 1990s increasingly began to focus on what would happen when terrorists struck the United States itself. In 1999, William Perry predicted what would happen if terrorists were able to strike hard at the United States:

An incident of catastrophic terrorism would abruptly and irrevocably undermine the fundamental sense of security of Americans, their belief that the United States is a safe place to live, to make plans, to raise a family. Americans have not experienced a similar shock of vulnerability in their own homeland since Joseph Stalin exploded the first Soviet A-bomb in 1949.[27]

On 11 September 2001, the United States experienced just such 'an incident of catastrophic terrorism', and the result was what Perry had predicted: a shock of vulnerability. The terrorist attacks on New York and Washington realised the risk that had shaped so much strategic

---

[25] Javier Solana, *The Development of a Common European Security and Defence Policy: The Integration Project of the Next Decade* (Berlin: EU-Commission/Institut für Europäische Politik, Press Release, 17 December 1999).

[26] The United States Commission on National Security/21st Century, *New World Coming: American Security in the 21st Century*, Phase I Report on the Emerging Global Security Environment for the First Quarter of the 21st Century (September 1999), 138.

[27] Perry and Carter, *Preventive Defense*, 150.

thinking up to then. When a risk is realised, however, it is a risk no more. The risk realised in a catastrophe is part of history, not a threat to the future. While catastrophic terrorism is no longer a risk but a specific threat, the attacks on New York and Washington made all the other risks dealt with in the scenarios of the 1990s all the more credible. The risk of al-Qaeda setting off a nuclear weapon in the downtown area of an American city was no greater in material terms on 12 September 2001 than it had been on the 10th, but the fact that al-Qaeda had been able to hit the financial district on Manhattan badly on the 11th made the prospect of an even worse attack, with al-Qaeda or some other terrorist group using nuclear or chemical weapons, more vivid and credible. In this sense the risk did go up, because risks are perceptions of future dangers, not material facts, and the terrorist attacks changed those perceptions. Deputy Secretary of Defense Paul Wolfowitz described the attacks on 11 September 2001 as 'a window into our future',[28] and he went on to argue that, 'along with the globalization that is creating interdependence among the world's free economies, there is a parallel globalization of terror, in which rogue states and terrorist organizations share information, intelligence, technology, weapons materials and know-how'.[29] Western societies defined themselves and their future in terms of globalisation, but according to Secretary Wolfowitz globalisation was not just furthering wealth and freedom. 'A parallel globalisation of terror' existed where the very processes that did Western societies so much good also put them in danger. Anthony Giddens refers to this as the 'dark side of modernity', which, he argues, is constituted by its 'high consequence risks', which he defines as follows:[30] 'In contrast to health dangers, high consequence risks by definition are remote from the individual agent, although – again, by definition – they impinge directly on each individual's life chances.'[31]

When the dust had settled over Manhattan, commentators began to point out that however terrible the events of 9/11 were, the probability of being a victim of terrorism was still very much lower than the risk of traffic accidents.[32] The probability does not define the risk, however. Giddens argues that although 'high consequence risks', like terrorist attacks, may not have a high probability, their consequences are so

---

[28] Paul Wolfowitz, *Building a Military for the 21st Century*, Prepared Statement for the House and Senate Armed Services Committees, 3–4 October 2001 (Washington, DC: US Department of Defense, 2001), §3.

[29] Ibid., §37.

[30] Giddens, *Modernity and Self-Identity*, 122.

[31] Ibid., 121.

[32] Gavin de Becker, *Fear Less* (Boston, MA: Little, Brown and Company, 2002), 120–1.

catastrophic that the risk of them occurring at all is probability enough for them to influence people's lives and the security policies that people demand from the politicians in order to be safer. Such risks become even more threatening because they are seen as part of the globalisation process. Therefore most people expect new terrorist attacks with the same everyday certainty as they expect it to rain some time in the future. Globalisation defines expectations for the future, and terrorism is defined as a consequence of globalisation. In other words, if the future turns out the way people hope and expect, then terrorism will be a part of that future.

In strategic terms, the consequence of 9/11 was that globalisation went from a strategic asset ensuring an international system, which created the structural conditions for Western military activism in the way described by the two Chinese colonels, to a strategic liability. In that sense 'unrestricted warfare' arrived on 11 September 2001. The 'high consequence risks' of globalisation are no longer something that has to be prevented from developing. The scenario has become reality, and now the risks have to be managed.

The US *Quadrennial Defense Review* (QDR) of 2001 states that 'managing risks is a central element of the defense strategy'.[33] But how is the government to manage risks? During the twentieth century, Western welfare states insured their citizens against risks. 'The story of government in the twentieth century', Michel Dean argues, 'might be understood as an attempt to find a mode of government able to offer an assurance of the life of the population.'[34] François Ewald argues that, in looking to the government for the assurance of their life chances, citizens came to regard their future and the society's future as intertwined. Doing well on your own was neither morally nor practically feasible – Ewald calls this a 'solidarist society'.[35] This underscores the point about high consequence risks. In a solidarist society, everybody feels that they carry part of the risk of a terrorist attack directed against their country, provided this risk is localised. For people living in the American Midwest, the Scottish Highlands or rural Germany, the likelihood of becoming a victim of terrorism is very remote indeed. Nationalism explains why people in the Midwest should feel touched by what happened in New York on 11 September 2001, but the solidarism that arises from the insurance state explains why they are afraid.

While terrorism poses a threat to individuals rather than the state, the state cares about these threats because its job is to insure its citizens.

[33] *QDR* 2001, 57.   [34] Dean, *Governmentality*, 176.
[35] Ewald, 'Insurance and Risk', 208–10.

The Health and Safety Executive, which manages the safety of places of work and dangerous installations, like nuclear power plants, in Britain, explains how citizens' demands on the government to manage risk have grown in recent years:

The end result is an apparent aspiration for a society free of involuntary risks, underpinned by a belief that the state has a duty to insulate people from harm. There is in consequence an increasing demand for explanation of how it is intended to protect against harm, both in general and in particular circumstances.[36]

This demand for a risk-free society and for the government to explain how it is going to protect its citizens is by no means new when it comes to strategic issues. National security was on government agendas long before food poisoning or pollution. Security issues were believed to be of a different nature from other government tasks because the threat was not directed against the state's citizens but against the state itself. Citizens might be targeted, as with strategic bombing during the Second World War, but only in order to undermine the state's morale and productive capacity. However, terrorism poses a threat to citizens first and the state second. As such, terrorism is a threat much like pollution, hazardous working environments and the other issues that the Health and Safety Executive has to deal with. And while citizens expect the state to be limited in its ability to act against foreign enemies, globalisation means that the threat of terrorism comes not from outside the state but from within it. Thus the normal expectations of safety apply to citizens who, in the words of the Health and Safety Executive, expect that 'the state should be proactive in protecting people from risks as distinct from reacting to events'.[37] People expect the same vigilance from the government in relation to terrorism as to pollution, but the government's problem is that it cannot offer a future free from the risk of terrorism. In 2003 Tony Blair told a House of Commons committee that he believed that a terrorist attack on Britain was 'inevitable'.[38] In 2005 he was proved terribly right when bombs exploded in the London Underground. The best that states can do is to manage the terrorist threat, but how are they to do that? This is the topic of the next section.

---

[36] The Health and Safety Executive, *Reducing Risks, Protecting People*, Discussion Document (London: The Health and Safety Executive, 1999), iii.

[37] Ibid., 5.

[38] 'Blair: UK Terror Attack Inevitable', CNN, 21 January 2003, www.cnn.com (7 October 2004). President Bush echoed this sentiment, acknowledging that 'we can neither predict nor prevent every conceivable attack'. George W. Bush, *Remarks by the President at the Signing of HR 5005 the Homeland Security Act of 2002*, 25 November 2002 (Washington, DC: The White House, Office of the Press Secretary, 2002), §30.

How to manage an unpredictable environment

If the citizens of Western democracies are increasingly demanding their governments to be as proactive in protecting them from international threats as from more traditional domestic security concerns, then we should examine more closely how strategies for dealing with the traditional number-one domestic security issue, namely crime, have developed in the past thirty years.

Where citizens have not previously expected governments to control the international system to an extent where they could prevent other states from posing a threat, prevention has been high on the criminological agenda at least since 1764, when Cesare Beccaria stated that 'it is better to prevent crimes than to punish them'.[39] Deterrence was the key concept in the paradigm of crime prevention that developed out of Beccaria's dictum. In Gordon Hughes' words, 'deterrence as crime prevention is about affording rational, self-interestedly calculating individuals reasons and opportunities not to commit crimes'.[40] This perspective was a means-end rational perspective on crime prevention. Utilitarians like Jeremy Bentham believed that crime was about choice: if the criminal believed he could benefit from committing a crime, then he would commit it. Crime prevention consisted in convincing the would-be criminal that his crime would not pay. The establishment of police forces in major European cities in the early nineteenth century took place in accordance with this paradigm of deterrence.[41]

With the rise of the welfare state, crime prevention was no longer solely a matter between the criminal and the police. With the rise of the solidarist logic of insurance as the basis of governance, the focus was no longer on deterring people from committing crime, but on how to prevent people from committing crimes by removing the factors that made crime part of their social environment. The question was not what the criminal would do, but what society could do for criminals. The criminological focus shifted from deterring crime to rehabilitating criminals in order to ensure that they did not commit new offences. By the late 1970s, however, the rise in crime rates in spite of all the rehabilitation work led to loss of faith. In 1980 Tony Bottoms concluded that 'no one now seriously pretends . . . that "rehabilitation" has any

---

[39] Quoted in Gordon Hughes, *Understanding Crime Prevention: Social Control, Risk and Late-Modernity* (Maidenhead: Open University Press, 1998), 30.

[40] Ibid.

[41] Les Johnston, *Policing Britain: Risk, Security and Governance* (London: Longman, 2000), 5–17.

utilitarian value in the general reduction of crime rates or in the prevention of the recruitment of recidivists'.[42] According to Gordon Hughes, the result was a 'crisis' in the practice of crime prevention.[43]

Beccaria's choice between punishment and prevention had come to be regarded as a false dichotomy because criminals were no longer believed to be rationally calculating individuals. For this reason, they could not be deterred by the threat of punishment. Having committed crimes that could not have been prevented, convicted criminals could not be prevented from committing new crimes, because efforts at rehabilitation were believed to be mostly in vain. Unable to choose between prevention and punishment, criminologists and the politicians they advised had to admit that they could no longer offer the choice of eradicating crime. This was a fundamental break with the modern belief that a more perfect society could be achieved by social engineering. Crime would have to be accepted as a part of social intercourse. 'The idea that crime can be effectively prevented', Hughes argues, 'thus seems to be in the process of being replaced by a widespread recognition that at best crime, given its routine social normality and presence, may be better understood as a risk to be managed.'[44] Acknowledging their inability to influence individual criminals, Home Office criminologists began to focus on crime management rather than crime prevention.

A term borrowed from economics may help us understand what this shift meant. Economists distinguish between 'stocks' and 'flows'. For example, 1,500,000 people are unemployed in 2005–6 in country X. If the number of unemployed is a stock, then exactly the same 1,500,000 individuals will be unemployed for all of 2005 and 2006 in country X. If the number represents a flow, however, then 2,500,000 people may be unemployed from time to time over the same two years. Whether the unemployment figure represents a stock or a flow makes a crucial difference in how to deal with the unemployed. In the case of a stock of permanently unemployed, active measures for stimulating the economy and getting them back to work may be needed. However, if the unemployment figures merely indicate a flow of temporary unemployment for people between jobs, then the figure might actually reflect the existence of a dynamic labour market.[45]

Similarly, when criminologists ceased to focus on the individual criminal, they stopped focusing on crime as a stock. It was no longer a

---

[42] Quoted in Hughes, *Understanding Crime Prevention*, 48.
[43] Ibid., 59.
[44] Ibid., 7. See also Johnston, *Policing Britain*, 52.
[45] David Begg, Stanley Fischer and Rudiger Dornbusch, *Economics*, third edition (London: MacGraw Hill, 1991), 217–18.

question merely of capturing fewer criminals: now crime prevention was about managing the environment in which criminals operated. One could not prevent criminals from committing crimes, but one could reduce their opportunities for doing so and thus give individual criminals incentives for leaving crime. First, the philosophy was that, since the government could not prevent all potential criminals from actually committing crime, crime prevention should focus on removing the criminal's 'targets'. Gary Marx refers to this as target removal, target devaluation and target insulation.[46] Secondly, where, in the final analysis, the authorities had very little ability to influence individual offenders, they had ample opportunity to shape the environment. This approach has been called 'situational crime prevention', that is, 'a pre-emptive approach that relies . . . on reducing the opportunities for crime'.[47] In American and British cities, the urban landscape is being remodelled in order to reduce the opportunities for committing crime. Open spaces and closed-circuit television (CCTV) quickly single out individuals who seem out of place. By removing benches from parks or bus stops, a new security architecture is installed that prevents people from stopping more than briefly, thus making the homeless and others who are hanging around public places much more visible.[48] The sense of visibility either makes them feel uncomfortable, so that they move away, or else directs other people's attention to them, thus making potential victims more alert.

While crime prevention was leaving the deterrence paradigm in the late 1970s, the Cold War meant that deterrence continued to be the predominant Western strategic doctrine until the early 1990s.[49] Just as the punishment of criminals did not leave the criminological agenda in the 1970s, the end of the Cold War did not mean that deterrence was completely abandoned. As in the case of crime prevention, however, international security threats were increasingly understood as a flow rather than a stock. In its Strategic Concept of 1991, NATO asserted that, 'The monolithic, massive and potential immediate threat' of a Soviet attack had disappeared.[50] In economic terms, this meant that the threat was no longer a stock. For this reason it was no longer as

---

[46] Quoted in Hughes, *Understanding Crime Prevention*, 70.
[47] Ibid., 60.
[48] Edward W. Soja, *Postmetropolis: Critical Studies of Cities and Regions* (Oxford: Blackwell, 2000), 303–12.
[49] Freedman, *Deterrence*, 14–25.
[50] NATO, *The Alliance's Strategic Concept*, Agreed by the Heads of State and Government participating in the meeting of the North Atlantic Council in Rome on 7–8 November 1991 (Brussels: NATO Handbook, NATO Office of Information and Press, October 1995), §6, 236.

predictable and the response no longer as clear-cut. NATO documents thus ceased to refer to the specific and unique threat presented by the Soviet Union. Instead, the headline for the security agenda that the Western allies discussed at NATO became 'security challenges and risks'.[51] NATO's Strategic Concept of 1999 thus concluded that the Alliance was 'subject to a wide variety of military and non-military risks which are multi-directional and often difficult to predict'.[52]

Perhaps the most striking thing about the policy documents produced on strategic doctrines in the 1990s is the frankness of their authors over how little they know about the new 'security challenges and risks' and their recognition that they are developing the doctrines to deal with them as they go along. As the strategic community looked around for new doctrines for a new security environment, it seems safe to assume that the strategists were influenced by other strategic practices in the society at large. As argued in Chapter 2, strategic practices are proliferating today, and it would only be natural for military strategists to look for new approaches to be inspired in some way by the strategic practices they encountered in their own societies. It is striking how the 'preventive defense' that former US Secretary of Defense Perry advocated in 1999 and the pre-emptive doctrines that President Bush sponsored in his National Security Strategy of 2002 resemble late modern strategies of crime prevention: they are both based on the premise that threats cannot be controlled, so must be managed.

When a security issue becomes a flow, the purpose of security policy is no longer to stop threats, but to 'filter' the really bad risks away. Where the metaphor of the Cold War was the wall – the wall in Berlin, as well as the protective wall of armour and nuclear weapons that NATO set up on the other side – the metaphor of the post-Cold War security environment is the filter. Governments now try to set up a 'risk filter' that screens their jurisdiction against the most dangerous elements coming from the flows of globalisation.[53] The most decisive policy question is how fine the filter should be. For example, numerous security specialists have pointed out the obvious tactic that terrorists might use global container traffic to smuggle a nuclear device into a Western country. In 2003, ABC demonstrated on television that it was possible to smuggle

[51] NATO, *Strategic Concept 1991*, §8, 236–7. NATO, *The Alliance's Strategic Concept*, Approved by the Heads of State and Government participating in the meeting of the North Atlantic Council in Washington, DC, on 23 and 24 April 1999, reprinted in NATO Handbook – Documentation (Brussels: NATO Office of Information and Press, 1999) §20, 411–12.
[52] NATO, *Strategic Concept 1999*, §20.
[53] I owe the term 'risk filter' to Thomas Gammeltoft Hansen.

a container with uranium through US customs.[54] This led to widespread calls for security checks on every container entering the United States. The problem in setting up such a fine risk filter is that it undermines the low transaction costs which are at the heart of globalisation. The roll-on-roll-off containerships are so easy to use for smuggling because they are so very effective in moving very large cargoes from one part of the globe to another. A fine risk filter in every harbour would reduce the risks, but only at considerable cost to macro-economic growth. The Organization for Economic Cooperation and Development estimated in 2003 that new security measures put in place after 9/11 placed an initial burden on ship operators at US$1,279 million, and at US$730 million per year thereafter.[55] In other words, there would be an increase in the transaction costs that globalisation is supposed to reduce.

The UK Health and Safety Executive calls the discussion of how fine the risk filter should be a discussion about 'tolerability', which it defines as 'a willingness to live with a risk so as to secure certain benefits in the confidence that the risk is one that is worth taking and that is being properly controlled'.[56] Traffic is a prime example of risk tolerability. Each year many people are killed or disabled in traffic accidents, but this does not lead to a ban on cars. Instead governments focus on legislation to make cars and roads safer, while government agencies sponsor costly awareness campaigns against drink-driving and other issues that affect people's behaviour on the road. When people attempt to put terrorism in perspective by pointing out that the risk of dying in a car crash is far greater than the risk of dying at the hands of terrorists, they are not only proving that security policy has become an everyday issue, but also arguing that the tolerability that makes us cope with the constant risks of everyday life should be applied to security issues.

This game of probabilities has been in the forefront of crime prevention for thirty years. As in the case of terrorism, the crime-prevention approach began because of rising crime rates – or at least the perception that crime, or terrorism, had become a 'high consequence risk'. Since then the level of crime has been an important indicator of the success of new crime-prevention initiatives and an important factor in local politics in the United States, where, for instance, the high-profile 'tough on crime' policies of Rudolf Giuliani made him a popular mayor in

[54] 'Border Breach? Customs Fails to Detect Depleted Uranium – Again', ABC News, http://abcnews.go.com/sections/wnt/Primetime/sept11_uranium030910.html (9 October 2003).
[55] OECD, *Security in Maritime Transport: Risk Factors and Economic Impact* (Directorate for Science, Technology and Industry, Maritime Transport Committee, July 2003), 3.
[56] The Health and Safety Executive, *Reducing Risks, Protecting People*, 1.

New York. The basis of such policies has been to 'reclaim the streets', that is, to establish control in order to be able to manage the situation. Given such control, people are much more willing to tolerate some crime or some insecurity, because they know that a single pickpocket does not reflect a general descent into urban chaos, but just an individual criminal who managed to get through the risk filter. One way to ensure overall control is through architecture, that is, CPTED, or 'crime prevention through environmental design'.[57] Another option is surveillance. In 2001 2.5 million CCTV cameras were operating in Britain, 150,000 in London. And gradually surveillance is moving from observation to prevention. Computers at Bristol University are being used to analyse videos of criminals' body language with the aim of developing software that can predict assaults before they begin.[58] The preventive capability of CCTV has also been tried out in fighting terrorists. In Britain trials have been conducted in order to establish whether it is possible to use traffic cameras to recognise faces in order to identify terrorist suspects.[59]

Like the software that will identify the beginnings of violent behaviour, Western intelligence services have closely watched states developing weapons of mass destruction. Where police officers use CCTV, intelligence services use satellites. The fact that these states are called 'rogue' states suggests an analogy between the rogue youths who create trouble for nice, upstanding citizens on a pedestrian street, and the regimes of North Korea, Iran or Iraq causing instability in their regions. What Giddens terms 'risk-profiling' becomes an important part of dealing with rogues, be they states or young people.[60] In the area of crime prevention, the question is whether the police or social services should deal with the young people terrorising the pedestrian street. When it comes to rogue states, the question is whether to bomb their weapons production facilities or to facilitate 'regime change' by force.

When intelligence officials ponder the meaning of their satellite images or police officers view CCTV tapes for clues, they are not just considering what the pictures show of what the rogues can do: their real concern is what to expect next. By designating people or states as rogues, values are made the central issue. A gang of young men are rogues

---

[57] Hughes, *Understanding Crime Prevention*, 62.

[58] Helen Carter, 'Eye Spy', *Guardian*, 1 August 2001.

[59] Mark Townsend and Paul Harris, 'Security Role for Traffic Cameras', *Observer*, 9 February 2003.

[60] Giddens, *Modernity and Self-Identity*, 119; for a similar argument, see Christopher Coker, *Globalisation and Insecurity in the Twenty-First Century: NATO and the Management of Risk*, Adelphi Paper 345, International Institute for Strategic Studies (Oxford: Oxford University Press, 2002), 63.

because they have deviant values, which are mostly regarded as irrational and for that reason cannot be deterred. There are two options in dealing with rogues like these: either their opportunities to commit crimes are reduced by surveillance, or else their values are changed. Risk-profiling is therefore becoming very important in crime prevention. When it comes to dealing with sex offenders, another group with deviant values, social workers and police can use a number of 'risk-assessment tools', which list a number of variables that officers can use in assessing the likelihood of sex offenders repeating their crimes, but they can also be used on people who have not in fact yet committed a crime.[61] This focus on values is re-emphasised in strategies for dealing with sexual and violent offenders. In therapy, whether in prison or in the community, sex offenders learn to change 'patterns of deviant sexual arousal', break the 'cycle of abuse', learn about the impact of abuse on victims and learn social skills to deal with other people in non-deviant ways.[62] In other words, this is about giving people new values, a new narrative of themselves, in the belief that this will make them act differently. The sort of person that therapists believe they are working with is not Beccaria's rational criminal, who can be deterred, but a reflexive individual who must be forced to reflect on his values and their risks for other people.

Values also matter in security policy. The means-end rational conception of strategy that thrived during the Cold War did not place great emphasis on values. Although Western countries never trusted non-democratic regimes, they were able to deal with them when the strategic need arose, and they did not regard such regimes as *ipso facto* unstable or dangerous. The end of the Cold War changed this. President George Bush Sr argued that the fall of the Soviet empire had shown that 'certain truths have, indeed, become evident: governments responsive to the will of the people are not likely to commit aggression'.[63] According to this theory of 'democratic peace', the post-Cold War peace was based on the absence of a non-democratic (and therefore aggressive) great-power challenger to 'the free world'.[64] To maintain the present peace, the West should therefore strive to establish what President Clinton called 'a world of thriving democracies that cooperate with each other and live

---

[61] Hazel Kemshall, *Risk Assessment and Management of Known Sexual and Violent Offenders: A Review of Current Issues*, Police Research Series, Paper 140 (London: Home Office, 2001), 23.

[62] Ibid., 40.

[63] George Herbert Walker Bush, *Remarks at the Texas A&M University in College Station, Texas*, 15 December 1992, The George Bush Presidential Library, College Station, TX.

[64] For a more elaborate version of this argument, see my *The West, Civil Society and the Construction of Peace*.

in peace'.[65] As John Lewis Gaddis points out, Clinton believed that the US merely had to guide this process by enlarging the international institutions of democratic peace like NATO, whereas his successor, George Bush, actively wants to promote and impose democracy.[66] Bush thus argued in 2002: 'As we defend the peace, we also have an historic opportunity to preserve the peace. We have our best chance since the rise of the nation state in the seventeenth century to build a world where the great powers compete in peace instead of prepare for war.'[67]

The difference between Clinton's and Bush's ideas of democratic peace reflects differences in the debate over crime prevention. The Clinton approach, of consolidating the secure nations against the general insecurity of the world, reflects the strategies of 'defensible space'[68] that have turned the architecture of cities like Los Angeles into a crime-prevention tool in itself.[69] This is also reflected in the phenomenon of 'gated communities', where fencing and security guards protect middle-class suburbia from the flows of insecurity coming from the city outside. 'These developments', Edward Blakely and Mary Snyder argue, 'in part reflect the notion of community as an island, a social bulwark against the general degradation of the urban social order.'[70] As the NATO Strategic Concept puts it, 'an important aim of the Alliance and its forces is to keep risks at a distance'.[71] This idea of fencing off the 'free world' against the 'unfree' and therefore dangerous world is also reflected in projects of integration like the European Union, an organisation that might be called the largest gated community in the world. Having completed the vision of a common market and a peaceful political community for all European countries, the EU seems increasingly to focus on how to prevent other people from entering it to enjoy the region's comfortable way of life. While common border controls and immigration regimes are among the most vibrant areas of joint EU policy, the EU's member states are in complete disagreement on how

---

[65] William Jefferson Clinton, *Address by the President to the 48th Session of the United Nations General Assembly*, The United Nations, New York (Washington, DC: The White House, Office of the Press Secretary, 1993).
[66] John Lewis Gaddis, 'A Grand Strategy of Transformation', *Foreign Policy*, www.foreign policy.com (11 December 2002).
[67] George W. Bush, *Remarks by the President at 2002 Graduation Exercise of the United States Military Academy*, West Point, New York, 1 June 2002 (Washington, DC: The White House, Office of the Press Secretary), §26.
[68] Quoted in Hughes, *Understanding Crime Prevention*, 60.
[69] Soja, *Postmetropolis*, 298–322.
[70] Edward J. Blakely and Mary Gail Snyder, *Fortress America: Gated Communities in the United States* (Washington, DC: Brookings Institution Press, 1997), 3.
[71] NATO, *Strategic Concept 1999*, §48.

to deal with the problems of the world beyond itself, the debate about the Iraq war in 2003 being a case in point. Not unlike a gated community in suburban America, EU member states can easily agree on the standards by which they should live, but the more perfect they make their own world, the less patient they become with the less perfect world outside the gates.

The withdrawal to the security of your own, fenced-off space works only so long as the rest of the world is unable to visit its insecurity on you. Zigmunt Bauman thus argues that 9/11 shows 'the annihilation of the protective capacity of space'.[72] President Bush's change to a more enterprising mode of building the democratic peace thus in part reflects the realisation that no democracy is an island. If the states and societies that surround the democratic world are not themselves in the process of becoming democratic, then the democracies can be as peaceful as they want, yet still not be at peace. President Bush thus initiated a new focus on spreading democracy to the Arab world in order to stop it exporting terrorism and radical Islamic ideologies to the West.

In sum, the Western doctrine is to leave deterrence behind in favour of managing risks that are believed to be inherent in a globalising world. In a world defined by change, the most important standard for measuring what risks are important and need to be dealt with are what kind of catastrophes they may cause in the future. The next section deals with this focus on the future.

The presence of the future

The most important part of a doctrine is to identify the threats and suggest when to act on them. The notion that Western governments perceive their strategic environment in terms of risk acquires credence from the fact that they increasingly measure their security in terms of future threats. John Adams explains that risk is most often defined 'as the product of the probability and utility of some *future* event'.[73] One might object that security thinking is about future threats as a matter of definition.[74] The point about security discourse, Ole Wæver argues, is that by identifying an object – whether the Soviet Union or Saddam Hussein's WMD programmes – as a security issue, a government is allowed to do certain things (invade Iraq, for example) which are beyond

---

[72] Zygmunt Bauman, *Society Under Siege* (Cambridge: Polity Press, 2002), 88.
[73] Adams, *Risk*, 30.
[74] Barry Buzan et al., *Security: A New Framework for Analysis* (Boulder, CO: Lynne Rienner Publishers, 1997), 26ff.

the bounds of normal politics.[75] In risk society, strategic thinking is proliferating beyond the confines of security policy. Today the type of emergency argument that Wæver identifies as the rhetorical base of security policy is used just as frequently by criminologists, environmentalists and social workers as by security specialists and defence ministers, all of whom argue their cases in terms of scenarios for what might happen if, for example, crime, the environment or children's welfare is not managed properly. In doing so, they argue their case in terms of a different understanding of the future than the understanding that traditionally defined the security discourse.

In the traditional security discourse, the future described in a scenario is a consequence of present inaction. This was the type of argument Kennan made about the Soviet Union in 1946: it defined the threat in a certain way and argued that, under these circumstances, the enemy would attack you in the future or prevent you from doing something you wanted if you did not change your policy. It was the insecure party that should act, whereas the threat was, in the words of NATO, believed to be 'monolithic, massive and potentially immediate'. This is a stock-type argument. Risks are flows: where risk is concerned, the danger is itself evolving. A risk is never a present danger: it only becomes a danger because of what it is expected to cause in the future. This argument reverses the causality of the threat. In Kennan's argument for a new US policy towards the Soviet Union, his suggested US reaction was an effect of the nature of the Soviet threat. A risk argument is the cause of a security challenge that does not exist outside the scenario and never will if the policy is successful. This does not make the risk unreal, because it is based on actual events, but the interpretation of what these events will lead to is more important than taking stock of what the enemy is capable of now. In Ulrich Beck's words, 'the concept of risk reverses the relationship of past, present and future'.[76]

Policies based on scenarios are essentially about preventing or pre-empting a process from coming into fruition. In 2002, the Bush administration made pre-emption a core concept in the US National Security Strategy, and this line of thinking was a crucial part of the argument for invading Iraq in 2003. For this reason, much of the passionate debate about the war turned into a surprisingly abstract argument about the possibility of foreseeing future risks and how to act upon them. The result of this debate has been paradoxical: at the same time as

---

[75] Ole Wæver, 'Securitization and Desecuritization', in Ronnie D. Lipschutz (ed.), *On Security* (New York: Columbia University Press, 1995), 54–7.
[76] Beck, *World Risk Society*, 137.

preventive arguments become the foundation of more and more policies, security policies based on prevention or pre-emption are becoming more and more controversial. This section uses the debate on the case for pre-emption with regard to Iraq as a way to explore the 'presence of the future' in strategic doctrine. The aim of this chapter is not to investigate the arguments for or against invading Iraq in 2003, but to describe strategic rationales. The debate over the Iraq war provided a glimpse into what key decision-makers think about such rationales. Having outlined the arguments for and against pre-emption in the case of Iraq, I go on to show how these arguments bear a striking resemblance to arguments for pre-emptive action in other policy areas, especially the 'precautionary principle' in environmental policy.

Iraq, anticipatory defence and judging risks

It was the United States' desire to invade Iraq which made 'anticipatory defence' – in the words of the then National Security Advisor, Condoleezza Rice – the main focus of a heated world-view debate on the doctrines involved in using armed force in a globalising age.[77] On 10 November 2002, President Bush addressed the UN General Assembly urging the international community to take decisive action against Saddam Hussein's regime, but the President left little doubt that if the Security Council did not authorise the use of military force against Iraq, the United States would invade it anyway.[78] The Security Council adopted Resolution 1441 that in effect read Saddam Hussein the riot act, but whether Saddam Hussein's behaviour merited a military intervention remained a hotly disputed question. Not since the Cuban Missile Crisis had the stakes at Security Council meetings been so high and ambassadors' and foreign ministers' rhetoric so highly pitched. Large-scale demonstrations against the war filled main squares in major cities on both sides of the Atlantic, while pundits fiercely debated the issue in the media. The American government lost this debate, at least in the international community, and most certainly as regards public opinion in France, Germany and a number of other European states, not to mention in the Arab world.[79]

---

[77] Quoted in Kamal Ahmed and Ed Vulliamy, 'United They Stand: The "Odd Couple" Offensive', *Observer*, 8 September 2002, 16. Christopher Coker refers to this as a new doctrine of 'preventive defence'; Coker, *Globalisation and Insecurity*, 54.

[78] George W. Bush, *President Bush Speaks to United Nations*, Remarks by the President to United Nations General Assembly, UN Headquarters, New York, 10 November 2001 (Washington, DC: The White House, Office of the Press Secretary, 2001).

[79] On the politics of the run-up to the war, see Keegan, *The Iraq War*, 88–125, as well as Murray and Scales, *The Iraq War*, 15–44.

The Bush administration's argument for why Iraq needed to be invaded rested on the belief that management of the residual risk which Iraq posed after the 1991 Gulf war, using 'routine bombings' and sanctions, had become increasingly untenable morally because of the terrible effects of sanctions on the Iraqi people, as well as being ineffective in their attempts to curb Saddam Hussein's ambitions and capabilities. It thus seems fair to assume, as many observers have done, that a war against Iraq was high on the Bush administration's policy agenda when he came into office in January 2001.[80] It was the events of 11 September 2001, however, that made a permanent solution to the 'Iraq problem' a strategic necessity in the eyes of the key policy-makers in Washington. Now the administration desperately needed to make a strategic move in the Middle East and, rightly or wrongly, considered Iraq to be the key to a new way of managing the risks of terror emanating from the Middle East. By invading Iraq, the United States could put in place a regime in Baghdad that did not support Islamic fundamentalism ideologically, as Saudi Arabia did, nor was a liability when it came to relations with the Arab world, like the other key American ally in the area, Israel. The US would have to produce its own piece in order to play the Middle East strategic chess game in a new way. Ulrich Beck has referred to this as a 'rule-altering' policy.[81]

From this perspective, focusing on Iraq's weapons programmes was primarily a way of demonstrating that Iraq was in breach of UN resolutions and that therefore the US should be given authority for an invasion. After 11 September 2001, however, the proliferation of WMDs (the weapons themselves, as well as technology and know-how) was considered a greater risk. If al-Qaeda could achieve such devastating results by using highjacked planes as cruise missiles, what could terror groups or indeed rogue states not achieve with WMD capabilities? Making the bomb might well be too complicated for terrorist groups, but could they buy them from North Korea or Iraq? That might not even be probable – selling WMDs would be very risky for these countries if they were caught – but was it a risk worth taking? In any case, Bush argued, if Iraq developed WMDs, the United States would no longer be able to manage the risk posed by that country. 'The dangers we face will only worsen from month to month and from year to year,' the President argued, 'and when they have fully materialized it may be too late to protect ourselves and our friends and our

[80] Hersh, *Chain of Command*, 163–201; Woodward, *Bush at War*, 49, 83–4.
[81] Beck, 'Reinvention of Politics', 34–6.

allies.'[82] Refusing 'to live in this future of fear', Bush argued that the United States needed to take action.[83] The President's National Security Strategy of September 2002 thus states:

> The United States can no longer solely rely on a reactive posture as we have in the past. The inability to deter a potential attacker, the immediacy of today's threats, and the magnitude of potential harm that could be caused by our adversaries' choice of weapons, do not permit that option. We cannot let our enemies strike first.[84]

The Bush administration was not able to make even some of its closest allies, like Germany, accept the case for 'anticipatory defence'. Prime Minister Blair was, as we shall see, a much more eloquent apologist of anticipatory defence, but even he was not able to convince the British people firmly that the invasion was necessary in order to reduce security risks. This was made abundantly clear in a number of agonising television programmes in which the Prime Minister defended his reasons for going to war in front of an audience that simply did not accept his rationale and directed most of their questions to confronting him with what they believed to be the real reasons for wanting to take the nation to war.[85] These reasons were based on means-end rational conceptions of why a government might want to go to war. Perhaps the best example of this was the argument that the war was about the control of Iraq's oil. Oil constituted a material reason, a thing you could physically control by conquering Iraq, and people were able to infer interests in oil production by pointing to the large Iraqi oil reserves.

There are many reasons for the opposition to the British and American governments' argument for invading Iraq. However, if one focuses on opposition to the concept of anticipatory defence itself, then one reason why British and American policy-makers were so unsuccessful in arguing the case for it might simply be that they were surprised that they had to: after all, the concept was not new, nor accepted only by Anglo-American policy-makers.

William Perry describes the Clinton administration's view that if North Korea developed nuclear weapons it would 'create intolerable risks'. President Clinton was prepared to launch air strikes against North

---

[82] George W. Bush, *President Bush Discusses Iraq with Congressional Leaders*, 26 September 2002 (Washington, DC: The White House, Office of the Press Secretary, 7 October 2002), §5.

[83] Ibid.

[84] *National Security Strategy*, 17 September 2002, 15.

[85] Andrew Marr, 'Blair's Masochism Makes Great Television – But Is It a Good War Strategy?', *Daily Telegraph*, 12 March 2003; Alan Cowell, 'Blair Hears Drumbeat of Dissent from Party', *International Herald Tribune*, 12 March 2003.

Korea's WMD production facilities, but settled for a political commitment from the regime in Pyongyang to discontinue the weapons programme. He did use military force against al-Qaeda training camps in 1998 in an unsuccessful attempt to kill the organisation's leadership. Clinton stressed that the attack was in response to the bombing of American embassies in Africa, but instead of settling for revenge as an argument for launching cruise missiles, he went out of his way to emphasise that military action was necessary in order to prevent future attacks on the United States. In his address to the nation after the cruise missiles had struck the camps – which al-Qaeda had apparently already abandoned, having been alerted to the US attack by Pakistani intelligence[86] – the President told the American people that 'the risks from inaction to America and the world would be far greater than action, for that would embolden our enemies, leaving their ability and their willingness to strike us intact'.[87] The President focused on opponents' capability and how further development of that capability was a risk in itself. In 2002, Vice President Cheney made exactly the same argument in relation to Iraq and, like President Clinton four years before, he concluded, 'the risk of inaction is far greater than the risk of action'.[88]

During the 2004 presidential campaign in the United States, Senator John Kerry strongly criticised President Bush for having eroded US alliances in the row about the invasion of Iraq. But when news anchor Jim Lehrer asked the Senator for his views on pre-emption in the first television debate between the candidates, Kerry would not reject the right to pre-emption, in spite of the fact that it would have made political sense for him to do so:

No president, through all of American history [Kerry said], has ever ceded, and nor would I, the right to pre-empt in any way necessary to protect the United States of America. But if and when you do it, Jim, you have to do it in a way that passes the test, that passes the global test where your countrymen, your people understand fully why you're doing what you're doing and you can prove to the world that you did it for legitimate reasons.[89]

Kerry did not reject the notion of pre-emption: he objected to the way in which the Bush administration had gone about pre-empting because 'the

---

[86] Clarke, *Against All Enemies*, 186–9.
[87] William Jefferson Clinton, *Address to the Nation by the President*, 20 August 1998 (Washington, DC: The White House, Office of the Press Secretary, 1998), §16.
[88] Richard B. Cheney, *Remarks by the Vice President to the Veterans of Foreign Wars 103rd National Convention*, 26 August 2002 (Washington, DC: The White House, Office of the Press Secretary, 18 September 2002), §41.
[89] *Transcript: First Presidential Debate*, 30 September 2004, from Coral Gables, FL. Text from FDCH E-media, www.washingtonpost.com (7 October 2004).

key is for America to lead: to build an international consensus for early preventive action, so that states don't even think of taking the nuclear road'.[90] Kerry thus argued for the expansion of programmes like the Nunn-Lugar initiative, which is aimed at preventing unemployed Russian nuclear scientists or unaccounted-for nuclear material from ending up in a rogue state. However, Kerry also suggested that the invasion of Iraq would have been a more credible deterrence to regimes in Iran or North Korea if it had been based on a global consensus.

While such a consensus had been impossible to reach in the particular case of Iraq, there seems to be a general acceptance of the doctrine of pre-emption. Russia opposed the US invasion of Iraq, but 'as for carrying out preventive strikes against terrorist bases,' stated Colonel General Yuri Baluyevsky, Chief of the Russian General Staff, 'we will take all measures to liquidate terrorist bases in any region of the world'.[91] Few people made a more passionate case against the US arguments for attacking Iraq than Dominique de Villepin, the French foreign minister in 2003, but in general the French government made it clear that 'the possibility of preemptive action might be considered, from the time that an explicit and confirmed threatening situation is identified'.[92]

The question was whether to apply the general principle of pre-emption to the particular case, Iraq. It was a matter of judgement – or so Blair argued in October 2004:

Here is the crux. It is possible that even with all of this, nothing would have happened. Possible that Saddam would change his ambitions; possible he would develop the WMD but never use it; possible that the terrorists would never get their hands on WMD, whether from Iraq or elsewhere. We cannot be certain. Perhaps we would have found different ways of reducing it. Perhaps this Islamic terrorism would ebb of its own accord. But do we want to take the risk? That is the judgement. And my judgement then and now is that the risk of this new global terrorism and its interaction with states or organisations or individuals proliferating WMD, is one I simply am not prepared to run. This is not a time to err on the side of caution.[93]

The Prime Minister was echoing a report by the Cabinet Office's Strategy Unit on how to improve the British government's ability to handle 'risk and uncertainty'. The report concluded: 'handling risk is at heart

---

[90] John Kerry, *Remarks of Senator John Kerry on Security and Strength for a New World*, Seattle, WA, 27 May 2005, www.johnkerry.com (4 June 2004), §40.

[91] Nick Pation Walsh, 'Putin Puts £6m Price on Rebels' Heads', *Guardian*, 9 September 2004.

[92] Quoted in Freedman, *Deterrence*, 94–5.

[93] Tony Blair, *PM Warns of Continuing Global Terror Threat*, 5 March 2004 (London: Prime Minister's Office, 2004), §§45–7.

about judgement'.[94] The Strategy Unit had been tasked with looking into the government's risk-management capabilities in the wake of the BSE scandal, in which government ministers had insisted that BSE-infected livestock were not dangerous, based on the lack of any scientific evidence to the contrary. Not only did later research prove this assertion wrong, but the government's position was clearly out of line with the public's risk perception. The public feared BSE when the government did not, just as the government feared Iraq when the public did not. This is an illustration of Ulrich Beck's argument that political discourse in risk society is defined by 'definitional struggles over the scale, degrees and urgency of risks'.[95]

Defining the scale, degree and urgency of risk is a strategic enterprise. The fact that the Cabinet Office has a Strategy Unit in the first place and that its strategic maxims are reflected in domestic as well as foreign policy demonstrates how much strategic thinking has proliferated. It also shows that strategy in both the domestic and international arenas is increasingly defined by questions of risk management. Blair's point about strategy is that formulating a strategy and acting on it is itself a risk. One only knows for sure when the risk is no longer a risk when it has become a catastrophe. Again the analogy with meteorology is suggestive. The meteorologist does not know what the weather is going to be like in a week's time, but the very usefulness of his profession is to make the prediction anyway. The evidence on the basis of which he makes his prediction is wrong by definition, but the scenario of next week's weather that the weatherman presents to his viewers is much better than not knowing anything at all. With a weather report, it is possible to make a choice: one can estimate the probability of it raining and act accordingly.

The real question is what kind of chances you are prepared to take – will you bring your umbrella to work only if the probability of rain is 100 per cent, or will 15 per cent do? In effect Blair is arguing that since WMD proliferation is much more risky than rain, one should not accept even a low probability.[96] By speaking in terms of probability, Blair is rejecting any criticism of the Iraq war in means-end rational terms. If the

---

[94] *Risk: Improving Government's Capability to Handle Risk and Uncertainty*, Strategy Unit Report, November 2002 (London: Cabinet Office, 2002), 6.

[95] Beck, *Risk Society*, 46.

[96] This theme was consistently present in Blair's strategic rationales from shortly after 9/11. Thus, when discussing the response to al-Qaeda's attack, he told the Labour Party Conference that 'whatever the dangers of the action we take, the dangers of inaction are far, far greater'; Tony Blair, *Prime Minister's Address to the Labour Party Conference*, Brighton, 2 October 2001, www.labour.org.uk (17 October 2001), §14.

war is regarded in terms of cause and effect, the fact that no WMDs were discovered in Iraq after the invasion invalidates the rationale for the war, which then became an effect without a cause. Hence the conspiracy theories on the *real* cause of the war, because it is only by identifying a materially existing cause (e.g. oil) that the effect (the war) can make any sense. From a risk perspective, the missing WMDs are of concern because, in the words of the Home Office, 'the key issue in risk assessment is accuracy, and the avoidance of either over-prediction or under-prediction'.[97] The fact that the intelligence reports were much less accurate than the typical weather report makes strategists concerned that what proved to be the over-prediction of Iraq's capabilities will lead to the under-prediction of other threats. The decision to invade Iraq, however, should not be judged in terms of whether it can be determined to be right post factum. 'In the risk society,' Joost van Loon explains, 'risks manifest themselves as particular symptoms of a virtual cause.'[98]

Risk judgements are not about right or wrong, as Hazel Kemshall argues in her study of how to treat potentially violent or sexual offenders. 'Defensibility' is the most important aspect because, like the weatherman, one is bound to be wrong.[99] When the purpose of strategy becomes one of managing risks, then one is dealing with 'real virtualities'[100] rather than realities. Blair and Bush had to choose which scenario they believed in and to act upon it. Dominique de Villepin chose another scenario and therefore recommended a different course of action. 'Obviously, for the crisis in Iraq is a major proliferation crisis,' the French foreign minister asserted, 'we decided to use a method, the United Nations inspections, to eradicate this risk, find out the truth and abolish all these weapons should they exist.'[101] If one follows the risk rationale, the fact that the UN could not have done the job because there was not much of a job to do in the first place does not prove that invading Iraq was the wrong thing to do. The risk perspective means that as soon as the Iraq war ended, the risk from Iraqi WMDs ceased to be important. What had been a 'real virtuality' became an 'inconsequential reality'. When scenarios 'cause' action, then past actions, whether mistakes or not, are not regarded as a prime concern. They might be of moral or political importance, but not of strategic importance. A risk that has not

[97] Kemshall, *Risk Assessment and Management of Known Sexual and Violent Offenders*, 13.
[98] Joost van Loon, *Risk and Technological Culture: Towards a Sociology of Virulence* (London: Routledge, 2002), 25.
[99] Kemshall, *Risk Assessment and Management of Known Sexual and Violent Offenders*, 21.
[100] Ibid., 136.
[101] Interview given by M. de Villepin during the *Complément d'enquête* programme on France 2, Paris, 24 March 2003, www.special.diplomatie.fr (27 March 2003), §2.

materialised is simply gone; what matters in the risk perspective on strategy is always the next thing on the horizon. Thus after the invasion, it became the risks arising from the occupation of Iraq that dominated the strategic agenda. The falsification of the WMD argument for invading Iraq also mattered less in a risk framework because, seen from that perspective, threats are not about the stock of WMDs that Iraq might or might not possess. The management of risk is about filtering the flows of risk. From this perspective, the mere existence of the will to develop a WMD capability and the know-how possessed by the Iraqi government made Iraq a threat because the regime intended to restart its programmes at the earliest opportunity. This opportunity would arise when sanctions were lifted, and that was basically the only strategic alternative to invasion. The sanctions had disastrous consequences in Iraq and were proving increasingly hard to manage. From this perspective, an invasion was a way to regain the initiative in Iraq, but also, argued the Bush administration, to achieve new management capabilities in the Middle East in general. It is on the success of these issues that risk strategists will focus.

In conclusion, one should note that the debate over the Iraq war has taken place on two completely different levels. The proponents of invading Iraq argued in terms of risk, while their opponents structured their arguments in terms of means-end rationality. From this perspective, the invasion was a strategic blunder based on bad intelligence at best, a conspiracy in order to ensure US economic and strategic interests and the President's re-election at worst.[102] From a risk perspective, the war should not be judged by the non-existing stocks of WMD, but on its ability to filter the flows of risks coming from the Middle East. It might come as a surprise that Blair's and Bush's arguments for 'anticipatory defence' did not pass the 'global test' that Senator John Kerry had asserted that US pre-emption should be able to pass, because their arguments actually have a lot in common with the 'precautionary principle' that is advocated as providing the basis of environmental law by Greenpeace and other 'friends of the earth'. This is what we turn to next.

Precautionary principles

The precautionary principle has become a cornerstone of Western environmental policy and is enshrined in international treaties, especially

---

[102] Michael Moore's *Fahrenheit 9/11* (Columbia, 2004) is perhaps the best-known example of this form of argument.

the Rio documents. The precautionary principle formed part of the short-lived EU constitution, and President Jacques Chirac has argued that it should become part of the French constitution. The precautionary principle is itself a result of the proliferation of strategic thinking. The principle is a way to define a doctrine for conducting environmental policy, a doctrine based on the 'better safe than sorry' principle that Blair advocated in his defence of the invasion of Iraq. Christopher Coker points out that the precautionary principle and 'anticipatory defence' really represent the same kind of doctrine.[103] President Bush outraged environmentalists by rejecting the Kyoto protocol, but in arguing in favour of invading Iraq he stated his case in terms of precaution. This similarity is not merely an analogy, it demonstrates how all strategic thinking in risk society is guided by 'the politics of urgency'.[104] The controversy that surrounds the precautionary principle might thus serve as a guide to the possible consequences of pre-emptive military doctrines.

The precautionary principle is based on scenarios for the future. The fear of global warming is a prime example. George Woodwell describes the scenario and suggests that policy-makers act accordingly:

The possibility exists that the warming will proceed to the point where biotic releases [of greenhouse gases] from the warming will exceed in magnitude those controlled directly by human activity. If so, the warming will be beyond control by any steps now considered reasonable. We do not know how far we are from that point because we do not know in sufficient detail about the circulations of carbon among the pools of the carbon cycle. We are not going to be able to resolve those questions definitively soon. Meanwhile, the concentration of heat-trapping gases in the atmosphere rises . . . If the process [of stabilising the composition of the atmosphere] is not undertaken, the erosion of the human habitat will proceed rapidly, with the full panoply of ecological and political consequences.[105]

John Adams demonstrates how Woodwell's argument works: 'he begins with a *possibility*, proceeds by an *if*, via doubts about *how soon*, to the *imperative for urgent action*'.[106] Now, compare Woodwell's argument in favour of the need for precautionary measures to stop global warming to President Bush's argument as to why precautionary measures are needed against proliferators of WMDs. In his State of the Union Address in 2002, Bush gave an assessment of Iran, Iraq and North Korea, and continued:

---

[103] Coker, *Globalisation and Insecurity*, 73–5.
[104] Van Loon, *Risk and Technological Culture*, 4.
[105] Quoted in Adams, *Risk*, 168.   [106] Ibid.

States like these, and their terrorist allies, constitute an axis of evil, arming to threaten the peace of the world. By seeking weapons of mass destruction, these regimes pose a grave and growing danger. They could provide these arms to terrorists, giving them the means to match their hatred. They could attack our allies or attempt to blackmail the United States. In any of these cases, the price of indifference would be catastrophic . . . We'll be deliberate, yet time is not on our side. I will not wait on events, while dangers gather. I will not stand by, as peril draws closer and closer. The United States of America will not permit the world's most dangerous regimes to threaten us with the world's most destructive weapons.[107]

The subject and rhetoric might be different, but the argument is the same. The President describes the possibility that Iran, Iraq and North Korea will develop WMDs, and he outlines what will happen *if* they succeed in acquiring these weapons and what will happen *if* they pass on this technology and know-how to 'their terrorist allies'. When exactly the axis of evil states, let alone 'their terrorist allies', are to acquire such weapons remains most unclear in the State of the Union Address. Elsewhere in his Address, the President tells the Congress about Iraqi attempts to acquire WMD technology,[108] but this is the only proof of the regime's intent to acquire WMDs; how and when this technology will result in a WMD capability remains unclear. Nonetheless, the Address left few in doubt that the United States would invade Iraq as soon as possible in order to prevent one of 'the world's most dangerous regimes . . . threaten us with the world's most destructive weapons'.

Two years later, Senator John Kerry challenged Bush's Iraq policy and the basis on which the President argued the case for war, but, as already mentioned, he did not seek to refute the precautionary argument. Indeed the Senator argued in precautionary terms himself when he made securing nuclear bomb-making primarily in the former Soviet Union a cornerstone of his foreign policy. In spite of the fact that there are virtually no reported cases of bomb-making material actually being smuggled from the former Soviet Union to Iran, Iraq or North Korea, Kerry essentially argued: the stuff is there; it might be used; if it is used it would be terrible; we ought to do something about it, now![109] The fact that Kerry challenged the specific reasons and the intelligence that President Bush had put forward for going to war, but did not challenge the logic itself (in spite of the fact that doing so would have been to his

---

[107] George W. Bush, *The President's State of the Union Address*, 29 January 2002 (Washington, DC: The White House, Office of the Press Secretary, 2002), §§20–2.

[108] Ibid., §§17–18.

[109] John Kerry, *Remarks by Senator John Kerry on New Strategies to Meet New Threats*, 1 June 2004, West Palm Beach, FL, §12–13.

political advantage, because Bush was vulnerable due to the lack of a global consensus on the risk-management argument), demonstrates how the precautionary argument has become established security doctrine in the United States.

The precautionary principle is accepted on the other side of the Atlantic as well. In spite of the huge differences of opinion between its member states over the Iraq war, the first EU strategic concept concluded in 2003 that the EU 'should be ready to act before a crisis occurs. Conflict prevention and threat prevention cannot start too early.'[110] The EU strategic concept brings the precautionary discourse full circle when it identifies the global warming 'predicted by most scientists' as a potential threat that the EU needs to prepare itself to address.[111] This environmental focus indicates why it is not surprising that the EU and the US both have pre-emption in their strategic policy papers, in spite of their differences on Iraq. By including the precautionary principle in the EU treaties and participating in global environmental regimes, the EU's heads of state and government have long since adopted arguments in terms of the precautionary principle. The United States, on the other hand, is reluctant to adopt the precautionary principle in environmental policy, even though it has adopted it in its security policy.

The precautionary principle may have been widely accepted as the basis for environmental policy, but there is also widespread concern about the consequences of such a doctrine. Bjørn Lomborg strongly criticises the 'politics of urgency' recommended by 'environmentalists' because the scenarios that these policy recommendations are based on are themselves grounded in flimsy empirical evidence. Lomborg thus believes the global warming debate 'to be yet another case of people arguing furiously in the dark'.[112] Lomborg demands that environmentalists must be able to establish a causal link, but this is exactly what the precautionary principle rejects. The 1987 Convention on the Protection of the North Sea thus states that 'a precautionary approach is necessary which may require action to control inputs of such substances even before a causal link has been established'.[113] The lack of a causal

---

[110] Javier Solana, *A Secure Europe in a Better World*, European Council, Thessaloniki, 20 June 2003 (Brussels: EU High Representative for the Common Foreign and Security Policy, 2003), 12.

[111] Ibid., 3.

[112] Bjørn Lomborg, *The Sceptical Environmentalist* (Cambridge: Cambridge University Press, 2001), 167.

[113] Quoted in Julian Morris, 'Defining the Precautionary Principle', in Julian Morris (ed.), *Rethinking Risk and the Precautionary Principle* (Oxford: Butterworth-Heinemann, 2000), 3.

link means that the precautionary argument 'hinges on the untold *if*', Lomborg argues, echoing Adams.[114] According to Lomborg, the result is that environmentalists keep making 'a lot of poor predictions, often based on little more than rhetorically pleasing arguments'.[115] According to those who put forward precautionary arguments, zinc will run out, or Iraq will produce nukes, but none of this turns out to be true.

Lomborg spends a lot of energy debunking the statistical foundation of environmentalist scenarios on future scarcities of raw materials, on global warming and similar issues, but his main charge is a philosophical one: the future will probably not be as good as we hope, but it will most certainly not be as bad as the pessimists predict. By thinking of our future in terms of worst case scenarios, we are, Lomborg argues, spending 'our resources and attention solving phantom problems while ignoring real and pressing . . . issues'.[116] In the terminology used in this book, Lomborg fears that environmentalists are falling into a 'preventive trap'. In the same way, former Vice President Al Gore lamented that the invasion of Iraq diverted attention from the, in his view, much more urgent task of capturing Osama bin Laden and stabilising Afghanistan.[117] After the war, Dominique de Villepin asked whether preventing a danger that was not there had in fact not turned out to be the cause of insecurity rather than a precaution against a gathering menace:

We too were concerned by the security threat of Iraq. But what were we talking about? Was it weapons of mass destruction? At that time there was an inspection system which we had constantly adapted and was working. Was it terrorism? At that time, there was no established link between Iraq and the al-Qaeda network. Today, in Iraq, terrorist groups, which hadn't been there before, are taking advantage of the inadequate border controls to infiltrate. Was it remodelling the Middle East region? Today we can all clearly see the concern of the neighbouring countries. Is the region more stable? Are we on the way to peace?[118]

Lomborg points out that most people are much more sceptical about arguments for increased defence spending on account of some distant threat than they are about logically similar arguments about the need to spend on environmental issues.[119] He also argues that one should always

---

[114] Lomborg, *Sceptical Environmentalist*, 27.
[115] Ibid., 29–30.
[116] Ibid., 5.
[117] Al Gore, *Iraq and the War on Terrorism*, 23 September 2002, www.commonwealthclub. org (13 October 2004).
[118] Dominique de Villepin, *BBC Dimbleby Lecture*, BBC News, www.bbc.co.uk (6 November 2003), §§99–105.
[119] Lomborg, *Sceptical Environmentalist*, 9–10. Cf. Adams, *Risk*, 169.

be sceptical about intervention in social life by means of environmental laws on the basis of the precautionary principle. The case he makes against intervention where there is a lack of evidence mirrors the case against the intervention in Iraq put forward by John Mearsheimer and Stephen Walt. While the Bush administration presented Saddam Hussein as 'a serial aggressor', Mearsheimer and Walt argued that 'the facts . . . tell a different story':[120]

It is not surprising [Mearsheimer and Walt continue] that those who favour war with Iraq portray Saddam as an inveterate and only partly rational aggressor. They are in the business of selling a preventive war, so they must try to make remaining at peace seem unacceptably dangerous. And the best way to do that is to inflate the threat, either by exaggerating Iraq's capabilities or by suggesting horrible things will happen if the United States does not act soon.[121]

The authors also point to what John Adams believes to be central to the precautionary principle. Whether it is nature or national security that needs to be protected, the object of protection is regarded as 'ephemeral'.[122] When one believes that nature is on the verge of collapse, there is no room to take a risk and hope that the invisible hand of the market or the power of new technologies will solve the problem in due course. Similarly, Deputy Secretary of Defense Wolfowitz regarded 9/11 as a 'window' to a risky future:

A future where new enemies visit violence on us in startling ways; a future in which our cities are among the battlefields and our people are among the targets; a future in which more and more adversaries will possess the capability to bring war to the American homeland; a future where the old methods of deterrence are no longer sufficient – and new strategies and capabilities are needed to ensure peace and security.[123]

If that is one's analysis, then there is no time to wait and little comfort in hoping for the best. Tony Blair puts it this way: 'this is not a time to err on the side of caution'.[124] This argument points to an inherent contradiction in the strategic notion of risk as a flow rather than a stock. In embracing the risk framework, one has to accept that not all risks can be prevented from materialising on the one hand, while on the other hand the policy-makers of the risk society seem unwilling to accept Aaron Wildavsky's point that 'relative safety is not static, but is rather a

[120] John J. Mearsheimer and Stephen M. Walt, 'An Unnecessary War', *Foreign Policy* (January/February 2003), 52.
[121] Ibid., 58–9.
[122] Adams, *Risk*, 34.
[123] Wolfowitz, *Building a Military for the 21st Century*, §4.
[124] Blair, *PM Warns of Continuing Global Terror Threat*, §§45–7.

dynamic product of learning from error over time'.[125] According to the risk strategists, threats are flows, but they are not willing to go with the flow. Perhaps the stakes are just too high. Wildavsky recognises as much when he carefully notes that 'trial and error is not a doctrine one would like to see applied to engaging in nuclear war'.[126] Unwilling to pay the price of insecurity, however, the risk strategists have to face boomerang effects that produce more risks than the initial action was intended to avert.

The boomerang effect

The main challenge to strategy in risk society is unpredictability. It has become a cliché for Western strategy papers to contrast the predictable and unitary threat from the Soviet Union during the Cold War with the unpredictable and multifaceted threats that characterise the post-Cold War period. Still, in order to act, one needs an idea of what is going to happen. Scenarios provide such a vision of the future and, as we have seen, policy-makers act on these visions. However, a scenario tells you only that something is likely to happen, it does not tell you when and where. Therefore the most obvious doctrine that follows from the focus on scenarios is pre-emption, that is, an attempt to rob the enemy of the capability to realise the scenario, thus also making redundant the questions of when and where. But what if pre-emption is not possible? This question is very much on the minds of those concerned with terrorism. One can strike at the finances, communications and training facilities of terrorists, and even target individual terrorists or the states that are harbouring them, but one can never be sure that another terrorist cell is not planning an attack. Terrorist scenarios thus include limited options for preventing attacks altogether, which leave strategists with no choice but to ask when and where attacks are likely to occur in order to strengthen defences at these points.

In the summer of 2003, the Pentagon planned to open a futures market for terrorist-watchers in order to obtain answers to the questions of when and where. 'Futures markets have proven themselves to be good at predicting such things as elections results,' a press statement insisted; 'they are often better than expert opinions'. The Pentagon's idea was to let people buy futures for when and where a terrorist attack

---

[125] Aaron Wildavsky, 'Trial and Error Versus Trial Without Error', in Julian Morris (ed.), *Rethinking Risk and the Precautionary Principle* (Oxford: Butterworth-Heinemann, 2000), 35.
[126] Ibid., 41.

would take place. The purpose was not for people to make a lot of money, for the futures were for very small amounts, but to engage many people with different information bases in joint scenario-making. In other words, the Pentagon strategists believed more in the rationality of the market than in that of individual analysts in the CIA headquarters in Langley, Virginia. The idea caused uproar and the website closed down even before trader registration could begin on 1 August 2003.[127]

By viewing terrorism in market terms, the Pentagon implied that terrorism was a risk beyond control. Instead it was a flow that could be managed, as one manages a market, by following trends. The knowledge the Pentagon obtained on terrorism could not be used to stop terrorism once and for all, because one does not close down a market – in the market place, knowledge merely makes one a better operator. Congress did not like the implication that terrorism would remain a largely uncontrollable feature of global politics, nor did the politicians like the implications of people being able to make money out of terrorism. The ethics of the matter was one thing, but what if terrorists bought futures on the attacks they themselves planned to carry out? This would actually be an advantage for the Pentagon's ability to predict, but to the politicians on the Hill it seemed obscene.

The fate of the terrorist futures market demonstrates some of the boomerang effects of pre-emptive doctrines. Congress's distaste for what strategists considered an innocent and perhaps rather creative way of obtaining greater knowledge about the unpredictable indicates that different risk cultures react differently to doctrines. This makes decisions on strategy difficult. The futures market also raises the question of how many risks it is possible to filter away. The underlying assumption of the futures market is that terrorism will not go away and that no final victory can be declared in the war on terror, a premise that was apparently politically unacceptable. Some claim that this is leading to excessively heavy preventive doctrines in a futile attempt to prevent what in the final analysis is unpreventable. From this perspective, learning to live with risks may be more important than preventing them. Finally, the uproar against the terrorist futures market also shows how much strategies based on 'real virtualities' depend on trust. If the legislature, the people or one's allies do not trust the basis of the scenario within which a government is proposing to act, then it will be difficult not only to carry out the required military actions, but also to summon support

---

[127] Carl Hulse, 'Pentagon Cancels Scheme for Wagering on Terror', *International Herald Tribune*, 30 July 2003.

the next time a security issue arises. The case of the invasion of Iraq illustrates this. I deal with these issues in what follows.

Living with terrorism

In the final analysis, the question of pre-emption boils down to what one expects of the twenty-first century. In the West, we expect the twenty-first century to be shaped by globalisation. After 9/11, the discourse on globalisation paid more equal attention to the dark side of globalisation (e.g. terrorism) as to its brighter promises (e.g. the spread of wealth and democratic peace). The question remains whether strategy should focus on pre-empting the ills or furthering the good sides of globalisation. Most politicians will argue that one can fight the bad while still acquiring the good things that globalisation brings with it. Sometimes this is even true and not only a way to avoid facing the electorate with hard choices. However, sometimes it is not true. When choices are to be made, the philosophical difference between those who feel that globalisation's bright side will prevail and those who fear the spread of darkness makes a real difference. Most of all, if we regard globalisation as the process that is shaping the West's future, then the good as well as the bad prospects are believed to be open ended: either there is no end to all the good that globalisation is going to achieve, or there is no end to the ills it is going to cause.

The most forceful criticisms of pre-emption thus come from those who believe that a focus on the dangers of globalisation is actually 'pre-empting' good things from happening. Following this line of thinking, Didier Bigo argues that, 'rather than the ambiguous discourse of politicians or experts who, in trying to reassure the public, conjure up an impressive list of vulnerabilities never imagined by this very public, we would do well to adopt the slogan of "living with terrorism"'.[128] Bigo is not arguing that one should condone terrorists' methods or motives, but that terrorism should be accepted as a fact of life. From this perspective, the comparison between the numbers of people killed in traffic accidents and those killed in terrorist attacks makes sense. Just as traffic accidents are an acceptable price to pay for our transport needs, so terrorism is an acceptable risk because of all the good things we otherwise achieve through globalisation. This line of argument is well known within risk research. Deborah Lupton calls reducing risks the

[128] Didier Bigo, *To Reassure, and Protect, After September 11*, www.ssrc.org/sept11/essays/ (1 December 2004).

mantra of the age, but 'there also exists a counter discourse, in which risk-taking is represented far more positively'.[129] One such 'counter-culture' is extreme sports, in which some people take risks for fun that other people desperately try to avoid.[130] This underscores Prime Minister Blair's point about risk assessment being a matter of judgement. One chooses the risks one is prepared to accept and acts to prevent those that one is not willing to accept. Blair recognises that making choices carries a risk in itself, a risk that is amplified because other people may regard the decision as being based on excessive risk-averseness. People belonging to different risk cultures will not accept the choices made by others.

During the debate about the Iraq war in 2002–3, many Europeans felt that Americans were following a far too risk-averse approach to the new security environment. They considered that Americans were preoccupied with the unattainable goal set out by Abraham Lincoln: 'So far as possible the people everywhere shall have that sense of perfect security.'[131] The US Congress protested against the futures market for terrorism because it rejected the idea of 'living with terrorism'. However, such perfect security can simply not be realised, the European argument went, and the rest of the world had been painfully aware of this for quite some time. Following this line of argument, Slavoj Zizek's comment on the death of some 3,000 human beings on 11 September 2001 was as post-modern as it was laconic: 'The US just got the taste of what goes on around the world on a daily basis, from Sarajevo to Grozny, from R[w]anda and Congo to Sierra Leone.'[132]

Some critics of the US demonstrated more compassion than Zizek, but they all showed the disdain of those willing to take risks for those who are not. They felt that the US should have accepted living with terrorism rather than waging war against it. From the American perspective, however, the risk-taker attitude of 'old Europe' was grossly irresponsible, if not downright cowardly, because, paradoxically, Americans found that 'old Europe' was not, in fact, willing to take risks. Americans scorned the French for not having the guts to take the risks of war when it was necessary. The different interpretations of the risks posed by Saddam Hussein led to different interpretations of where the risks

---

[129] Lupton, *Risk*, 148–9.   [130] Ibid., 149–50.

[131] Abraham Lincoln, *First Inaugural Address*, 4 March 1861, www.libertyonline.hyper mall.com/Lincoln/Lincoln-1.html (3 December 2004). Cf. John Lewis Gaddis, *Surprise, Security, and the American Experience* (Cambridge, MA: Harvard University Press, 2004), 7–33.

[132] Slavoj Zizek, *Welcome to the Desert of the Real!*, The Global Site, 16 September 2001, www.theglobalsite.ac.uk/times/109zizek.htm (18 February 2002).

lay.[133] One reason why the Bush administration failed to persuade key European allies to support pre-emptive action against Iraq was this difference in risk cultures, a difference which was made only more marked by the fact that the WMDs the Bush administration were so fearful of did not turn up in Iraq, but instead risks arose from the occupation itself.

Pre-emption makes it worse

When a risk is averted, it disappears along with the scenario that pre-emptive action has now made impossible, but then the pre-emptive action itself may become a risk. A possible boomerang effect was very much on the war-planners' minds just before the war began. 'We still do not know how US forces will be received,' a so-called senior official told the *New York Times* in February 2003; 'will it be cheers, jeers or shots? And the fact is, we won't know until we get there.'[134] As it turned out there were some cheers, but many more shots. Instead of an Iraqi people grateful to the US troops for having liberated them from Saddam Hussein's dictatorship and ready to be the beacon of democracy in the Middle East envisioned by US strategists, the situation in Iraq soon deteriorated into guerrilla warfare. When electioneering began for the US presidential election one and a half years later, the challenger, Senator John Kerry, argued that 'the president's policy in Iraq precipitated the very problem that he said he was trying to prevent'.[135] This is a rather precise definition of a boomerang effect. The President wanted to create stability and new strategic options in the Middle East. Instead 140,000 US troops became bogged down in insurgency operations that did not seem to produce any final results. As a part of the 'war on terror', the Iraq war did not impress people either: 49 per cent of Americans polled by the German Marshall Fund thought that they had become more insecure because of the war; 72 per cent of Europeans thought that a war they had not supported in the first place made them more vulnerable to terrorism.[136] This corresponded to Dominique de Villepin's fears from before the war:

---

[133] Cf. Jordan Tama, 'Is Europe Too Cautious?', *Foreign Policy* (January/February 2004), 88–90.
[134] David E. Sanger and Thom Shanker, 'War Planners Begin to Speak of War's Risks', *New York Times*, 18 Feburary 2003.
[135] John Kerry, *Kerry Lays Out Iraq Plan*, 20 September 2004, New York, transcript *Washington Post*, www.washingtonpost.com (22 September 2004), §67.
[136] German Marshall Fund, *Transatlantic Trends 2004 – Topline Data*, www.transatlantic-trends.org (16 January 2005), 52.

There is indeed a risk of seeing unrest, that's been our worry from the outset. The risk of a new upsurge of terrorism, of seeing societies becoming inflamed. States threatened with destabilization by this crisis. We obviously hope it won't happen, but, given the situation today, there's a risk which must be taken into account in the whole management of the crisis.[137]

After the war, de Villepin argued that the war had challenged international order because, in his view, it had been waged without a proper UN mandate. Moreover, this crisis in global governance was mirrored in the destabilisation of the Middle East which the war had brought about. 'The world seems to be out of control,' the French foreign minister concluded.[138] Few things are worse from a risk perspective than a breakdown of management capabilities. By tying up most of its armed forces in Iraq and straining relations with its allies, the war had severely limited the immediate operational capabilities of the United States.

The war had therefore also limited the management capabilities it was designed to enhance, but it had also limited the US ability to make and gain acceptance for its strategies. In his 2002 State of the Union Address, President Bush had argued that Iraq was just one member, albeit the most dangerous, of an axis of evil. Having dealt with Iraq, however, the President had little or no capabilities left to deal with the other axis members, namely Iran and North Korea. It was probably no coincidence that Iran's nuclear programme seemed to pick up speed following the war in Iraq, which on the one hand stimulated the Iranians' desire to develop a deterrent against the 140,000 US troops next door to them in Iraq, while on the other hand giving Iran an opportunity, given that US troops had become bogged down in insurgency operations in Iraq. In the winter of 2004, Secretary of State Colin Powell presented new intelligence on Iran's weapons programme and strongly implied the need for urgent action to pre-empt the country's development of nuclear weapons. However, Powell's statement was met with an uproar. Representative Gary Ackerman told the *Los Angeles Times*:

After crying wolf for so long about Iraq, how are we going to have any credibility on this? People in the Arab world won't believe it and say we have a bad track record and just want to invade another country in the Middle East. How do we expect anybody to believe us, even if we know it is true? This is the disaster we created for ourselves in lying about Iraq.[139]

---

[137] Villepin, Interview, §23.
[138] Villepin, *BBC Dimbleby Lecture*, §6.
[139] Quoted in Sonni Efron, Tyler Marshall and Bob Drogin, 'Powell's Talk of Arms Has Fallout', *Los Angeles Times*, 19 November 2004.

The policy agenda had moved on, following the flow of risk, but policy-makers had lost the trust of the American people and the allies, not to mention governments and peoples who are no longer prepared to give the US the benefit of the doubt. When strategy is based on scenarios, the credibility of these scenarios is the most important issue for policy-makers when they are seeking the agreement of the electorate and their allies for a particular strategy. The problem is that scenarios cannot be based on clear-cut evidence, because the risk logic dictates that, by the time such evidence has become available, it is too late to act. 'The dangers we face will only worsen from month to month and from year to year,' President Bush had stated before the war; 'to ignore these threats is to encourage them'.[140] After the war, however, dissuading other states from developing WMDs had become harder because the lack of trust in the administration's intelligence on Iraq made it more difficult to sell military action to the electorate, and the US's enemies knew it. Instead of functioning as a deterrent that demonstrated what would happen if one did not comply with the non-proliferation regime supported by the US, the invasion of Iraq actually opened new possibilities for the Iranian government. The US had lost the all-important strategic goal of 'decision-superiority'.

Discussing the boomerang effect thus leads one to ask when it is better to let sleeping risks lie rather than awaken them with pre-emptive action. To answer this question is the true role of politicians in a time of pre-emptive doctrines. If the commander's job is to identify risks and devise ways to pre-empt them, the commander-in-chief's job is much more complicated: he has to weigh the strategic requirement for pre-emption against its possible boomerang effects. If he gets the balance wrong, either he might cause the risks to become actual attacks, or he might find that the risks caused by pre-emptive action actually end up outweighing the risks which he wanted to pre-empt in the first place. Since both the risks he wants to pre-empt and the risks that might arise from pre-emptive action are based on scenarios, neither of them are real in any way that can be measured or assessed with any finality. This means that strategy is no longer the means-end, rational, scientific enterprise of Clausewitz' definition. Instead, strategy has once again become the art that Machiavelli wrote about – a way of doing politics that is different from other policy areas only in the fact that the stakes are far too high to allow any of the boomerang effects which the politician in risk society knows are bound to follow from a decision.

---

[140] Bush, *President Bush Discusses Iraq with Congressional Leaders*, §5.

Conclusions

The development of risk society has been marked by a transformation in the enforcement of policy from deterrence to the management of risks. Perhaps this is most clear in respect of the prevention of crime, but it is also true of a plethora of other policy areas. A central feature of management as a means of governance is the pre-emptive doctrines that managers come to use in order to maintain control over the issues they manage. The concept of management springs from a realisation that in risk society one cannot produce final results – crime will not be abolished, nor can terrorism be prevented. The task for the managers of risk society is to be able to control the situation in such ways that there are no unmanageable levels of pollution, crime or terrorism. In order to maintain the control required to preserve a manageable environment, the threats that might erode control in the future must be pre-empted. If one reacts only when the risk has become a reality, control will probably be lost and one will no longer have the resources to manage crime, terrorism, pollution or the proliferation of WMDs.

This move from deterrence to management came late in security policy because the Cold War kept the West focused on deterrence. Perhaps it is not too sweeping a generalisation to call the final decades of the Cold War a case of strategic symbiosis. The anachronistic nature of the Soviet regime, which made it incapable of change and therefore doomed it as a social system, kept Western security policy focused on doctrines of deterrence that seemed exceedingly anachronistic compared to the innovations in governance on the domestic front. In Phillip Windsor's words, 'deterrence became its own institution, its own form of rationality, its own bureaucracy'.[141] Post-Cold War security thinking is characterised by the breakdown of this rationality in the face of new risks, but because the means-end rationality of deterrence was enshrined in institutions and bureaucracies – such as one finds them in strategic concepts, military doctrine, university reading lists and scholarly conventions – the breakdown has been agonisingly slow. It took the terrorist attacks of 11 September 2001 to make the new risks that the policy of scenarios was based on seem real, but as we have seen, these scenarios are by no means universally accepted among either policy-makers or academics.

However, most Western policy-makers, academics and others who represent society's collective understanding of what globalisation is and

---

[141] Windsor, *Strategic Thinking*, 169.

what it will become agree that it is changing the economic, social and political foundations of Western society; 11 September 2001 made key policy-makers believe that globalisation also had a dark side in the shape of terrorism and the spread of WMDs. The very different ideas on how to deal with new security threats arise to a large extent from different perceptions of whether the bright side of globalisation is stronger than the dark side. If the darker forces are stronger, much pre-emptive action is needed; if the brighter forces are stronger, then more gentle management techniques will suffice. At this point it becomes clear just how much the environmental debate over the precautionary principle and the debate over pre-emptive security strategies have in common.

Neither President Bush nor environmentalists would probably like to have so much in common, but actually it should not surprise them. The American President and grassroot environmentalists are equally parts of late modern Western society and they think accordingly. This does not mean that they agree on policy, but they do agree on the principles involved in conducting policy. If they did not recognise these principles, they would not be effective political operators. It is surprising, however, that although applying the precautionary principle to security strategy has proved very unpopular, environmentalists' arguments for the pre-cautionary principle have captured the imagination of Western publics. The arguments against using the precautionary principle for environmental issues and the debunking of the scenarios on which the principle is based by people like Bjørn Lomborg are at best marginal and at worst discredited as something approaching the immoral for large sections of public opinion. When it comes to security policy, however, arguments like Lomborg's are widely accepted. In strategic studies, many if not most scholars are unconvinced by pre-emptive doctrines, whereas natural scientists dealing with environmental issues are appalled that anyone should dare to challenge the precautionary principle.[142]

It is fortunate that people remain critical about strategic precautionary principles, because the doctrine of managing the flows of insecurity by occasional pre-emption makes it almost impossible to hold policy-makers accountable for their policies. When the strategic goal is to avoid risk, success can never be measured because a risk prevented will never materialise. It is equally impossible to establish when the pre-emption of risk fails because the focus on flows makes the original action unimportant compared to the new risks that have arisen. Of course, parliamentary

---

[142] On the scientific establishment's responses to Lomborg, see 'Misguided Math About the Earth', *Scientific American* (January 2002), 61–71. For a description of the debate, see 'The Litany and the Heretic', *Economist*, 31 January 2002.

commissions and newspaper editors will focus on the immediate results of certain spectacular actions, like the 2003 Iraq war or whether US intelligence could have prevented 9/11, but a strategy cannot be reduced to single events, nor can its evaluation. If a strategy cannot be evaluated, how is the electorate supposed to reward or punish a government, how can parliament control the government and how can the government itself adjust its strategy so that it becomes more effective?

Former Vice President Al Gore captured this concern in September 2002: 'The doctrine is presented in open-ended terms . . . the implication is that wherever the combination exists of an interest in weapons of mass destruction together with an ongoing role as host to or participant in terrorist operations, the doctrine will apply.'[143] Gore's concern was that if Congress approved the Bush administration's doctrine for going to war with Iraq, would Congress be able to say when the authority ended? When one fights flows of risk, the fight goes on forever, and forever is beyond the effective control of most politicians. This depoliticisation first showed itself in the 'routine wars' of the 1990s. The sanctions against Iraq, the occasional air raids on Iraqi air defences and Serb forces in the Balkans, the 'humanitarian interventions' in Third-World countries were all characterised as the incremental results of policies that were never put to a real democratic test.

This is a consequence of using military force to manage the international security environment. Management is conceptually different from the wars imagined by the founding fathers of virtually every Western constitution. The elaborate safeguards for when and under what authority a nation's armed forces can go to war simply do not apply to the military management of the post-Cold War world. This phenomenon began during the Cold War itself, when, for example, the US Congress gave President Johnson sweeping powers to deal with Vietnam, but today this is the exception rather than the rule. Michael Ignatieff points to the paradox that, in the case of the Kosovo war, there was great controversy about whether military action had been sanctioned by the UN or not, but almost no attention was paid to 'the decay of institutional checks and balances on the war-making power of the executive'.[144] Ignatieff goes on:

Formal debates in representative bodies subject military aims to the kind of detailed scrutiny that they cannot expect to receive through opinion polling. The institutional checks and balances of a democratic system help, in other

---

[143] Gore, *Iraq and the War on Terrorism*, §22.
[144] Michael Ignatieff, *Virtual War: Kosovo and Beyond* (London: Chatto and Windus, 2000), 181.

words, to clarify the goals and purposes of war. When military operations are unsanctioned and undeclared, as they were in Kosovo, their objectives changed from week to week, depending on what our leaders decided they should be.[145]

Ignatieff's observations are equally true of the 2003 Iraq war and, perhaps especially, the agonising insurgency that followed. Perhaps the democratic ideals that Ignatieff writes about are simply unattainable because the management process does not present concrete threats that one can deal with in the 'yes, we will do something about it' or 'no, we should not' type of arguments that parliaments best like to discuss. This problem is hardly unique to strategy, however, and most issues facing Western democracies are no less complicated and no less the result of risk society than issues like whether Iraq should be invaded or Iran's WMD facilities bombed. The point is that most of these issues (environmental issues and crime are good examples) are the subject of continuous debate in representative bodies, as well as among the public at large. People simply know more about them, or are at least more familiar with the problematic, than is the case with security issues, which are still treated as exceptional issues dealing with the exceptional circumstances of the international system. Therefore they are not subject to the everyday dialogue that constitutes the foundation of a democratic debate. When it comes to strategic issues, today's concepts and arguments would be instantly familiar to people who debated them at the beginning of the twentieth century. This would not be the case for environmental issues or crime. Perhaps it should not be the case in terms of security either.

While scepticism towards precautionary principles is a value in itself, it is less fortunate when one rejects the need for precautionary measures because one insists on doing strategy in the old-fashioned, means-end rational way. The way in which most of the Bush administration's arguments for going to war with Iraq were rejected in favour of what were not much more than conspiracy theories – simply because these fitted a cause-and-effect argument rather than the reflexive risk argument made by Bush and Blair – is not conducive for a democratic debate either. This does not mean that anyone adopting a risk frame of mind will automatically experience an urge to invade other countries. On the contrary, one of the most important points about the risk approach to strategy is that different risk cultures dictate different responses. This chapter has shown this to be the case in the Iraq debate as well. Accepting the risk framework means entering into a debate over scenarios. The

---

[145] Ibid., 180.

only way to obtain democratic scrutiny of which scenario should guide policy is for policy-makers and the opposition to accept the premise of risk society: nobody knows for sure, but everybody has to face the risks.

But who exactly are the people behind the risks? This is the subject of the next chapter, as we turn our attention to the changing nature of the forces against which the West is creating strategy.

5 Agents: the UN approach and the terrorist approach to warfare

'US Secretary of Defense jailed on war crimes charges in Germany.' This headline was never printed, but for a few weeks in February 2005, newspaper editors entertained the notion that it might be. The US Secretary of Defense, Donald Rumsfeld, was due to give a speech at the security conference held every year in Munich, but his aides said that he would not travel to Germany unless he received assurances that he would not be arrested to face war crimes charges. He was quickly given such assurances and went to Germany without incident.[1] One interesting element in this story is that it was not the German government that made charges against Rumsfeld, but the New York-based Center for Constitutional Rights acting on behalf of four Iraqis who claimed to have been abused by American soldiers in Abu Ghraib prison in Iraq: they invoked German legal statutes enforcing certain treaties on war crimes in an attempt to have the German authorities detain Rumsfeld.[2]

This indicates that, at the beginning of the twenty-first century, war is no longer a means that a government can choose merely because the use of armed force fits its political ends. In the years since 1945 the 'UN approach' to warfare has negated the doctrine by which Clausewitz defined war. War was no longer an uncomplicated means to pursue political ends. The Charter is but one of a whole corpus of treaties and norms that make up the laws of war and that have grown up since the nineteenth century, but since 1945 the laws of war have developed within the discursive framework defined by the UN Charter. The UN approach to warfare defines states' use of armed force with reference not to states' national interests or the monopoly of violence that is said to characterise them, but to their obligations under international law, customs and norms. Often governments will try to assert their right to make political judgements on strategic issues, but they will find

---

[1] 'German Prosecutor Refuses Rumsfeld Probe', *Washington Post*, 11 February 2005.
[2] 'German Prosecutor Rejects Investigation of Rumsfeld', *Los Angeles Times*, 11 February 2005.

themselves bound by laws and norms which are based on the premise that the use of armed force is inherently problematic, no matter what ends it is being used for. While some governments will actively promote these views, it is NGOs, international lawyers and, indeed, the UN itself which are the most vocal advocates of the UN approach. Still, the UN approach defines the state as a strategic agent because it defines what is legal and legitimate when it comes to the use of armed force and thus shapes the rules of engagement which guide how armed force is used on the micro-level of the particular combat event. Though the UN approach finds war problematic, it recognises the need occasionally to have recourse to war to ensure 'international peace and security'. To be legal, any use of armed force must have the enforcement of international order as its end and must be used solely for the execution of international organisations' – most importantly the UN's – authoritative interpretation of international law, custom and norms. In short, according to the UN approach states use military force rationally when they follow the rules of the international community. However, arguing for the UN approach therefore also makes states the only legitimate *users* of military force, because in this respect only states are the subjects of international law.

The premise of the UN approach is that war is a risk in itself. On the one hand, any use of armed force is regarded as suspect because it puts people at risk. On the other hand, governments that choose to use armed force run the risk that Rumsfeld did – their actions may be found to be illegitimate or downright illegal. Thus war is no longer a continuation of politics with the addition of other means, but instead has become the continuation of law by other means. Clausewitz understood war as something that statesmen could decide to wage on the basis of their own political judgements; today war is something statesmen administer in the way bureaucrats administer the laws of the state. This is yet one more example of how strategy is becoming more like 'normal' politics.

The bureaucratisation of warfare has evolved during the twentieth century, from the movement to outlaw war in the 1920s to the International Criminal Court established in 2002. The fact that Rumsfeld's actions were seen to be so violently at odds with the laws of war indicates the extent to which warfare has been bureaucratised. The UN approach to warfare seems to have successfully closed the chapter on war between great powers as a legitimate and politically viable way to alter international order. Today a world war is a risk buried in the past, and the UN's role and aim is to keep it buried there. As we have seen, war between great powers is not high on the Western security agenda. Most Western politicians believe that, if globalisation is managed successfully, then such wars can be at least postponed indefinitely, and perhaps be made impossible by the spread of democracy and markets. It is the rise of non-state actors like al-Qaeda and the proliferation of weapons technology that are shaping future scenarios for risk societies.

While the UN approach to warfare may have closed one chapter of the history of warfare in the West, the West fears that the emergence of al-Qaeda is proof that another chapter has been opened. The terrorists' approach to warfare is seen as being of a different order from the threats of the past. Thus just as the laws and rules of war have become more strict than perhaps ever before, the enemies that the West expects to fight in the future are increasingly seen as being outside these laws and rules. In dealing with the terrorist approach to warfare in this chapter, I am not seeking to define either terrorists or terrorism, but rather to describe how the West regards terrorist organisations like al-Qaeda as symbols of the enemies it is going to face in the twenty-first century. From this perspective, the terrorist approach to warfare might thus be defined as asymmetrical warfare fought by enemies with an organisation and rationality that are radically different from those of Western armed forces. The terrorist approach is thus a reflection of the West's fears more than a description of actual terrorist networks.

The preventive doctrines that are seen as necessary in order to manage the risks posed by al-Qaeda and other new agents are either not addressed or in various degrees forbidden under existing international law. Perhaps Rumsfeld should not have been surprised to hear about the threat of indictments against him, since the way he, as the Secretary of Defense, was waging the 'war on terror' placed him and his Commander-in-Chief beyond international law and morality in the eyes of many. In this chapter I argue that managing the risk of war through the UN approach is now colliding with scenarios regarding *who* Western countries are going to fight in the future. The result is a boomerang effect of the bureaucratisation of warfare, which opens up new ways of fighting against those who are perceived to be a new type of enemy, the chief example of whom are those described as terrorists. This does not mean that the existing laws of war will collapse, but as this boomerang effect unfolds in the future, it will probably mean that these laws will cover less and less of the strategy that Western societies engage in.

The term 'agent' is used in a number of different ways in this chapter. The chapter describes how international law and the UN approach to warfare defines who the legitimate agents in fighting wars are and how they are to fight them (agency). The chapter then goes on to deal with how the West perceives itself as an agent using military force and how this self-reflection is to a great extent determined by how the West regards the agents it is fighting. In this case one crucial difference is the belief of many Western observers that in the twenty-first century the West will face enemies with a different rationality and different mode of organisation from the means-end rational nation states which were its enemies in the twentieth century. Finally, the chapter goes from the organisational level to the individual level by focusing on the soldiers' motives for fighting.

In the description of these different layers of agency, Max Weber's theories are again invoked to describe the modernisation of strategy and thus as a way to determine at which point the modern means-end rationality ceases to explain strategic actions. Thus the chapter begins with a description of how the risk of war has been managed following the Second World War by means of Weber's characteristics of bureaucracy. After analysing the bureaucratisation of warfare, I turn to the 'presence of the future'. In the future, Western strategists do not expect their enemies to operate through means-end rationality. The way in which al-Qaeda's 'reasons' for operating are discussed provides insights into how it is believed that future adversaries in general will be operating. Having concluded that bureaucracy no longer provides an adequate answer to the scenarios of the future, the boomerang effect, described as the negation of Weber's characteristics of bureaucracy, is discussed in the last third of the chapter.

Management

During their advance on Baghdad in March 2003, troops of the 101st Airborne Division set up camp in the Al-Kufa Factory for Soft Drinks and Healthy Water, 20 miles from Karbala. Here the military historian Rick Atkinson found the soldiers high on the sugar and caffeine of the Kufa version of Coke, while they were trying to wash the desert sand off their uniforms with the Iraqi Healthy Water. Obviously a lot of soft drinks had been consumed. After the war, the division's lawyers tracked down the owner of the soft-drink factory and paid him US$12,600 for the soft drinks.[3] Imagine the Roman legions compensating Gaul farmers for everything the legionaries got their hands on after a battle, or British officers paying Zulu chiefs compensation for a devastated village. The Romans and British accepted war as a state of emergency in which force ruled everything. The spectre of meticulous US Army

---

[3] Rick Atkinson, *In the Company of Soldiers: A Chronicle of Combat in Iraq* (London: Little, Brown and Company, 2004), 243.

lawyers travelling the Iraqi countryside to identity the owner of a soft-drink factory illustrates a different approach to war, one in which force is ruled by law. Clausewitz regarded armed force as a means of policy different from the other means available to a government and thus governed by different and less stringent rules. Today, Western governments increasingly regard military force as a means equal to other political means. As we have seen in the previous chapters, the result of this view is that military force is being used more frequently. This normalisation of warfare also means that war has come to be guided increasingly by the law, rules and administrative practices that define civilian instruments of government. In short, war has become bureaucratised.

Max Weber found bureaucracy to be the quintessential means-end rational mode of organisation. 'The fully developed bureaucratic mechanism', Weber stated, 'compares with other organizations exactly as does the machine with the non-mechanical modes of product.'[4] The modernity of Western armed forces is most often explained in terms of their mechanisation. From that point of view, the RMA (revolution in military affairs; see Chapter 3) marks a high point in the development of wars fought by machines. Indeed, one scenario for how the RMA will develop envisages warfare being fought entirely by machines. However, Western armed forces have also become machines in the sense that Weber alludes to: they have become bureaucracies.

The RMA promises to shed the Light of Reason on the battlefield, but in doing so it is addressing a demand made because of bureaucratisation. Western armed forces would be no more interested in fighting zero-casualty wars with minimal collateral damage than the Romans were was it not for the fact that the Western way of warfare is increasingly being guided by rules and regulations that demand such low casualties and such high precision. The more warfare is regarded as a means similar to civilian means, the more the 'friction' and violent uncertainty of war becomes a risk that needs to be managed by rules and regulations. And the more war is managed, the more the reasons for going to war are subject to judicial review rather than assessments of national interest. This does not mean that war is ceasing to be a political means: on the contrary, it is making the use of armed force even more political and the motives and justifications for going to war are being disputed more and more. It has become increasingly difficult to justify action in terms of an inherent military logic. War is slowly losing the 'grammar' which, according to Clausewitz, gave it an inherent logic that politicians

---

[4] Max Weber, *From Max Weber: Essays in Sociology*, ed. H. H. Gerth and C. Wright Mills (London: Routledge, 1997), 214.

should not meddle with.[5] Now the very use and usefulness of military force can be challenged. Opposition to a military action can be raised in the UN Security Council on the basis of law, rather than opposed by diplomats, military posturing or other old-fashioned methods.

This part of the chapter will deal with these issues in terms of the three characteristics by which Weber defined bureaucracy: (1) fixed areas of competence; (2) fixed duties; and (3) sole employment of professionals.[6]

Bureaucracy I: outlawing war

According to Weber, the first characteristic of a bureaucracy is the way its areas of competence are fixed by the rule of law. What the bureaucrat can and cannot do is carefully defined and subject to legal review. Thus a bureaucratic institution is unique in the history of executive power by not being able to use any means it sees fit to realise any goal it wishes to define. Instead the relationship between means and ends is carefully defined by law. Clausewitz did not believe that such restrictions applied to war. 'Attached to force', he claimed, 'are certain self-imposed, imperceptible limitations hardly worth mentioning, known as international law and custom, but they scarcely weaken it.'[7] Actually, any social enterprise is governed by rules, including war.[8] In Clausewitz' time, however, the rules of war enabled most other social and legal constraints to be put aside in the name of the expediency of war. In modern times, Ole Wæver suggests, arguing that the state was under threat constituted an argument for leaving normal considerations of legality, morality and politics aside in favour of the needs of the state in a time of emergency.[9] In other words, war was a risk the state would have to take, and was constitutionally allowed to take, in order to secure its vital interests. Since the Second World War, states have allowed themselves to take fewer and fewer risks, and international law has come to reflect their risk-aversion.

Since the Second World War, therefore, war has been regarded as a risk that is best avoided. Nuclear weapons underscored this, but the point was really made by the horrors of the two world wars. War could never be a risk-free means again. The way the Axis powers had worshipped the virtues of war made it easier to separate war as a means from the ends it was used for. Any war, no matter how worthy its ends, was

---

[5] Clausewitz, *On War*, 605–9.
[6] Weber, *From Max Weber: Essays in Sociology*, 196ff.
[7] Clausewitz, *On War*, 75.
[8] Martin van Creveld makes this case most strongly in his *On Future War*.
[9] Wæver 'Securitization and Desecuritization', 50–4.

now seen as suspect, and the UN Charter promised to 'save succeeding generations from the scourge of war'.[10] According to Martha Finnemore, the result is that 'interstate uses of force are increasingly shaped by Weberian rational-legal authority structures, specifically legal understandings and the rules or norms of international organizations'.[11] The most important norm-setting organisation has been the United Nations. The UN Charter thus states that 'all Members shall refrain in their international relations from the threat or use of force against the territorial integrity or political independence of any state, or in any other manner inconsistent with the Purposes of the United Nations'.[12] The Charter allows member states to defend themselves, whether alone or with the help of other states,[13] but after 1945 war was no longer a means a state could justifiably use at its own discretion. The Charter was the culmination of the movement to outlaw war, which among other things had resulted in the Kellogg-Briand Pact in 1928. Those arguing for the legal abolition of war knew full well that war would not disappear because a piece of paper said it should; they regarded outlawing war as a process of rationalisation which would gradually make a war an illegitimate means. Those arguing for the outlawing of war were fond of drawing an analogy with the outlawing of duelling, because duelling too had gone on, despite being outlawed. In 1547, fifty years after duelling had been outlawed in France, 4,000 men were said to have been killed in duels, and King Henry II granted 14,000 pardons for duelling. In spite of less-than-perfect beginnings, however, the ban eventually worked, and duelling came to be regarded as murder. It was not only illegal, it was wrong.[14]

After the Charter no analogy to duelling was needed. War had been outlawed, but this has not meant that wars have not occurred since 1945, just as duels were still fought in sixteenth-century France, but since the adoption of the UN Charter war is no longer just a political means that states can take recourse to just as they please. War has been objectified as a problem in and of itself. Risk researchers will recognise this as a typical problem of risk society in which a previously unproblematic political means becomes a theme and problem in itself. One example of this is how, upon the outbreak of the Iraq war in 2003, the

---

[10] UN Charter, Preamble, www.un.org/aboutun/charter (26 January 2005).
[11] Martha Finnemore, *The Purpose of Intervention: Changing Beliefs About the Use of Force* (Ithaca, NY: Cornell University Press, 2003), 21.
[12] UN Charter, Article 2(4).
[13] Ibid., Article 52(1).
[14] Quincy Wright, 'The Outlawry of War and the Law of War', *American Journal of International Law* 47 (July 1953), 369.

German foreign minister, Joschka Fischer, told the Bundestag that 'war is the worst of all solutions'.[15] On the one hand this statement equates war with other 'solutions' to policy problems, but on the other hand Foreign Minister Fischer made it clear that, no matter what the circumstances, war will always be the worst choice. This is not a pacifist statement, since Fischer also implies that, even though war is a bad solution, it might be the only solution in certain circumstances. However, the foreign minister rejected entirely what to Clausewitz would have been obvious: that war is the only solution to certain problems between states. This rejection of war as a fact of life is now widely shared. A UN high-level panel set up by the Secretary-General in the wake of the Iraq war concluded that the fact 'that force *can* legally be used, does not always mean that, as a matter of good conscience and good sense, it *should* be used'.[16]

This points to a useful distinction between war in the legal sense and war in the material sense, which Quincy Wright introduced in the 1950s when he tried to gauge the consequences of the Charter's abolition of war. The use of force is legally possible only if sanctioned by the UN; Wright thus suggested that a UN-sanctioned use of military force does not really constitute war in the traditional sense of the term as a specific legal situation between two sovereign states. In the UN approach, one party would be an aggressor breaking the law, while the other party would be enforcing it. This at least was the legal theory, but strategic practice soon showed that wars occur regardless of their illegality. To Wright the Korean war proved that, in a material sense, war would not cease to exist simply because of the UN Charter. However, Wright's point was that states follow the laws of war even when the wars they fight are illegal in the strict sense. They fight wars in the material sense and follow the rules of war in doing so, but they do not recognise these conflicts as war in the legal sense.[17] Sometimes the gap between law and practice, or war in the legal and material sense, can be overcome. The 1991 Gulf war was an example of this. The 2003 Iraq war is an example of a state of affairs that has been much more common since 1945, in which the gap between law and practice becomes a battleground in its own right. Because war has been objectified, it is perceived as a risk in its own right. Thus a government arguing for the need to

---

[15] Joschka Fischer, *Speech by Federal Foreign Minister Fischer in the German Bundestag on 20 March 2003 on the War against Iraq* (Berlin: German Foreign Ministry, 2003), §1.

[16] *A More Secure World: Our Shared Responsibility*, Report of the Secretary-General's High-Level Panel on Threats, Challenges and Change (New York: United Nations, 2004), 61.

[17] Wright, 'The Outlawry of War and the Law of War', 365. Cf. Arend, 'International Law', 99–100.

use military force has to convince not only its own legislature and people that military action is required, but also the 'world community' (in practice the Security Council) that a war will not jeopardise international peace and stability. Thus war is not just a means that can be put into action by political fiat: the choice of war as the means required to solve a given problem becomes immensely political, so political in fact, that choosing war as the continuation of politics by other means becomes a risk in itself.

Qiao Liang and Wang Xiangsui argue that the creation of what they term 'supra-national combinations' is a way to contain the risk of choosing war.[18] According to the Chinese colonels, a supra-national combination gives the use of military force legitimacy by having an international organisation – preferably the UN – underwrite it, though such a legitimising organisation is only one element in a coalition that mobilises other states and NGOs in supporting military action. The more 'combinations' there are, the lower the risk of going to war. The Chinese colonels explain how the United States' ability to make such combinations is a key to its power. Worldwide legitimacy makes it possible for the US to use its military force.[19] Apart from legitimacy, 'combinations' also make it possible to maintain decision superiority.[20] With worldwide backing a government is allowed to make decisions about the use of military force which would otherwise be constantly questioned. This was exactly the problem the US faced the second time it went to war against Iraq. In 2003, it did not have the worldwide base for going to war as it did in 1991, and therefore the war itself was something that had to be justified every day during the campaign.

Not only the rationality behind using war as a means, but also the conduct of war itself becomes immensely political. Technological developments allow these political concerns to penetrate every level of command. Thus the soldiers of the 101st Airborne cannot just loot a soft-drink factory – the Army has to reimburse the owner of the factory. This example shows that wars are still fought and soldiers still behave as they have done for centuries, but these material facts of war aside, war has become a completely different legal entity. In Iraq US forces had more than seventeen lawyers at division level and each brigade had a BOLT or Brigade Operational Law Team.[21] This reflects the way in

---

[18] Liang and Xiangsui, *Unrestricted Warfare*, 183.
[19] Ibid., 184–5. Cf. G. John Ikenberry, *After Victory: Institutions, Strategic Restraint and the Rebuilding of Order After Major Wars* (Princeton, NJ: Princeton University Press, 2001), 215–56.
[20] *QDR 2001*, 37.
[21] Atkinson, *In the Company of Soldiers*, 46.

which legal concerns have in many ways come to guide combat. Another example is General Wesley Clark's description of how targets were approved during the 1999 bombing campaign against Serbia:

In the US channel, we would need a complete analysis of each individual target – location, military impact, possible personnel casualties, possible collateral damages, risks if the weapon missed the target, and so forth. This analysis then had to be repeated for different types of weapons, in search of the specific type of weapon and warhead size that would destroy the target and have the least impact elsewhere. And this had to be done to my satisfaction, then sent to Washington where it underwent additional levels of legal and military review and finally ended up on President Clinton's desk for his approval.[22]

This immensely complicated process seems to prove Niklas Luhmann's observation right, that an ability of a political system to identify risks is inversely proportional to its ability to manage them.[23] In other words, one can never increase one's resources to deal with risks at the same pace as one identifies new risks. Each action on the battlefield opens up new risky scenarios and new legal dilemmas. The only way to maintain just a minimum of effectiveness is to predefine carefully when war is legal and what rules of engagement can be allowed. This striving for predictability is what we turn to next.

Bureaucracy II: predictability

Creating predictability is the second characteristic of bureaucracy according to Weber, who argues that 'the peculiarity of modern culture, and specifically of its technical and economic basis, demands this very "calculability" of results'.[24] Government by bureaucracy means that people know their rights and duties and know that these will not change through the whim of the rulers. For example, 'predictability' makes it safe for a company to invest in research and development because it knows that the tax-breaks offered by such investments will remain. In the language of risk theory, bureaucracies can be described as institutional risk-reducers. Since they are in the business of reducing risks, it is not surprising that they are risk-averse organisations. Since the bureaucrats' job is to maintain the status quo, too much innovation and creativity on their part will be seen as a risk in itself. Luhmann describes the result: 'bureaucratic behaviour is notoriously risk-averse'.[25]

Weber had already pointed out that bureaucratic decision-making takes place by means of 'a system of rationally debatable "reasons"

---

[22] Clark, *Modern War*, 201.   [23] Luhmann. *Risk*, 145.
[24] Weber, *From Max Weber: Essays in Sociology*, 215.   [25] Luhmann, *Risk*, 190.

[which] stands behind every act of bureaucratic administration, that is, either subsumption under norms or a weighting of ends and means'.[26] Ideally, bureaucrats do not decide to act because they or their organisation can gain from doing so, but because it is the rational thing to do. This is another reason why Weber described the bureaucracy as a machine: it acts automatically in many ways. Given particular circumstances, the rules dictate that certain actions are required.

Military force is increasingly regarded as something that creates predictable results. The RMA gives expectations that one can muster the precise means to achieve the precise ends that have been identified as necessary for prevailing in battle. Moreover, in viewing military force in terms of the RMA, Western governments and publics expect their armed forces to be so superior that they can assume their success in any military contest. In other words, technology reinforces a belief that military means can be calculated and that calculation will produce a favourable result. At the same time, it follows from the focus on doctrines for managing a benign security environment that military force can be regarded as a way to manage the rules of the international system. This tendency is underscored by the increasing legalisation of war discussed above. From this point of view, the use of military force should be machine-like and should simply implement the wishes of the international community as expressed by the Security Council.

The conclusions of the International Commission on Intervention and State Sovereignty set up to discuss when and how 'humanitarian interventions' were justified shed some light on this question. Taking its point of departure in the laws of war, the Commission argues that military force should be used only as a last resort and used proportionally. So far the Commission is merely reporting on the state of international law, but then it adds yet another standard which is to be met before intervention can be undertaken: 'reasonable prospects for success', which the Commission defines as follows:

Military action can only be justified if it stands a reasonable chance of success, that is, halting or averting atrocities or suffering that triggered the intervention in the first place. Military intervention is not justified if actual protection cannot be achieved, or if the consequences of embarking upon the intervention are likely to be worse than if there is no action at all.[27]

Clausewitz would never have expected the light of reason to shine so brightly that one would be able to foresee the result of military action.

---

[26] Weber, *From Max Weber: Essays in Sociology*, 220.
[27] International Commission on Intervention and State Sovereignty, *The Responsibility to Protect* (Ottawa, ON: International Development Research Centre, 2001), 37.

His central insight concerning military force was the fact that friction makes war unpredictable. Thus according to Clausewitz waging war is always risky. The Commission on Intervention assumes the opposite: that one can determine whether or not wars are risky. On the one hand this reflects the technological superiority of the West: if enough resources are invested, the US and its allies will prevail. But one cannot be certain of success, as the cases of Baghdad and Mogadishu show. If non-risk is a condition for intervention, then few of the situations in which military force will be most needed to impose order will qualify for intervention. Such situations are risky by definition, which is why armed force is needed in the first place.

The Commission's argument reflects the way war has become a bureaucratic duty rather than a political instrument. The Commission not only argues that it is possible to assess the risks of war: the second part of its argument is that it is only when this risk assessment concludes that military action will have no, or very few, boomerang effects that military action *should* be undertaken. It is a true hallmark of bureaucratic reasoning that one makes the probable outcome rather than the desirable outcome the standard by which decisions are made. Even if the odds are against you, it does not necessarily follow that you should not fight. At Thermopylae the Spartans knew full well that the danger of fighting the Persians on their own was overwhelming, but they fought nonetheless. The Spartans accepted the danger as a part of their code. The danger of Britain fighting on after the fall of France in 1940 was very great indeed, but Churchill's government chose to fight on nevertheless. The government accepted the danger of war because they made a political decision. The Commission, however, is seeking to define bureaucratic rules for when to use war. Because their recommendations are therefore based on predictability, they are risk-averse.

To Clausewitz war was about wanting something you could obtain only by using military force. For that reason he spent page after page discussing the 'will' of the antagonists. The kind of war the Commission on Intervention is describing is not 'willed', not the result of a political desire to achieve certain ends, but rather a duty that governments have to perform not for their own sake, but for the maintenance of certain standards laid down by the international community. This is a bureaucratic kind of war, and as a result, an equal obligation is placed on all members of the international system. Thus the Danish, Polish and Australian governments argued that it had a duty to help the United States and Britain invade Iraq in 2003, in spite of the fact that their military contribution made little military difference. The US appreciated these allies' participation because they constituted one of the 'supra-national combinations' that the Chinese colonels referred to. From the point of view of Denmark, Poland and Australia, however, participating in the Iraq war was a way to confirm their place in the international community, just as *not* participating in the invasion became a way for other states to confirm their interpretation of their duties to the international community. In other words, participation in the war became a matter of bureaucratic duty rather than political interest. In fact one of the most popular slogans against the war was 'no war for oil', which was meant to offend the leaders of the coalition, which it duly did. From the traditional Clausewitzian conception of strategy, being accused of fighting for a material interest like oil was not an insult but a proof of sound strategic judgement. Wars have been fought for much less valuable resources than oil, but in those days war was a political choice, not a bureaucratic duty.

Bureaucracy III: professionalism

When the word 'bureaucrat' is mentioned, most people probably think of people in suits behind desks rather than people in uniform driving a tank, but actually the army was one of Weber's chief examples of bureaucracy. As a reserve army officer himself, Weber clearly saw that 'only the bureaucratic army structure allowed for the development of the professional standing armies'.[28] Clausewitz' understanding of the armed forces as an instrument used to realise the will of the government followed this line of thinking. The armed forces were guided by law and rules and had fixed duties to perform. This bureaucratic mode of organisation is also reflected in the organisation of the armed forces themselves. A strict hierarchy with a clear chain of command means that Western armed forces closely resemble the ideal type of the bureaucracy that Weber described.

While Machiavelli wanted soldiers to be driven by their passion for the motherland,[29] the modern, Weberian soldier is a much more rational creature. Today soldiering is perhaps best described as a career. However, while soldiering is a chosen profession for officers, for most privates and NCOs it is a relatively short-term occupation. Like the civil servant, the soldier is a professional who knows the rules and regulations he must follow and has some expert knowledge of the area he is dealing with. The difference between the civil servant and the soldier is that

---

[28] Weber, *From Max Weber: Essays in Sociology*, 222. On Weber's military career, see 'The Man and his Work', in ibid., 6–7.
[29] Machiavelli, *Discourses*, 209–11.

the soldier's professionalism ultimately rests on his willingness to put his life on the line to realise an objective. He not only uses particular means to attain the ends of the bureaucracy, he is himself a means. When it comes to weighing the risks for or against taking a certain action, the soldier is thus not only an expert – he, or his comrades, are those who are going to take the risks and, possibly, pay the price.

Weber pointed out how in a bureaucracy 'the "political master" finds himself in a position of the "dilettante" who stands opposite the "expert"'.[30] The generals who advise politicians are such experts, but they also speak on behalf of the soldiers who are taking the risks of military action. This often gives them a moral as well as a professional superiority over their political masters, especially given that very few of today's politicians have personal experience of fighting wars. This was true of President Clinton, who notoriously did his best to avoid military service during the Vietnam war. It was therefore very hard for him indeed to ask soldiers to take the sorts of risks he had not been willing to take as a young man. If the military did not want to engage in missions that the President was considering, like sending troops to Bosnia, as described above, it could avoid doing so to a large extent. Clinton's advisor on terrorism, Richard Clarke, recalls how the President pulled him and General Hugh Shelton aside after a cabinet meeting. 'Hugh,' the President said to the General, 'what I think would scare the shit out of these al Qaida guys more than any cruise missile . . . would be the sight of US commandos, Ninja guys in black suits, jumping out of helicopters in their camps, spraying machine guns. Even if we don't get the big guys, it will have good effect.'[31] General Shelton 'looked pained', according to Clarke's account of the events, and nothing more came of it. Instead, the US fired a volley of cruise missiles at al-Qaeda's Afghan training camps, with little effect. Only after 9/11 did the Pentagon agree to put troops on the ground in Afghanistan, but even then it was with some reluctance.[32] This may seem odd. From a purely institutional point of view, one might imagine the Pentagon relishing the opportunity to put al-Qaeda on its to-do list, thus potentially being able to attract more funding and exert more influence on the national security decision-making process. In this case, as in the case of almost all the other new security risks that the US has faced after the Cold War, the Pentagon's reaction was the opposite. The generals went to great lengths to avoid becoming involved in new missions like peace-keeping

[30] Weber, *From Max Weber: Essays in Sociology*, 232.
[31] Clarke, *Against All Enemies*, 189–90.
[32] Woodward, *Bush at War*, 43–4, 247.

or fighting terrorists. When politicians have finally persuaded the military to become involved in these situations, the military was able to define rules of engagement in such a way as to minimise the risk for the troops involved, but also to minimise the impact the troops could have on the ground. For example, the Pentagon insisted on a very narrow mandate for the NATO troops who were to implement the Bosnia peace accord in 1998. The generals did not want their headquarters in Bosnia, did not want to confiscate heavy weapons and did not want their soldiers to engage in 'police work'. In other words, they would deploy to Bosnia, but not do everything that the mission required. In the end the civilian side made the military engage itself rather more, which proved to be enough to stabilise the country, but the architect of the peace agreement, Richard Holbrooke, despaired that too little use was being made of the implementation.[33]

This reluctance to take on new missions is by no means limited to the US military: most Western armed forces share this reluctance. Fifteen years after the end of the Cold War, the bulk of European armed forces are still organised in ways that suit territorial defence against a Soviet armoured attack, even though this is of little relevance in the post-Cold War world.

True to form, the reluctance was even given its own abbreviation: MOOTW, meaning 'military operations other than war'.[34] As Thomas Barnett notes, this phrase was basically a way for the military to point out that such operations were temporary in nature and should in no way influence the core mission of the US armed forces, namely to win and fight wars. In Barnett's words, 'who, after all, joins the military to do things other than war?'[35]

What Western armed forces do is war, and war is narrowly defined to suit the bureaucratic organisation of the armed forces themselves. In the twentieth century, armed forces were tasked with developing the structures to fit continental-wide mechanised warfare. This required a huge logistical base and large-scale divisional bureaucracies to organise the movement of thousands of men and machines. During the Cold War, it was total war on this scale that Western military forces trained for. By the end of the Cold War, the wars they were fighting had become

---

[33] Richard Holbrooke, *To End A War*, revised edition (New York: The Modern Library, 1999), 216–23, 335–7.
[34] This is the NATO abbreviation. The Allied Joint Doctrine defines this concept as 'a wide range of activities where military capabilities are used for purposes other than large-scale combat operations'; NATO, *Allied Joint Doctrine*, September 1998.
[35] Thomas P. M. Barnett, *The Pentagon's New Map: War and Peace in the Twenty-First Century* (New York: Putnam, 2004), 103.

completely different. These wars did not fit established rules and procedures, and therefore were not wars in the military's eyes. In fact,
these conflicts became a risk to the professionalism of the military
bureaucracy. Either a new professional ethos had to be developed,
which eschewed the 'big war' in favour of the 'small war', or else the
new conflicts had to be defined as something that military professionals
did not deal with.

As a first-time presidential candidate, George W. Bush pandered to
the US armed forces' unwillingness to engage in MOOTW. Bush criticised President Clinton for squandering US military resources on small
wars from Haiti to Bosnia. It was time, Bush argued, for the armed
forces to concentrate on what he perceived to be their core function: to
'fight and win wars'.[36] Bush's presidency was only nine months old when
the President himself embraced a 'new kind of war' in the fight against
terrorism following the 9/11 attacks on New York and Washington.

From the point of view of those who argue for a new military organised to fight new wars, the reluctance to deal with MOOTW is a risk
to the security of the Western world. For example, Thomas Barnett
argues that '9/11 elevated military operations other than war to grand
strategy'.[37] The risk literature identifies the ability to maintain management capabilities in the face of risk as a pivotal element of strategy. If
the agencies responsible for managing military threats simply will not
recognise them, then this ability is lost: new enemies will constantly be
fought using old means. On the other hand, those who believe that the
military should be assigned to deal with terrorism, nation-building and
similar missions because no greater threats exist in the post-Cold War
world fear that the Western armed forces are wasting their energies on
temporary projects. Transforming the armed forces to meet the new
threats means risking all the tried and learned ways of organising armed
forces. Since bureaucracies are risk-averse, they tend to see the risk of
change as greater than the risk of inertia. This does not mean that the
US in particular or Western armed forces in general will not change their
ways: on the contrary, the RMA is placing transformation on the institutional agenda. But the bureaucratic nature of the military helps to
explain the slow pace of transformation. The bureaucratic logic also
enables one to predict that the real problem of transformation will occur
at the point when new enemies or new technologies necessitate a different organisation of the armed forces. That will be the true test of the
transformation paradigm and of the extent to which the armed forces

[36] Bush, *Governor Bush Addresses American Legion.*
[37] Barnett, *The Pentagon's New Map*, 105.

have turned 'post-modern', that is, left behind their bureaucratic, means-end rational understanding of themselves.

The continuation of law by other means

In sum, it is one of the paradoxes of strategy in the late modern age that Western militaries are transforming themselves on the technological and doctrinal levels while remaining very much the same on the organisational level. In fact, the RMA probably reinforces the tendency to think of war as a rational enterprise managed by a bureaucracy because information technologies hold the promise of a battlefield lit up by the light of reason – a battlefield that suits the bureaucratic mind perfectly. It clearly identifies means and ends, is predictable and therefore makes it possible to avert many of the traditional risks of war. However, one of the insights of the risk literature is how the perfection of modern rationales in fact implies their ultimate breakdown. While reinforcing the bureaucracy on the one hand, the RMA is breaking its rationale down on the other. The promise of a completely rational Clausewitzian war is, as we have seen, ultimately self-defeating, because full information shifts the focus on to asymmetrical strategies. Such strategies can either deal with information or take up terrorism or insurgency. In either case a bureaucratic organisation will be less than perfect to deal with them.

The greatest paradox of the bureaucratisation of warfare, however, is the way in which an increasingly more means-end rational approach to war is making it a more legalistic enterprise. Clausewitz would have expected otherwise. His claim that war was a continuation of politics by other means was part of an argument with those who claimed that the military should run their own war, if not the entire foreign policy of the state. Clausewitz believed that the army knew best how to use military means, but that the government knew best how to define the political ends. Today means and ends are being merged, but on the government's terms rather than the military's. Clausewitz would never have imagined that the rationalisation of warfare would make the relationship between states resemble a national political community. Nevertheless, making war a law-governed activity is a logical consequence of regarding it as a political end, at least when the standards for conducting politics are set by societies that are much more governed by the rule of law than Clausewitz' Prussia, as well as being much more closely in interaction with one another on many more levels because of globalisation. Thus on the one hand one of the oldest modes of international interaction, namely war, has become more thoroughly rule-regulated than perhaps ever before. On the other hand, however, globalisation means that a plethora of new modes of interaction and new actors in conducting them are developing, most of which are not regulated by international law to the same degree as war. It is in these new, globalised phenomena that risk societies see the new dangers lying, and bureaucratic rules and procedures cannot adequately guide responses to them.

The presence of the future

Who do you expect to fight? The answer to that question is central to strategy. The battles one expects to fight shape both doctrines and weapons development. In other words, the expectations of one's enemies shape the armed forces that a government maintains in order to remain secure. For most of the twentieth century the answer to 'who do you expect to fight' would be fairly simple: 'the country we fought in the last war'. Perhaps this reflects the truism that armed forces plan for the last war, but actually geopolitics made it reasonable for Germans to expect to fight the French and the Russians, for the British to expect to fight the Germans, and for the Americans to expect to intervene in a European war on the side of Britain and France against first Germany and then Russia. The predictability of the enemy's identity suited the bureaucratic approach to warfare. At the same time, the legalisation of warfare reflected very narrow expectations regarding exactly how a crisis would evolve into a war.

Enemies are no longer exclusively defined by history because risk society does not expect history to guide it in the twenty-first century. In risk society decisions are based on scenarios. The strategy they suggest is that non-state actors like al-Qaeda will be a central feature of the strategic landscape of the twenty-first century. Taking their point of departure in this expectation, Western societies debate the rationality of al-Qaeda because most people see al-Qaeda as the symbol of a new type of enemy operating on the basis of a different rationality from the West's. When strategy is based on different rationalities, the basis for the bureaucratisation of warfare is seriously challenged. Identifying the enemy is no longer a question of means and ends, but of values.

Before we discuss how people in risk society regard their enemies, we must consider how they regard identity in general. The first two sections deal with this question by identifying late modern man as 'protean man', who chooses different identities and then shows how this notion of identity does not permit people to identify with Islamic fundamentalist terrorists. This means that the enemy cannot be seen as an innocent means doing his government's bidding, as soldiers were previously seen. 'If our enemy is not like us, then what *is* he like?' Following 9/11, this question has been answered with reference to three different conceptions of the terrorist's rationality: he is irrational, of a different rationality, or perfectly rational but evil. Having dealt with these concepts of rationality, this part of the chapter ends by considering how identifying enemies has itself come to be considered a risk.

Protean man

Al-Qaeda could have found no method of terrorism more frightening to the citizens of risk society than the suicide bomber. In late-modernity, our present lives are defined by the future they are to realise. We define ourselves by the choices we make. If there is such a thing as a late modern personality, then it is captured in Robert Jay Lifton's phrase, 'protean man', one who is defined by his choices, which can always be remade.[38] Because identity is a choice, Jonah Goldstein and Jeremy Rayner argue, 'the idea of authenticity has become more and more central. Because identity-claims are not subject to a common measure, they cannot be negotiated away in the same way as interests; only I can shape and re-shape who I am.'[39] Most people are prepared to accept the most outrageous lifestyle choices of other people if these choices are believed to be based on people's true desires. The singer Sheryl Crow captures this sentiment in the line, 'If it makes you happy, it can't be that bad.'[40]

People in risk society respect choice and find it hard to condemn any choice as unethical. For that reason, the suicide bomber places the citizens of late-modernity in the uncomfortable position that they can identify with the way he chooses to define his life by his actions and they can somehow respect his insistence on authenticity. Still, the suicide bomber insists on the authenticity of values defined by opposition to everything that the citizens of risk society hold dear, his choice being bloody murder. In so doing, the suicide bomber challenges protean man's fundamental belief in the inherent justice and aesthetics of choice. While late modern persons can identify with the insistence on authenticity and choice, they cannot accept the fundamentalists' insistence on only one authentic belief dictated by God and therefore only one right type of choice. Furthermore, protean man cannot accept the lethal finality and the costs of his choice that this belief leads the fundamentalist to make.

[38]   Robert Jay Lifton, 'Protean Man', *Partisan Review* (Winter 1968), 13–27.
[39]   Jonah Goldstein and Jeremy Rayner, 'The Politics of Identity in Late Modern Society', *Theory and Society* 23 (June 1994), 368.
[40]   Sheryl Crow, 'If It Makes You Happy', *Sheryl Crow*, A&M Records, 1996.

What makes the suicide terrorist truly appalling to the citizens of risk society, however, is the way his acts rob other people of their futures. When life is not defined by some inherent and shared meaning but has to be defined and redefined by each individual, then one cannot argue that the true quality of life is measured by what you do in it rather than by the length of it. The shorter your life, the fewer the choices you can make. But not only does terrorism rob its victims of their future, it also becomes part of the possible futures that the citizens of risk society have to choose between. The possibility that their life will be cut short or tragically changed by the loss of a loved one because of terrorism becomes a part of their future.

The nature of the terrorist attacks on New York and Washington in 2001 thus made it clear to protean man that one of the most fundamental choices he was facing by the beginning of the twenty-first century had become how to define his enemies. If terrorists can make choices that are unacceptable, then their way of choosing must be different from how ordinary people make choices in late modern Western society. In other words, they have to act using a different rationality. Thus the terrorist attacks on New York and Washington exploded the notion that the enemy was a means-end rational bureaucracy like the Pentagon. The attack on the Pentagon itself was not directed by the general staff of a nation state, but carried out by a terrorist cell in a loose network called al-Qaeda. The question President Bush asked afterwards in order to explain to his people why the US had been attacked was not what al-Qaeda's interest had been in attacking the US, but instead 'Why do they hate us?'[41] Bureaucratic warfare simply has no response to that question. Therefore the President concluded: 'the enemy is a different type of enemy'.[42]

Defining what type of enemy al-Qaeda is has become a debate about why terrorists make the choices they make. It is a debate about rationality. But it is also a debate about the future, because the response to terrorism depends on whether the terrorists are deemed irrational, rational or just evil beyond any concept of rationality. The debate about the rationality of the new enemies thus defines Western strategy at the beginning of the twenty-first century. The definition of terrorist

---

[41] George W. Bush, *Address to a Joint Session of Congress and the American People*, 20 September 2001 (Washington, DC: The White House, Office of the Press Secretary, 2001), §24.

[42] George W. Bush, *President Pledges Assistance for New York in Phone Call with Pataki, Giuliani*, Remarks by the President in Telephone Conversation with New York Mayor Giuliani and New York Governor Pataki, 13 September 2001 (Washington, DC: The White House, Office of the Press Secretary, 2001), §33.

rationality also defines the West. The difference between the actions of the terrorists and the military action the Pentagon has undertaken in response to them clearly illustrated the difference between the means-end rational war-fighting bureaucracy and the al-Qaeda network.

Who are you and who is your enemy?

The bureaucratic conception of warfare gives you no reason to hate your enemy. Weber describes it as the 'special virtue' of bureaucracy that 'it succeeds in eliminating from official business love, hatred, and all purely personal, irrational, and emotional elements with escape calculation'.[43] The reason for this is the separation of means and ends. According to bureaucratic reasoning, one can be passionate about ends, but one ought to be purely professional about means. Clausewitz defined ends as existing beyond the purview of the soldiers. In this view, soldiers can, of course, be motivated by the ends for which they fight, but how they fight is not determined by the political ends they are fighting for. The honour and virtue of soldiering come from not becoming personally and emotionally involved. Of course, it is difficult, indeed verging on the impossible, for people not to get emotionally involved in something as dangerous and decisive as war. This is yet another area where Protestant self-restraint became an important part of Clausewitz' writings: duty should come before passion. This is also the point of the laws of war, which stipulate that a soldier is not a murderer because he does not kill for his own ends but for the ends of the state. The moment he starts defining his own ends and fights for his own benefit, however, he forfeits his status as a means and thus becomes culpable. So long as a soldier does not commit such crimes, he is to be treated as a means: he is not to be prosecuted, but 'stored' in a prisoner-of-war camp until hostilities are over and the enemy can no longer benefit from using him as a means. Then he is to be released. In 1762, Rousseau formulated this doctrine thus: 'War is not, therefore, a relation of man to man but a relation of state to state, in which individuals are enemies only by accident, not as men or even as citizens, but as soldiers, not as members of the homeland, but as its defenders.'[44]

---

[43] Weber, *From Max Weber: Essays in Sociology*, 216.

[44] Jean-Jacques Rousseau, *On Social Contract or Principles of Political Right*, in *Rousseau's Political Writings*, trans. Julia Conaway Bondanella, ed. Alan Ritter and Julia Conaway Bondanella (New York: W. W. Norton, 1988), 90. It is worth emphasising that this concept of the soldier as a political means is a true Weberian ideal type, and that many, if not most, modern wars had serious problems living up to these ideals. This was especially the case when one side believed itself to be racially superior to the other, as

Following 9/11, the US government engaged in an exercise of strategic pedagogics in which it tried to explain the nature of al-Qaeda in order to justify the steps the United States would be taking later against the terrorists. The President thus emphasised that al-Qaeda was a different type of enemy from those the United States had faced during the twentieth century: 'our coalition is opposing not a nation, but a network'.[45] In his speech to Congress following the 9/11 attacks in 2001, the President went on to describe how such a network operated: 'Al Qaida is to terror what the mafia is to crime. But its goal is not making money; its goal is remaking the world – and imposing its radical beliefs on people everywhere.'[46] What made al-Qaeda especially dangerous, the President argued, was the fact that it does not have rational ends. One can understand the mafia: it wants money. In President Bush's view, however, al-Qaeda's goal is much more ambitious and much more dangerous. 'These terrorists kill not merely to end lives', the President argued, 'but to disrupt and end a way of life. With every atrocity, they hope that America grows fearful, retreating from the world and forsaking our friends. They stand against us, because we stand in their way.'[47] While the danger of terrorism was new to most Americans in September 2001, President Bush did not describe the terrorists in a new way. Indeed, in many ways his speech echoed what President Clinton had said about al-Qaeda in 1998:

> The groups associated with him [bin Laden] come from diverse places, but share a hatred for democracy, a fanatical glorification of violence, and a horrible distortion of their religion to justify the murder of innocents. They have made the United States their adversary precisely because of what we stand for and what we stand against.[48]

It is clear from Clinton's description of al-Qaeda that what the West sees when it looks at the organisation is mostly itself. Al-Qaeda is not defined

---

the Germans did on the Eastern Front during the Second World War. This did not make war any less instrumental, but the 'barbarisation of warfare' meant that one army was able to treat the enemy's army and civilians as means only, without any humane considerations. War became even more machine-like because the soldiers could no longer identify with their opponents. Furthermore, the idea of an equal opponent still existed, and it was on this basis that the Allies prosecuted German officers after the war. For a description of the 'barbarisation of warfare' on the Eastern Front, see Omer Bartov, *The Eastern Front, 1941–45: German Troops and the Barbarisation of Warfare* (London: Macmillan, 1985).

[45] George W. Bush, *President Thanks World Coalition for Anti-Terrorism Efforts*, The South Lawn, 11 March 2002 (Washington, DC: The White House, Office of the Press Secretary, 2002), §20.

[46] Bush, *Address to a Joint Session of Congress and the American People*, §14.

[47] Ibid., §26.

[48] Clinton, *Address to the Nation by the President*, §8.

on its own terms, but in terms of its opposition to the United States. If 'they stand against us, because we stand in their way', then one way to avoid confrontation would simply be to step aside and let al-Qaeda have its way in the Middle East. Even if this would be acceptable in power-political terms, however, appeasement is not regarded as an option, because the ambitions of this opponent are believed to be limitless. Al-Qaeda's ambition is not thought to be limited by interests; its ends are not to realise political ends, it is argued, but to impose values.

In this analysis, the fight against terrorism has moved beyond the carefully regulated and predictable environment of bureaucratic warfare. The rules do not apply in this case because the enemy is not a state bureaucracy and does not regard the struggle in terms of means and ends. In 1998, President Clinton recognised that al-Qaeda had declared a war against the United States that went beyond the established conventions. 'A few months ago, and again this week, bin Laden publicly vowed to wage a terrorist war against America, saying – and I quote – "We do not differentiate between those dressed in military uniforms and civilians. They're all targets. Their mission is murder and their history is bloody."'[49] In referring to how al-Qaeda defines the struggle, policymakers clearly realise that they can no longer define the terms of the conflict. Thus debating al-Qaeda's reasons for acting becomes the way to define the new enemy and thus set the rules of the new battleground. This is the question we turn to next.

New terrorists, new rationalities

It is not only the fact that this particular network has proved able to strike at the Western world that makes al-Qaeda a significant military phenomenon: it is the implications for the future that matter most from a strategic perspective. Al-Qaeda is widely regarded as the first of a new breed of terrorists who are able to exploit the flows of globalisation to their advantage.[50] From this perspective, al-Qaeda is merely the first of the terrorist groups of the future. In the eyes of Western strategists, these terrorist groups are able to operate because of the new capabilities which globalisation gives any group or state that aspires to use armed force. From this perspective, the capabilities that al-Qaeda has demonstrated seem to prove that existing, state-based enemies, such as rogue states, may also become more dangerous. This is not only because of the new

---

[49] Ibid., §4.
[50] David C. Rapoport, 'The Fourth Wave: September 11 in the History of Terrorism', *Current History* (December 2001), 419–24.

capabilities that the proliferation of technologies give any agent – state or non-state – in the globalising system, but also because the different means and ends that al-Qaeda represents have led some to question whether in fact all states should be regarded within the means-end rational framework of national interests.

Thus in many ways al-Qaeda is the symbol of a process rather than a genuine object of analysis, because in risk society the real strategic debate is not about present dangers but about how these dangers will proliferate in the future – and with the future in mind, al-Qaeda looks even scarier. How the West responds to the new strategic actors in the making depends on how it perceives the strategic rationales of its new enemies. 'What can we expect?' is an urgent strategic question, and the answer seems to depend on what kinds of rationality new enemies like al-Qaeda are believed to be operating by. Debating rationality is, in other words, no longer merely the pastime of sociologists; strategists are having a heated debate about rationality too. In this debate three views manifest themselves. Al-Qaeda, and groups like it, is either believed to be irrational, of a different rationality, or perfectly rational but without justifiable aims, or in President Bush's phrase, 'evil-doers'.[51]

Irrational

Irrationality is scary from a risk-society perspective because an irrational agent does not attempt to manage risks: instead he thinks little about the future and does not care much about boomerang effects. This is not just a very risky risk culture, because risk-takers know they take risks – that is what drives them. Irrationality represents the negation of culture; it is an anti-culture that breaks down the institutions on which risk society depends because it refuses to share late modern Western society's concern for risk. Chancellor Schröder described the events of 9/11 as 'barbaric attacks'[52] because from this perspective the Islamist terrorists are barbarians who are seeking to destroy a civilisation they hardly understand.

Roxanne Euben describes how the Islamic fundamentalism that motivates al-Qaeda is regarded in the West: 'Fundamentalism has in many ways become a negative mirror reflecting back on Western life that which

---

[51] These views should not be seen as mutually exclusive: for example, the Bush administration has made all three arguments. President Bush has repeatedly referred to the terrorists as 'evil-doers', he probably did so for the first time a few days after 9/11, see George W. Bush, *Remarks by the President on Arrival*, 16 September 2001 (Washington, DC: The White House, Office of the Press Secretary, 2001), §2.

[52] Gerhard Schröder, *The Terrorist Attacks in the United States and the Decisions Taken by the United Nations Security Council and NATO* (Berlin: Bulletin der Bundesregierung, No. 61/1, 19 September 2001), §10.

it would leave behind; it signifies the resurgence of the irrational in what much of Western culture has come to regard as the age of rationalization.'[53] Euben explains that the ideology behind al-Qaeda is regarded as a by-product of social change.[54] In this view, globalisation makes terrorists react to what they regard as an infringement of their values. As such they are revolting against nothing less than human progress, against the future – including their own future. Globalisation, and the modernisation that follows from it, promise their children a better life, it is argued, just as they promise children in Western societies a better life. Thus the terrorists are not only a risk to Western societies, but also a risk to the Islamic societies that they claim they want to rescue. In other words, the terrorists have got it horribly wrong. Their views are unacceptable, their reasoning flawed. Therefore, 'the terrorists are beyond reason', as presidential candidate John Kerry put it in 2004.[55]

When one cannot reason with a barbaric, irrational enemy, one has to fight him, because only thus can the future be saved. According to Prime Minister Blair, there is simply nothing to be expected from a scenario in which the terrorists prevail. Where globalisation defines an ever brighter future, fundamentalism offers no future at all when seen with Western eyes. In the absence of rationality there can be no way of defining progress, and thus the steady progress of modernity will be replaced by chaos. In Blair's words, 'the threat is chaos'.[56]

The danger associated with the terrorists, however, is inversely proportionate to the respect the West gives its terrorist enemy. One example of this is the Chairman of the US Joint Chiefs of Staff arguing that it was necessary to restrain detainees being transported to Guantanamo Bay because 'these folks are ready to chew through the hydraulic wires of a C-17 to bring it down'.[57] These opponents are regarded as berserks motivated by a personal rage. They will not stop at anything and therefore they cannot be treated as a means in the service of a state. To them, it is believed, the fighting provides its own reason. As President Bush told the German Bundestag, 'we oppose an enemy that thrives on violence'.[58]

[53] Roxanne L. Euben, *Enemy in the Mirror: Islamic Fundamentalism and the Limits of Modern Rationalism* (Princeton, NJ: Princeton University Press, 1999), 44.
[54] Ibid., 30.
[55] Kerry, *Kerry Lays Out Iraq Plan*, §5.
[56] Blair, *Prime Minister's Address to the Labour Party Conference*, §38.
[57] Quoted in Rupert Cornwell, 'Just Retribution or an Abuse of Human Rights? A Big Question, with Only One Answer in the US', *Independent*, 18 January 2002.
[58] George W. Bush, *President Bush Thanks Germany for Support Against Terror, Remarks by the President to a Special Session of the German Bundestag*, The White House, 23 May 2002 (Washington DC: The White House, Office of the Press Secretary, 2002), §25, www.whitehouse.gov/news/releases/2002/05/print/20020523.2.html (24 May 2002).

When the enemy is believed to enjoy violence for its own sake, it transcends the all-important distinction in the laws of war between using violence as a means and using violence for one's own ends or indeed for one's own pleasure. One is not supposed to like war: if the enemy is actually enjoying himself, then he has no claim to one's respect. On the contrary, he is extremely dangerous, because if he actually likes the pain of war, then the threat of military force is not going to deter him, nor will he lay down his arms if there is nothing more to be gained by fighting. He will fight to the end and enjoy it, therefore he ceases to be a means for political ends. There is little to learn from an enemy who is believed to be irrational. In fact, believing the enemy is irrational only reinforces one's belief in one's own moral purpose. In this perspective, the fight against terrorism is a fight to restore the world to its proper balance and to defend progress and civilisation against barbarism.

The belief that the enemy is irrational introduces a vital distinction between the individual terrorists and the capability of the terrorist group as such. The individual terrorist is a madman who will fight regardless of risk. Such terrorists cannot be persuaded to surrender; they will have to be defeated one by one. While the individual terrorist is thus a dangerous enemy, the irrational understanding of terrorism sees it as less dangerous. There ought to be some upper limit to how many people a fundamentally flawed idea can inspire. Furthermore, if the thinking of one's opponent is so flawed, then one should have a fair chance of outwitting him. From the 'irrational perspective', victory in the war on terrorism is therefore a foregone conclusion. If one believes that terrorists are as rational as oneself but that they are following a different rationality, they are altogether more dangerous.

A different rationality

The notion that the enemy has a different rationality is used to describe states as well as terrorists as enemies, but its main focus is actually not the enemies whom it describes, but the West's perception of these enemies. 'I think the greatest mistake is assuming that people will behave,' Deputy Secretary of Defense Paul Wolfowitz explains; 'well, it's a version of mirror imaging, I guess, [to assume that] people will be rational according to our definition of what is rational'.[59] The West will do well to remember, the argument goes, that not all societies are risk societies and that not all social groups are risk-averse. As pointed out in the discussion about the RMA, one of the few ways to defeat Western

---

[59] Deputy Secretary Wolfowitz, Interview with Sam Tannenhaus, *Vanity Fair*, Friday 9 May 2003, Transcript (Washington, DC: US Department of Defense, 2003).

forces is to be willing to accept risks that the West is not willing to take. In other words, Western strategists can no longer assume that their opponents will be risk-averse bureaucracies guided by means-end rationality and following the laws of war. All the established truths about what one can and cannot do are up in the air.

Thus this argument stresses the existence of different risk cultures, but it also points beyond thinking in terms of risk at all. In adopting this perspective, strategists must accept that not only is their rationality changing from means-end to risk, but their enemies' rationality will change from case to case. This dual uncertainty is another reason for capability-based defence planning (see Chapter 3), because if one really cannot figure out what an opponent will do, at least one can establish what he is able to do. And if it becomes clear that a regime, like Saddam Hussein's in Iraq, has acquired weapons of mass destruction, then one should assume the worst. As President Bush concludes in a discussion about weapons of mass destruction, 'If these regimes and their terrorist allies were to perfect these capabilities, no inner voice of reason, no hint of conscience would prevent their use.'[60] Kenneth Pollack made this argument even more unambiguously in relation to Saddam Hussein:

This is not to argue that Saddam is irrational . . . Nevertheless, Saddam has a number of pathologies that make deterring him unusually difficult. He is an inveterate gambler and risk-taker who regularly twists his calculation of the odds to suit his preferred course of action. He bases his calculations on assumptions that outsiders often find bizarre and has little understanding of the larger world.[61]

In other words, Saddam Hussein was a risk because he was unpredictable. Pollack argued that the best way to manage the risk of Saddam Hussein was to eliminate him from the equation and thus restore management capability by making the region more predictable, if no less dangerous. The challenge is for Western decision-makers to establish the nature of their enemy's calculations and study his assumptions about the world, and then decide what risk the enemy in question poses, as well as the proper response to it. But how can this response be guided by the bureaucratic rules of the military and the laws of war when, as a matter of definition, the enemy does not think according to those rules? The history of armed conflict demonstrates that it is wars between societies of different cultures that are fought the most

---

[60] Bush, *President Bush Thanks Germany for Support Against Terror*, §26.
[61] Kenneth Pollack, 'Next Stop Baghdad', *Foreign Affairs* 81 (March/April 2002), 36.

ruthlessly. The bureaucratisation of warfare has gone a long way in removing such perceptions of difference, but the rejection of the underlying assumption of a shared rationality reintroduces cultural difference in warfare. Thus defining the enemy as of a different rationality means creating much greater scope regarding what can be done to him. If more and more enemies are believed to be outside the bounds of means-end rationality, then armed conflict can become much more ruthless.

When the rationality of the enemy is different from one's own, it is difficult to establish criteria for victory. How does one know what the outcome of a particular battle means to the enemy? If the enemy defines the terms of the conflict differently from oneself, then one fights him at the risk of fighting a war that is a success according to one's own criteria, but which has very little impact on him. This is a traditional problem in guerrilla warfare, where the guerrilla avoids conventional Western-style battle in favour of a more localised and prolonged struggle. In order to win against such enemies, Western militaries will have to escape the established rules and procedures of bureaucratic warfare and define the criteria for victory from case to case. In doing so, however, they risk fighting wars that may be a success in local terms but cannot be recognised as such back home. They also risk betraying the very rules and procedures that define their professionalism.

Evil-doers

Perhaps the most common description of al-Qaeda's reason for using terrorism is that the terrorists are evil and that the way they commit their acts of terror proves just how evil they are. President Bush has thus described the perpetrators of 9/11 as 'evil-doers'[62] and 'a few dozen evil and deluded men'.[63] When the enemy is described as evil, he is placed beyond reason. Weber distinguished between instrumental and value rationality in order to demonstrate that what the modern Western mind believes to be rational (instrumental rationality) might in fact be irrational from another cultural or value-based perspective. The point about al-Qaeda for those who describe the terrorists as 'evil-doers' is that it represents on the one hand a recognition that they are different, but on the other hand a rejection of their different values as a legitimate reason for acting. An irrational enemy acts on the basis of his passions – he does not know any better. That is why he is a barbarian. An evil

---

[62] Bush, *Remarks by the President on Arrival*, §2.
[63] Bush, *Remarks by the President at 2002 Graduation Exercise of the United States Military Academy*, §15.

enemy knows better, but he chooses not to do good. He is perfectly rational, perhaps even means-end rational, but he does not care about any other ends than his own evil ends. If one regards one's enemy in this way, there can be no justice to the enemy's cause and nothing can legitimise his actions. Prime Minister Blair expressed this sentiment when he described a meeting with relatives of some of the 9/11 victims, including the mother and father of one victim, and went on to say, 'There is no justification for their pain. Their son did nothing wrong.'[64] From this point of view, one should find the reason for their actions in the terrorists' biography, because it is their evil minds that lead them to terrorism, not the social factors that define rationalities. One might study them and even admire their skill, as Sherlock Holmes did with Professor Moriarty, but there can be no compromise with evil. Thus argued Tony Blair in the run-up to the Afghanistan war:

> The action we take will be proportionate; targeted; we will do all we humanly can to avoid civilian casualties. But understand what we are dealing with . . . They have no moral inhibition on the slaughter of the innocent. If they could have murdered not 7,000 but 70,000 does anyone doubt they would have done so and rejoiced in it? There is no compromise possible with such people, no meeting of minds, no point of understanding with such terror. Just a choice: defeat it or be defeated by it. And defeat it we must.[65]

From this perspective, one can either argue that the fight against terrorism is the Armageddon of the twenty-first century – the ultimate struggle between good and evil – or that terrorists are merely criminals who do not deserve to be dignified as combatants in a war. President Bush followed the Armageddon line when he described the events of 9/11 thus: 'In a single instant, we realised that this will be a decisive decade in the history of liberty, that we've been called to a unique role in human events. Rarely has the world faced a choice more clear or consequential.'[66] President Bush declared the attacks on 9/11 'acts of war',[67] thus responding to the al-Qaeda declaration of war against the US which President Clinton had merely referred to in 1998. Michael Howard argues that declaring war against terrorism is 'a terrible and irrevocable error' in ontological as well as epistemological terms. On the ontological level, Howard believes that by declaring al-Qaeda capable of conducting

---

[64] Blair, *Prime Minister's Address to the Labour Party Conference*, §5.
[65] Ibid., §§24–7.
[66] Bush, *The President's State of the Union Address*, §62.
[67] George W. Bush, *Remarks by the President in Photo Opportunity with the National Security Team*, The Cabinet Room, The White House, 13 September 2001 (Washinton, DC: The White House, Office of the Press Secretary, 2001), www.whitehouse.gov/news/releases/2001/09/20010912-4.html (9 December 2001), §2.

acts of war and taking up the challenge to fight a war with the terrorists, the Bush administration is taking part in a Hegelian struggle for recognition. This will legitimate al-Qaeda at a time when the core of the strategy to defeat the terror network ought to have been to remove its legitimacy.[68] Howard also claims that the ontological misconception of the status of the terrorists leads to a misunderstanding of the epistemology of terrorism: '"Terrorism" is itself simply a technique for waging war, so it makes little sense to talk about "waging war" against it,' he argues.[69] The *Independent* has supported this argument, concluding that if George Bush could declare war on 'terrorism' following 9/11, then President Roosevelt ought to have declared war on bombing following Pearl Harbor.[70]

The two different conceptions of 'the war on terror' are based on different beliefs in how definitively evil can be stamped out. George Bush declared war on terror in order to signal that, 'Our war on terror begins with al Qaida, but it does not end there. It will not end until every terrorist group of global reach has been found, stopped and defeated.'[71] Those who oppose declaring war on terror do so exactly because they believe that a total defeat of terrorism is unachievable. Evil will always exist, they argue; the aim should be to minimise the risk of terrorism, not to eradicate the terrorists. This argument links up with the 'living with terrorism' argument discussed in the previous chapter.

In either case, the struggle against terrorism does not fall within the normal bureaucratic rules of modern strategy. If one regards the struggle against terrorism as a global law-enforcement operation, then national notions of how to capture, convict and punish criminals are pushed into the international realm. If one turns one's focus from the terrorists to those hunting them, then this view suggests that there are no 'soldiers' in the fight against terrorism, only 'policemen'. Therefore no one can claim the extraordinary 'licence to kill' that the laws of war give soldiers. Furthermore, prisoners should be tried in a court of law, not interned. Many of the widespread protests against the US prison camp at Guantanamo Bay should be seen in this light.[72] If one regards the fight against

[68] Michael Howard, Speech at the Conference New Policies for a New World, RUSI, unpublished, London, November 2001.

[69] Michael Howard, 'Terrorism Has Always Fed Off its Response', *Times*, 1 September 2001.

[70] 'It is Meaningless and Dangerous to Declare War Against Terrorism', Leading Article, *Independent*, 17 September 2001.

[71] Bush, *Address to a Joint Session of Congress and the American People*, §23.

[72] I have elaborated on this in 'The Prisoner's Reflection: Identity and Detainees in the "War on Terrorism"', in Mikkel Vedby Rasmussen, Sten Rynning, Kristian Søby Kristensen and Bertel Heurlin (eds.), *The Revolution in Military Affairs* (Copenhagen: Institute for International Studies, 2003), 213–28.

terrorism as a battle between good and evil, however, one has little time for the finer nuances of the law, whether domestic or international. In this view the terrorists are seen as outlaws who have placed themselves beyond the norms of civilisation. In this case it makes little sense to give them the rights that are normally granted to soldiers.

No matter how one regards al-Qaeda's rationality, the more Western strategists speculate about the terrorists' reasons for acting as they do, the more they are regarded as a new type of enemy, one that will redefine the terms under which the West will fight the wars of the future. Thus in spite of the fact that the numbers of terrorists are far, far lower than the numbers of soldiers in modern, bureaucratic armies around the world, it is terrorism and other 'asymmetric strategies' that Western strategists are thinking of when they reflect on the future of warfare, and in risk society the future is all that matters. The ways in which Western perceptions of the laws of war as well as the conditions for victory and defeat in the armed conflicts of the future are being challenged by the perception of new enemies show how defining one's enemies is a pivotal strategic decision. Strategists are acutely aware that, by choosing to define enemies and the future of battle in particular ways, they are risking producing as much conflict as they describe. This reflexive feature of risk strategy is described next.

The risks of defining enemies

From a means-end rational perspective, defining an enemy is the sensible thing to do. If another state has both hostile intent and the means to carry it out, then identifying this threat is a necessary condition for devising a strategy to defend oneself against it. Constructivist students of strategy even argue that identifying an enemy is a precondition for shaping your own identity: one needs to identify an 'other' in order to establish one's self.[73] From both perspectives, identifying al-Qaeda as an enemy should be text-book stuff. In the 9/11 attacks, the terrorist network has proved it had both the means and sinister ends. From a constructivist point of view, one could hardly ask for a more clear-cut case of an 'other' than Muslim fundamentalism in relation to late modern society inhabited by protean man. Still, neither the rationalist/realist perspective nor the constructivist, self–other perspective seems able to explain the anxiety with which Western governments have set out to define exactly who the war on terror was being fought against.

---

[73] For an example of this argument, see Klein, *Strategic Studies and World Order*, 5–6.

To protean man, it is very clear that defining an enemy is a choice. In late modern society, the rather abstract notion of identity created in the relationship between 'self' and 'other' has become a piece of cocktail-party wisdom for people who have become increasingly used to changing their own identities. The more identity becomes a choice, the more conscious people become of the reaction to such choices. Thus defining enemies is known to have consequences, and as the shock of 9/11 wore off, these consequences seemed to loom much larger to many people than the threat posed by the terrorists themselves.

Thus instead of launching a crusade against Muslim fundamentalism, Western leaders have gone out of their way to reject the 'self–other' distinction. They have done so in a *sotto voce* debate with Samuel Huntington and his thesis of a 'clash of civilisations'.[74] To Huntington 9/11 was a vindication of this thesis. The importance of scenarios of proliferation in the present strategic debate is underscored by the way Huntington argues that the West and the Muslim world clashed because conflict within the Muslim world proliferates. 'Contemporary global politics is the age of Muslim wars,' Huntington argues; 'Muslims fight each other and fight non-Muslims far more often than do peoples of other civilizations. Muslim wars have replaced the cold war as the principal form of international conflict.'[75] This analysis has been thoroughly rejected by Western political leaders. German Chancellor Schröder spoke for all of them when he asked, 'Is this the "clash of civilizations" that has so often been spoken of? My answer is clear. It is "no".'[76] One can, of course, debate how widely shared this view is or to what extent it is merely rhetorical, but in any case it is noteworthy that Western leaders are so careful in defining their enemy. Defining one's enemy is a risk in its own right. If the 'clash of civilisation' thesis were accepted politically, this would mean creating divisions in the world, a world which Western leaders firmly believe is being made one by globalisation. Thus from a Western point of view, accepting that there is a clash of civilisations would mean agreeing with al-Qaeda's worldview. The Western concept of civilisation is not exclusionary: on the contrary, it is based on the notion of civilisation as a journey to greater reason, freedom and prosperity that should be shared by all mankind. The West is in the vanguard of this journey, to be sure, but everybody

---

[74] Samuel Huntington, *The Clash of Civilizations and the Remaking of World Order* (London: Touchstone Books, 1998).
[75] Samuel Huntington, 'The Age of Muslim Wars', *Newsweek*, Special Davos Edition (December 2001–February 2002), 8.
[76] Schröder, *The Terrorist Attacks in the United States*, §§2–3.

can and ought to join in.[77] From this point of view, al-Qaeda is regarded as a conspiracy against the future. If al-Qaeda were to be defined as an 'other', then Western leaders would implicitly be acknowledging that there is an alternative to the progress of civilisation into a more globalised world, and that they cannot manage the risks that globalisation carries with it.

From this point of view, the concept of a 'war on terrorism' means exactly what it says. Terrorism offers an alternative to the state's monopoly of violence. According to this analysis, the state will face serious competition from transnational networks like terrorists in the twenty-first century. If this challenge is not met, then the state system itself might be at risk. When President Bush spoke to the UN General Assembly following the 9/11 attacks, he was therefore speaking as one head of state to other heads of states:

> Every civilized nation here today is resolved to keep the most basic commitment of civilization: we will defend ourselves and our future against terror and lawless violence . . . Every nation has a stake in this cause. As we meet, the terrorists are planning more murder – perhaps in my country, or perhaps in yours. They kill because they aspire to dominate. They seek to overthrow governments and destabilize regions.[78]

In arguing thus, President Bush is echoing the conclusion of the Chinese colonels who argue that non-state forces are 'the natural enemy of the international community, and especially large nations'.[79]

Whom do you expect to fight?

Western societies expect to fight enemies different from themselves in the future, and because they have become risk societies, identifying these enemies becomes a risk in its own right. Is the government identifying the right enemies, and does it understand how best to fight them? Is one risking creating more conflict by identifying enemies? These are the questions that have come to dominate the strategic debate. The date 9/11 has become a potent symbol for the risks that new, non-state actors pose. However, 9/11 has also become a symbol for how dangerous a 'clash of civilisations' can be. The fact that people of Arab descent who

---

[77] For descriptions of this Western conception of civilisation, see Norbert Elias, *The Civilizing Process* (Oxford: Blackwell, 1978 (1939)), and Christopher Coker, *Twilight of the West* (Boulder, CO: Westview Press, 1998).
[78] Bush, *President Bush Speaks to United Nations*, §§1, 9.
[79] Liang and Xiangsui, *Unrestricted Warfare*, 131.

had lived and studied in the West could turn into suicide terrorists made many in the West question their own societies. The question became, 'What have we done to make them hate us so?', those asking it being extremely reluctant to identify enemies in a 'war on terror'. This shows the reflective nature of risk societies, which do not just fear their enemies, they also fear identifying them. When enemies are identified, their nature can by no means be taken for granted. The debate about terrorism that followed 9/11 made al-Qaeda a symbol of new security agents with a rationality different from that of the nation state. Identifying enemies as different from oneself represents a fundamental break with the traditional, Clausewitzian conception of warfare. Enemies of a different rationality are subject to different rules from those codified in bureaucratic warfare. Thus at the same time as the laws and rules of war have become stricter than perhaps ever before, the enemies whom the West expects to fight in the future are increasingly seen as being outside these laws and rules.

The boomerang effect

War has become the continuation of law by other means, but Western societies do not expect their enemies to continue to fight by the means or for the ends presumed by the laws of war. The enemies of the future are believed to be very different from the bureaucratic Western armed forces. Thus it turns out that the perfection of the means-end rational approach to warfare, which can be described as the bureaucratisation of warfare, leaves risk societies with armed forces which they fear will not be able to meet the threats of the future. The perfection of the means-end rational approach thus becomes a risk in its own right. When the means, ends and organisation of the armed forces thus become a theme and a problem in themselves, then the armed forces become redefined. This is the boomerang effect of the bureaucratisation of warfare, which breaks down the modern armed forces, but it also makes it possible to fight conflicts that do not fall under the restrictive rules that stem from the UN Charter.

In the section on management, I analysed the bureaucratisation of warfare in terms of the three characteristics of bureaucracy identified by Max Weber. In the following I shall examine how professionalism, predictability and rules are redefined by the boomerang effect. One should note that, although the variables are the same in this section as in the section on management, the three characteristics of bureaucracy appear in a different order.

Bureaucracy I: the professionals

During the Kosovo campaign, the British Chief of the Defence Staff, General Sir Charles Guthrie, argued that, 'The simple truth is that late-20th century Western society is not very well adjusted to the prospect of fighting.'[80] Guthrie wrote this in response to calls for a ground invasion of Kosovo in order to stop the 'ethnic cleansing' going on there, but the General felt that the means and ends of war no longer correlated. The liberal elites of Britain, or any of the other NATO countries engaged in the Kosovo conflict, wanted the military to end the Albanians' suffering in Kosovo, but they were not, the General predicted, prepared to accept the means by which this could be achieved militarily. The same pundits who demanded action today, the General ventured, would demand an inquiry and an immediate withdrawal when British troops began to kill and get killed once they had been deployed to liberate Kosovo. Consequently, the General preferred to fight the Kosovo campaign from the air.

The RMA has given air forces the impression that war can finally be fought and won from the air. Perhaps it would be more accurate to say that in most armed forces, the air force is the only service which is still able to fight modern warfare on the bureaucratic terms that all the services used to fight it. The air force is a very modern, industrial service created in the mid-twentieth century when technological developments made strategic bombing a real possibility. As such, an air force has always been an industrial enterprise applying the power of machines to warfare. This has made the service quite ready to embrace the RMA. For the US Air Force, at least, the RMA has for the time being removed the threat to the bomber. Today, the US bomber almost always gets through. Where World War II bomber crews were highly vulnerable and suffered tremendous casualties, today's bombers run only a slight risk of being shot down. Thus, NATO was able to fight the Kosovo campaign without a single combat casualty because precision bombing could be carried out at altitudes well above the range of Serbian anti-aircraft weapons.

Colonel Warden's writings on strategy, however, show how the air force approach to the RMA is to pursue the light of reason – that is, to create the perfect Clausewitzian battle. The RMA means that the air force can fight purely modern wars, even if the conditions on the ground

[80] Charles Guthrie, 'Why NATO Cannot Simply March in and Crush Milosevic', *Evening Standard*, 1 April 1999.

and the wider strategic context continue to be governed by the logic of risk. The air force has become a decisive part of the wars that risk societies fight precisely because the risks of using warplanes are so low. However, this means that the air force is operating with a different logic from the rest of the forces engaged in the war. The air force is as much a part of the boomerang effect of the RMA calculus of war as army ground forces on the strategic level, but on the tactical level of operations the air force need not concern itself with asymmetrical strategies as the army has to. Mark Bowden captures this aspect in his description of the F-15 crews that fought the war in Afghanistan in 2001. Bowden tells how the Bold Tigers, as the crews operating out of a base in Kuwait referred to themselves, were

> in awe of the guys on the ground, who were so far from anything friendly, huddled down between rocks and cold mountain sides, eating their packaged meals (or bugs and snakes) and sleeping in bags on hard terrain, while the Bold Tigers dined on steak and lobster, watched European MTV, and slept in air-conditioned comfort.[81]

The F-15 crews did take risks in operations over Afghanistan, but they did not experience war as something completely different from their everyday lives. Their war was not as brutish, nasty and short as the British Chief of the Defence Staff had suggested war would be. On the contrary, the Bold Tigers had air-conditioning and MTV. The risks were acceptable, and the comfort approximated to the standards they were used to back home. This was not the case for the US national guardsmen and reservists who had been called up to serve on the ground in Iraq. In the experience of these part-time soldiers, the contrast between everyday life in late modern Western societies and conditions in war could not be more apparent. And their reaction seems to vindicate General Guthrie's view. When National Guard units and reservists did not expect to be sent overseas, they could meet their recruitment targets, but when the occupation of Iraq began to take its toll, this was no longer possible. The National Guard could not recruit in the way it used to, and many reservists did not re-enlist.[82] Perhaps this is what could be expected of part-time soldiers; what should worry the US military a great deal more is that its professional soldiers seemed to want to bail out too. In October 2003, a poll by the US armed forces paper *Stars and Stripes* concluded

---

[81] Mark Bowden, 'The Kabul-ki Dance', *Atlantic Monthly*, November 2002, www.theatlantic.com (18 January 2005).
[82] James Fallows, ' Hollow Army', *Atlantic Monthly*, March 2004, www.theatlantic.com (18 January 2005).

that 48 per cent of the soldiers in Iraq found it not likely or very unlikely that they would re-enlist.[83]

One should not place too much confidence in such figures, but they seem to suggest that when modern armies are *not* deployed as was intended – in divisions in order to achieve massed force – they will disintegrate when, for a longer period of time, they are deprived of the decisive battles they have been trained to fight. In other words, the professionalism fostered by the modern bureaucracy is itself at risk in combat situations where the relevance of the professional ethos comes to be questioned by the conflict itself. This was what happened to the American army in Vietnam. As Christopher Coker points out, 50 per cent of American soldiers were taking drugs in order to cope with the situation. Some had their drugs administered by army doctors, while the rest turned to pushers for their fix.[84] The American servicemen dropped out of the war, just as their successors in Iraq intend to when their contracts run out. In the meantime, US soldiers are finding that their very professionalism is being challenged. The scandals of the US-controlled Abu Ghraib prison outside Baghdad, where prison guards seemed to have been given a free hand with the prisoners, not only resulted in revulsion in civilian circles. General Peter Pace (Vice Chair-man of the Joint Chiefs of Staff) told CBS: 'This brings discredit and dishonour on all of us who serve in the military and brings discredit on our country. And we don't like doing that to ourselves, to our country, certainly not to our president.'[85] In the General's view, the culprits had betrayed their own comrades by violating the armed forces' professional ethos.

Thus it seems that using the armed forces for exactly the kind of enemies that Western societies expect to fight in the future is not only a risk in terms of the asymmetrical counter-strategies that the enemy might use (terrorism etc.), it also places the armed forces themselves at risk. Thus when General Guthrie remarked that 'late-20th century Western society is not very well adjusted to the prospect of fighting', perhaps he should have added that twentieth-century-style Western armed forces are not very well adjusted to fighting the wars of the late twentieth and early twenty-first centuries.

[83] Terry Boyd, 'Service Members Weigh Many Options in Deciding Whether to Re-enlist', *Stars and Stripes*, European Edition, 20 October 2003.
[84] Christopher Coker, *The Future of War: The Re-Enchantment of War in the Twenty-First Century* (Oxford: Blackweu, 2004), 105.
[85] General Peter Pace, Interview with Hannah Storm, CBS, Early Show, 5 May 2004, transcript (Washington, DC: US Department of Defense, 2004), www.defenselink.mil (6 April 2005).

The bureaucratic reaction is to reject the notion that any adjustment is necessary. We have seen how both the US and European armed forces have tried to defend their professionalism by declining to engage in new wars. In the long run, this strategy of bureaucratic survival will prove untenable because it does not square with the scenarios for the future. Thomas Barnett suggests that it was possible for the US armed forces to avoid focusing on how to fight terrorism or other counter-strategies to the RMA as long as the prospect of a 'peer-competitor' loomed large in the scenarios for the future. After 9/11 the scenario of the 'peer-competitor' remains, but it is situated much further in the future. Now, the scenarios that matter in military planning are about terrorism and low-intensity conflict.[86] With such scenarios driving the strategic imagination, the armed forces will have to devise ways of fighting them, and the success of generals will depend on their willingness to do so.

The new military operations will call for a new willingness to take risks. If one follows General Guthrie's analysis, then the risk society is unable to meet this demand for risk-takers. Writing about 'post-heroic' warfare, Edward Luttwak argues that, in order to be able to fight wars, Western societies will have to embrace the RMA in order to give all the services the air force's ability to project overwhelming firepower at a safe distance, quickly enough for the servicemen and women to be home for their favourite soap opera on television.[87] Looking to the future, another technological fix would be to use drugs or, in time, genetic manipulation to make soldiers willing to accept risks.[88] Both approaches are attempts to maintain the means-ends rationale for fighting wars. It is assumed that Western societies will continue to have the same ends for which they wish to use military force, but having a risk-averse population may mean that the means to do so will not be forthcoming. In order to solve the problem, the RMA will produce fighting machines, while gene therapy will turn people into fighting machines. In fact risk societies might produce people who are willing to take risks without technological fixes being required.

It is true that Western societies have become risk-averse, but it does not follow that every citizen of risk societies is unwilling to take risks. On the contrary, the risk literature points out that not only do societies obsessed with risk produce people who are risk-averse, but the obsession with risk itself produces people who are obsessed with taking risks. Every

---

[86] Barnett, *The Pentagon's New Map*, 96–106.
[87] Edward N. Luttwak, 'A Post-Heroic Military Policy', *Foreign Affairs* 74 (July/August 1996), 33–44.
[88] Coker, *The Future of War*, 75–9.

parent knows that telling small children how dangerous, for example, a hot oven is may make the children step back at first, but the danger will also be so fascinating that it soon draws the child closer and closer to the oven. One reason why the child wants to take the risk of burning itself is that most small children fortunately live very safe lives, but in order to test life itself they need the challenges of risk. In the same way, some people find the safety of contemporary Western societies boring. While most people are glad that their lives are not as dangerous and eventful as they could have been during, for example, the Second World War, some people long for the challenges and excitement of danger and therefore take risks. The rise of 'extreme sports' and other activities, whose sole purpose is the taking of risks, is one example of this, which Deborah Lupton terms 'edgework': 'Edgework is also characterized by an emphasis on skilled performance of the dangerous activity, involving the ability to maintain control over a situation that verges on complete chaos that requires, above all, "mental toughness", the ability not to give in to fear.'[89] Such 'mental toughness' is what every recruiting sergeant wants, and that is what he will get. Risk societies may be post-heroic, in the sense that people are not lining up to join the armed forces and public opinion does not accept soldiers dying in large numbers. The point of the RMA calculus of war is, however, that soldiers do not need to die in great numbers in order to achieve military results. During the First World War, only the force of numbers could achieve attrition, but, as we have seen in Chapter 3, today technology is increasingly able to project the force and suffer the casualties that men previously had to. So it is not so much that heroes are in short supply, but rather that fewer heroics are needed.

However, Western governments still demand boots on the ground to occupy and stabilise countries or hit the nodal points of the enemy's network. But such forces need not be organised in divisions or trained for pitched battles. They are, in Lupton's phrase, working on the edge of the modern military bureaucracy. They depend on the old-style structures to supply firepower, whether in the form of the air force's F-15s or the army's main battle tanks. In terms of engaging with the risks on the ground, such bureaucratic structures are too great a liability. For such missions, the armed forces will need people willing to take risks. Perhaps paradoxically this argument unites two communities which have not traditionally generated great mutual respect: non-governmental organisations (NGOs) and special forces.

---

[89] Lupton, *Risk*, 151–2.

Special forces are special because they are not part of the bureaucratic organisation of the armed forces as such. Symbolic of this is the way they prefer to choose their own weapons and to don their uniforms with personal details like the baseball caps in fashion among US Special Forces who fought the Iraq war in 2003.[90] Thus they work on the edge of traditional military hierarchy, but their own fighting does not depend on the operation of weapons systems in concert with other soldiers, such as guns or tanks. They fight on their own initiative – in other words, they embrace the risks of war. Investigating cases of 'altruistic suicide' among recipients of the Congressional Medal of Honor, Jeffrey Reimer concluded that 54 per cent of the soldiers who died to save their comrades were from special forces units – a vast overrepresentation given how small a part of the armed forces such units are.[91] The most common form of altruistic suicide in combat is to throw yourself on a grenade in order to save your comrades. While the psychology behind heroic acts like this is immensely complicated, it seems safe to conclude that one will embrace death in this way only if one has embraced the logic of combat entirely. In combat your side wins by your sacrifice, so it is only by risking your life that you can fight war to the fullest. In other words, you can only fully experience war if you are willing to risk your life. In a battlefield wired up by technology, this experience of risk and combat is difficult to achieve for any but the special forces. Where other soldiers place their lives at the mercy of the system and thus fear risks, the special forces embrace risks because they can still choose to fight, and find death, on their own terms.

The staff of NGOs such as Médecins Sans Frontières, who operate in high-risk environments, actually have a lot in common with special forces. NGO work is often edgework. NGO workers are often more in harm's way than most regular soldiers. In the Balkans, lorry-drivers for NGOs were shot at while delivering supplies, while UN peacekeepers were ordered to prioritise the protection of their own forces. Casualties among soldiers were a greater risk to governments than casualties among aid workers were to NGOs. One reason was that the NGO workers chose the risks themselves. The dangers that NGO workers face make sense to them in the same way that danger makes sense to the special forces. They felt that they could influence world events and do the right thing, and only the risks they took proved it worthwhile.

[90] For a description, see Atkinson, *In The Company of Soldiers*, 204.
[91] Jeffrey W. Reimer, 'Durkheim's "Heroic Suicide" in Military Combat', *Armed Forces and Society* 25 (Fall 1998), 113.

While the aid community and the special forces community find themselves to be in completely different businesses (taking lives versus saving lives), their risk calculus is similar, as is their ethos. Aid workers and special forces are both edgeworkers. This has led to an increased focus on how to integrate the work of special forces and aid workers. At this point one should remember that special forces are not only the guys in Ninja outfits spraying the enemy with machine-gun fire that President Clinton imagined. Because of their special skills, they are very often used to train allied forces or guard sensitive operations. Moreover, while some special forces outfits, like the US Army Delta Force, are highly exclusive and very small, special forces such as the US Army Rangers can be quite large: 33,520 American soldiers are designated special operations forces in the International Institute for Strategic Studies' *Military Balance* for 2004.[92] Special forces thus have the potential to be used in large-scale operations to pacify a country if backed by the firepower of the regular forces. In such stability operations, it is vital that cooperation between the armed forces and civilian aid workers is maintained in order to manage the risks of a failing state or of wherever the intervention is taking place. Strategists thinking in terms of risk appreciate the need to establish a stable socio-political environment as well as to conduct military operations.

To sum up, in imagining their future enemies as different from themselves, Western armed forces realise that they risk their future relevance if they do not organise themselves differently. The RMA will allow them to maintain forces organised on bureaucratic lines because technology allows, for example, the air force to keep its distance from the boomerang effects of undertaking operations other than the Clausewitzian war they are trained for. Infantry units are not that lucky; and so we will probably witness the special forces, who are prepared to accept risks, fighting one type of battle, while the larger part of the armed forces that can fight at a distance will be fighting another. The forces that fight at a distance will continue to define their professionalism in Weberian terms, while those engaging in close infantry combat will define their professionalism through their ability to handle risks. They will share this risk-professionalism with NGOs. Where special forces will increasingly be fighting non-state actors unlike themselves, they will increasingly work alongside non-state actors with an ethos a lot like their own.[93]

---

[92] International Institute for Strategic Studies, *The Military Balance 2002–2003* (Oxford: Oxford University Press, 2003), 24–5.

[93] The rise of 'private military companies' may strengthen this trend. These firms often fulfil roles that Western militaries do not have the manpower to perform or would rather

Bureaucracy II: predictability

The bureaucratisation of warfare has led Western societies to expect both wars and battles to be predictable. Prediction rests on the ability to calculate means and ends, but the concept of future enemies with different rationalities breaks this down – Islamic fundamentalists or Chinese colonels do simply not compute. Thus the way in which the West has chosen to manage the risks of warfare and the risks that Western societies believe the future holds collide. The boomerang effect of this 'collision' between the past and the future has replaced the focus on war as a duty – rather than seeing it as the product of calculation of interest – with a set of more eclectic reasons for going to war. At the same time, the view of military force as something that produces predictable results and can be planned with 'reasonable prospects of success' is increasingly becoming regarded as unviable when the opponent is expected to be unpredictable because of his different rationality.

The concept of war as a duty depends on the predictability of the strategic environment – what you are supposed to do is predictable because what others do is predictable as well. It is difficult to define a duty under international law if the circumstances under which that duty is to be carried out are constantly changing. The notion of the presence of the future thus undermines the bureaucratic concept of war as a duty, at least if duty is defined by law, because law is by necessity based on the past. Hence the importance of precedents in judicial arguments. A duty does not need to be defined as a legal obligation, however – a duty can also arise from a set of values. Values are much less post factum than law. Because they are much less precise, they offer ways to analyse one's options and obligations rather than fixing duties. Furthermore, in thinking in terms of values, one is able to place present concerns and scenarios for the future in relation to the past by means of a narrative which is much more flexible than the legal narrative. Whereas a legal narrative insists on projecting past experiences into the future, a value-based narrative can project expectations for the future back into the past and thus rewrite history to suit the concerns of the future. From this perspective, it is not surprising that the West is turning back to

not risk. Thus during the occupation of Iraq, around 15,000 private contractors were employed, in effect providing almost another division of occupying troops. Such companies often fulfil roles that fall between NGO work and traditional military operations. See 'Private Contractors in Iraq', *Economist*, 7 April 2004; David Shearer, *Private Armies and Military Intervention*, Adelphi Paper 316 (Oxford: International Institute of Strategic Studies, Oxford University Press, 1998).

values for guidance on how it should deal with the prospect of new types of enemies.

President Bush has spent a lot of energy placing terrorism and other threats of tomorrow into a narrative of the past. 'We have seen their kind before,' the President concluded, when describing al-Qaeda in September 2001: 'They are the heirs of all the murderous ideologies of the 20th century.'[94] A student of the history of ideas will probably tell you that al-Qaeda has little or nothing in common with communism or fascism, but if one views these ideologies not in terms of their internal logic but in terms of how, for very different reasons, they negated democratic society, then they are indeed the same.[95] Faced with the unpredictable, the President turns to the values of liberal society as the one thing that remains the same amid the turmoil of history. The challenges of communism and fascism are then used to show how the West has been challenged before by powerful opponents, while the victories in the world wars and the Cold War are used to prove that the West (i.e. the United States) will prevail in the future too. Thus it is democratic values that create a coherent history to explain and console the American people when they are facing the unpredictable. It is also a narrative that invokes great risks, however. By elevating the war on terror to the level of the world wars and the Cold War, the President was also seeking to mobilise his people. If they do not face up to this danger like their forefathers did, then the world will not be safe for democracy in the future.

The means-end rationale of duty is thus replaced with a narrative of values. Such values can be as universal as the duties that the UN places on states, but they are not as automatic, nor are they defined by the legitimacy of the decision-making process that defined them in the way that formal rules, like laws, are defined. From this perspective, war becomes a question of what is right rather than what is legitimate.

Bureaucracy III: rules

The 'UN approach to warfare' has been based on the notion that war is a risk in itself and therefore better avoided. As the United States painfully realised after invading Iraq in 2003, the fact that war is outlawed means that, if you run the risk of fighting war, you risk the legality and legitimacy of your cause. At the turn of the twenty-first century, however, it seems that war is on its way back. This does not mean that

---

[94] Bush, *Address to a Joint Session of Congress and the American People*, §27.
[95] For a version of this view, see Francis Fukuyama, 'Their Target: The Modern World', *Newsweek*, Special Davos Edition (December 2001–February 2002), 58–63.

the UN approach to war is being abandoned – on the contrary, the ban against interstate warfare is as strong as ever. One reason for this is the way in which nuclear weapons enforce this ban in the material sense. Great powers have nuclear weapons and therefore the risk they face in fighting each other is so huge that it merits outlawing great-power war itself. While material facts support the rules against interstate warfare, other material facts support the breakdown of the rules of war. The rise of new agents of war like al-Qaeda, who are believed to be of a different rationality, challenges the relevance of the rules of war when it comes to fighting them. In fact this opens new spheres of warfare that are not covered by the UN framework. The beginning of these new spheres of warfare was observed when various US presidents declared war on poverty and drugs. Though these 'wars' were not intended to be fought with aircraft carriers and ICBMs (intercontinental ballistic missiles), these presidents applied the logic of war to other areas. President Bush did the same by declaring a war on terror. Although this war certainly covers actual combat, it also embraces various other resources, being, as the President said, 'a new kind of war' compared to that defined by the UN approach. Thus new battlefields are being created in the material sense with little reference to existing legal definitions.

The absence of international law does not mean that wars are being fought without rules. They cannot, as Martin van Creveld explains. Combatants need to know who to fight and how to fight them, and they also need to understand the rules for the side that wins the battle.[96] These rules change with the combatants who fight wars, however, and when new agents define new battlefields, then the rules change. What is happening at the moment is that Western governments and their enemies are looking for rules regarding how to fight each other.

The focus on values, which is at the heart of President Bush's definition of the war on terrorism, shows how the 'new wars' are being made legitimate on the basis of values rather than laws. The material reality of such value-based wars will be quite different from the material reality of wars fought under the UN approach. Where the latter regards war strictly as a means to realise the ends of peace and stability for the international community, value-based wars are about making the world secure for certain ideas (democracy, for example). Value-based warfare makes the UN assumption that not all combatants are created equal much more radical. This assumption is based on the fact that the 'aggressor' is acting unlawfully and that other combatants are duty-bound to

---

[96] Creveld, *On Future War*, 1–32.

uphold the law in fighting the 'aggressor'. If one adopts the value perspective, it is acceptable to be an aggressor if the act of aggression will further the right set of values. For this reason, Richard Perle celebrated the 'death of the UN', which was brought about when the United States invaded Iraq without unequivocal backing from the Security Council. In doing so, Perle argued, the US had shown that values were more important than law. In his view, the Bush administration had shown its commitment to creating not only a more secure, but also a better world. Perle argued that the actions of the Bush administration should not be subsumed under a predefined set of values, as the Weberian model for bureaucracy would have it: the Bush administration should define its own rules.[97]

Al-Qaeda would also like to make conflict a test of rules and also believes that security is ensured by spreading the values which Osama bin Laden and associates hold dear. In many ways one can argue that the only thing al-Qaeda offers its members is the opportunity to fight for their ideals. No one in their right means-end rational mind will expect al-Qaeda to prevail over the US armed forces, but that is not the point. For much of human history, people have fought not to achieve something, but to prove something. What kind of rule can govern conflicts between combatants who seek to reaffirm their own values when fighting? It is often pointed out that wars between different cultures (i.e. different rule sets) are the most vicious. In such a conflict both sides need victory not only to achieve certain interests, but to reaffirm or perhaps even achieve a certain identity. In the terminology of risk society, it is wars that are worth the risk, because not fighting them would be seen to be a betrayal of certain values. Such conflicts are authentic to protean man – he will choose to fight them.

Protean man will choose to fight for his values because he sees the antithesis of these values embodied in certain persons. While the UN approach to fighting wars deals exclusively with the subjects of international law (states), this approach focuses on individuals who must be held responsible for their actions. In 1991 Martin van Creveld wrote that 'in the future there will be a tendency to regard such [enemy] leaders as criminals who richly deserve the worst fate that can be inflicted on them'.[98] In the years that followed, the conflicts the West has engaged in have been personalised exactly in the way Creveld described. The conflicts in the Balkans were about Slobodan Milosevic, the conflicts in the Gulf about Saddam Hussein, the struggle against

[97] Richard Perle, 'Thank God for the Death of the UN', *Guardian*, 21 March 2003.
[98] Creveld, *On Future War*, 200.

international terrorism about Osama bin Laden. These individuals play a powerful role in the popular imagination. Thus when the Bold Tigers watched MTV on their base in Kuwait, they probably saw one of 2002's hit music videos featuring the rapper Eminem dressed up as Osama bin Laden.[99] By that time the news media had started to blame the Bush administration for not having captured Osama bin Laden in order to bring him to justice in the way Slobodan Milosevic had been brought to justice. Only when the personalised enemy has been convicted of his crimes will the war be over, because only then will it have been conclusively demonstrated that it is our values and our rules that run the world.

It is important to note that the West's enemies put the West on trial too. In 1999 Yugoslavia attempted to indict NATO for war crimes and aggression at the International Court of Justice. Though the parading of Western hostages on video-clips shown on the Internet is hardly comparable to the due process of a court of law, hostage-takers in Pakistan, Iraq or elsewhere clearly intend their videos to send messages about the evil designs of the West, and not simply the just retribution that they will mete out to their victims. These 'courtroom dramas' are important because the second feature of these conflicts is that they establish legitimacy in their own right. The conflict is used to justify a cause, whether it is spreading democracy throughout the Middle East or re-establishing a Caliphate there. To borrow a term from Ulrich Beck, we now have 'rule-altering' conflicts, in which the combatants use force to change a political system. Where the wars that Clausewitz described were about making another state do something it did not want to do, these conflicts are about redefining the nature of political communities themselves. As a result, symbolism becomes very important. Al-Qaeda attacked the World Trade Center in order to attack globalisation itself. Similarly, the United States places great importance on holding elections in Iraq following the occupation in order to prove that democracy is being promoted in the Middle East.

Non-UN warfare

In 1945 the UN Charter promised to remove the scourge of war from the globe. At the beginning of the twenty-first century, however, many people no longer consider war a scourge. To the al-Qaeda terrorist, waging war against the West is a way to define an identity, while to a

---

[99] Eminem, 'Without Me', *The Eminem Show*, Shady/Interscope Records, 2002.

soldier in a special forces unit war holds out the excitements that risk societies have otherwise been careful to abolish. The NGO aid worker will probably agree that war is a scourge, but he will nevertheless find that, in the words of the US Army recruitment posters, he can only be all that he can be by taking huge personal risks when delivering aid in a war zone. The bureaucratisation of warfare turned war into a risk rather than a meaningful political instrument in the way that Clausewitz imagined. While the West accepts that bureaucratic rules should guide conflicts between major powers, the fact that Western governments believe that they are facing enemies who see war as an opportunity rather than a risk means that Western strategists feel the need to be able to use armed force more freely than the bureaucratic rules allow. Bureaucratic warfare itself has become a risk, as it stands in the way of dealing with the threats of the future.

Once the bureaucracy has been taken out of war, then war ceases to be a scourge. Christopher Coker calls this the 're-enchantment of war'.[100] The challenges and risks of war have been enchanting for most of human history. 'War, far from being merely a means has very often been considered an end,' Martin van Creveld notes, 'a highly attractive activity for which no other can provide adequate substitute.'[101] This does not mean that risk societies will turn into military garrisons. Because of the RMA, modern Western societies do not need to mobilise their societies for total war in the way European powers did in the nineteenth and twentieth centuries. Actually fewer and fewer people are needed to do the actual fighting, as the RMA ensures that devastating firepower can be delivered with great precision at great distances. The fewer the soldiers who are needed, the more these soldiers can be allowed to be on the edge of society. Moreover, the fascination with risk in late modern society means that a lot of people will want more rather than fewer risks. The challenge for risk societies will not be to provide the special forces but to integrate these forces with aid workers and others in order to put together units that can manage occupations or failed states. Such forces will be non-bureaucratic and only loosely networked with the remaining modern elements of the armed forces, such as the air force.

Conclusions

We often forget how much the legitimacy of war changed following the Second World War. At the beginning of the twentieth century, war was a

---

[100] Coker, *The Future of War*, xii.   [101] Creveld, *On Future War*, 218.

legitimate political choice in the way that Clausewitz described it – not only because it was believed to be just to wage war but also because war was believed to settle political disputes effectively. However, the experience of the First World War left the West disenchanted with war, to use Christopher Coker's phrase. War was no longer a way to settle political questions – it had come to be questioned itself. It is important to note that some still answered the question in favour of war by arguing that war was a superior moral activity. That view was thoroughly discredited during the Second World War, as a result of which war was outlawed by the UN Charter. As we have seen in this chapter, the result of outlawing war was not the end of armed conflict, but the bureaucratisation of war. As this process of bureaucratisation unfolded in the latter half of the twentieth century, the ends for which war could be used became more and more limited, and the means that a government could use in war fell more and more under scrutiny. At the beginning of the twenty-first century, war is no longer an activity which governments find it natural or indeed legal to use in order to further their interests.

The bureaucratisation of warfare thus challenges the basic premise of many modern writings on strategy – that states conduct international politics in the knowledge that they can ultimately resort to war. Not only are international law and international organisations playing a more important part in defining the legitimate means and ends of war, but Western states no longer expect to fight wars only against other states. This challenges yet another traditional assumption: that because of their monopoly of organised violence, states are the only agents of international security. The rise of terrorist organisations like al-Qaeda has led peoples and their governments to expect that the main security challenge of the twenty-first century will not come from other states but from various non-state actors. The final challenge to the modern strategy paradigm is the fact that these actors are not believed to be means-end rational but are believed to operate in accordance with a different rationality. Therefore, the well-known security strategies deployed against state enemies (e.g. the balance of power) cannot automatically be assumed to be as effective a part of the strategist's tool kit in the twenty-first century as it was in the nineteenth and twentieth centuries.

The main boomerang effect of the bureaucratisation of warfare is thus that it questions the effectiveness of warfare as a political instrument. The twenty-first century has thus begun with the same kind of question that people were asking by the beginning of the twentieth century. A hundred years ago this question was asked in order to outlaw war; today the established approaches to strategy and the laws of war are being questioned in order that people may be allowed to fight wars again. Non-state actors like al-Qaeda will not accept that the 'UN approach' to warfare gives them no right to state their claims in a globalising world just because they are not sovereign states. Al-Qaeda not only wants to be able to influence international politics, however – the terrorists also want to use the fight against 'Western values' as a way of confirming their own identity and values. By objectifying war as a scourge in itself, the UN approach has done away with the Hegelian notion of war as a struggle for recognition. The terrorists want recognition, but they want to fight for their identity and to define their identity by fighting the West.

Western risk societies still see war as a risk, but that does not necessarily mean that all Westerners shy away from war. The risk literature stresses that the obsession with risk in Western society means that some people turn fear into fascination by seeking out all the risks they can find, and indeed the risk society's focus on defining your identity through choice encourages them to do so. Such people will choose to go to war and will look forward to the risks of fighting. The risk perspective thus puts a different spin on the debate about 'post-heroic warfare' which has dominated the Western debate about whether risk societies have the will to fight and thus whether the Cold War was the last 'war' that Westerners would fight.

From a risk perspective, the issue is not that heroes are in short supply, but rather that Western governments no longer demand heroics from their soldiers. Recent campaigns have provided countless examples of bravery and valour, but in risk society the role of the soldier is not to die for king and country. No risk society would honour the charge of the Light Brigade. Soldiers not only regard themselves as professionals, they are also seen as professionals by society at large. Professionals are expected to get the job done, but not to get themselves killed in doing it. When they do get killed, however, society's reaction is a curious mix of complacency and outrage. Most politicians fear the outrage and the 'body-bag syndrome', but actually Western public opinion has largely accepted continuous casualties. It is interesting to note that many of the Americans who protest against the occupation of Iraq and its human costs are National Guard members or reservists or their families.[102] The public do not expect them to run risks and are outraged when they die because they are not professionals. So troops destined to carry out routine work or routine missions are not expected to get killed in the

---

[102] Brian Knowlton, 'US Toll in Iraq War Starting to Hit Home', *International Herald Tribune*, 19 March 2005.

public mind, and the public react strongly when such troops are exposed to risks when they should not be or when missions turn out to be riskier than the politicians have promised. However, the public seem quite willing to accept that special forces units risk their lives.

Instead of heroes, the soldiers of risk society are either risk-averse bureaucrats placed far behind the lines or high up in a warplane, or else they are a new breed of professional risk-takers in special forces units. It is the operations of the risk-takers that are going to define the ways of war in the twenty-first century.

6   Conclusions

Strategy began as a way to rationalise the new military technologies of the seventeenth century. For muskets and guns to be militarily effective the activities of a lot of people needed to be coordinated. Because muskets were not very accurate and because they could produce a continuous rate of fire only if a large number of soldiers lined up and fired in salvos, soldiers had to operate in close formation. This required drill and discipline, as well as what we today call command and control, at a level not seen in Europe since the Roman empire. The new weapons not only required better training for soldiers and more elaborate operating procedures for armies. At this point military technology began to become fundamentally different from the tools and weapons of civilian life. Now, becoming a soldier, and most certainly an officer, demanded training in operating the new weapons systems. Finally, the need for powder and bullets as well as food and other provisions for the new, larger armies placed new demands on military logistics. Strategy provided rational solutions to all of this, and the military academies set up to teach officers how to operate the new military system taught their pupils to think of strategy in modern terms – in terms of means-end rationality.

Today, the RMA means that the demands for operating mass armies are diminishing. Or perhaps the point is rather that organising logistics and thinking strategically are less demanding today – on a conceptual level at least – because of the rationalisation process which has been going on for 300 years. The armed forces know how to instruct crews in operating weapons, how to calculate the impact of a bombardment and how to identify a centre of gravity. These parts of modern military mindset will still be with us in the twenty-first century. By perfecting the modern way of warfare, however, the RMA is closing one chapter in the history of strategy and opening another. Because how does one rationalise the boomerang effects of the RMA in the shape of asymmetrical counter-strategies to Western military power such as terrorism? How do military forces operate if fire is delivered from far away and attrition carried out by autonomous weapons platforms?

These boomerang effects mean that the RMA cannot be regarded in terms of technological changes only. Just like the technological innovations which lead to new military technology must be regarded within a social context, so must the RMA capabilities be analysed with regard to the fundamental principles by which armed forces put these capabilities to use. This focus on doctrine shows how the pre-emptive logic of risk society is becoming a part of strategy. Obviously military force has been used pre-emptively countless times in history. What is new is that in risk society the future is present in strategic decisions – it is the presence of the future that makes pre-emption the overarching strategic principle. This means that strategy has come to resemble crime prevention and environmental protection – areas where policy-makers have long given up on producing final results (no crime, no pollution) in favour of managing risks. This approach came late and piecemeal to strategy because the Cold War kept the West focused on deterrence, but 9/11 put new doctrines firmly on the agenda. Perhaps because of the sudden switch in focus from deterrence to pre-emption this is by no means as universally accepted as the precautionary principle is in environmental policy. Another reason for the public reluctance towards pre-emptive doctrines is the boomerang effects. Pre-emptive action occurs before a danger has materialised and therefore the only visible result of such actions is the boomerang effects. Strategists are not only struggling to justify pre-emption, they also fear instances where it might not be able to pre-empt threats because they cannot be foreseen. Who knows when and where terrorists will strike next? Who knows exactly how far developed North Korea's nuclear weapons programme is? How exactly will China translate its economic growth and technological know-how into military power?

In the beginning the concept of strategy helped to define how the modern state fought its enemies. Strategy specified that war was a contest of interest decided by military capability. Interests were defined by politicians, and military capabilities were used by soldiers who served as the instruments for achieving the politicians' ends. Following the Second World War these rules were codified in the UN Charter which realised the ambitions of liberals in the nineteenth and twentieth centuries to radically limit the scope for which states could use war. War was outlawed because the decision to use armed force was no longer in the hands of an individual government but in the hands of the Security Council. Of course wars did still take place, but the outlawing of war was only one element in a 'bureaucratisation of warfare' which makes war the continuation of law with other means. Although the peaceful intentions of the UN might seem counter to the logic of strategy, this bureaucratisation is in fact the culmination of the means-end rational logic. When faced with enemies which the West believes to be operating by another rationality, this logic breaks down and so the 'UN approach' to warfare is left guiding only a part of the strategic landscape – the part believed to be of less and less importance by Western governments who focus on the future where terrorists like al-Qaeda or states with a different strategic tradition like China seem to be the greatest dangers. This is the boomerang effect of the bureaucratisation of warfare and this boomerang effect opens a new way for soldiers to understand their role. They are no longer merely instruments. Or rather, the soldiers in the front line are increasingly special forces who operate on a risk logic, while their colleagues far behind the front, who operate the RMA fire power that makes special forces an adequate substitute for infantry divisions, still work on bureaucratic lines. Soldiers in special forces units not only accept the risks of war, they actively seek out these risks; because while most people in risk society fear risks, some cannot get enough. Thus risk society can actually produce soldiers willing to risk their lives in the wars of the twenty-first century. The question is how this willingness to risk war fits the laws of war – will the new wars be fought in a legal vacuum or will international law change?

These are the new questions which strategy – as an academic discipline and as a political practice – needs to answer. Thus we find strategy to be back where we started; by the beginning of the twenty-first century strategy is again an activity in search of rules to guide it.

Ulrich Beck believes that faced with the security challenges of the twenty-first century risk societies will find that security can be found only in a cosmopolitan community. The problems of risk societies are to a large extent transnational, Beck argues with reference to pollution, and therefore he believes that the logic of risk challenges the political logics inherent in the principle of sovereignty. Beck believes that risk societies will eventually form a cosmopolitan political community that transcends present national boundaries.[1] Beck thinks that terrorism confirms this analysis. In his analysis terrorism becomes one more transnational risk which results in 'the transnational invention of the political through networking and cooperation'.[2] Because in Beck's view 'the only path in the face of the threat posed to national security by global terror (as well as financial risks, climatic catastrophe, organized crime etc.) is transnational cooperation'.[3]

---

[1] Beck, *What Is Globalization?*
[2] Beck 'The Silence of Words', 263.   [3] Ibid., 264.

That cooperation should be the *only* possible result of the challenge of terrorism is clearly at odds with the logic of risk society itself. As we have seen, politics in risk society is defined by the debate between different scenarios. This also applies to strategic issues, and the debate on 'the war on terror' in general and the Iraq war in particular clearly showed how different scenarios lead to different calls for action. Add to these differences diverging risk cultures and it becomes clear that the debate about the degree and urgency of risk does not create a transnational, cosmopolitan consensus. What is also challenging Beck's view is the fact that the pre-emptive logic, which he believes makes international cooperation a foregone conclusion, apparently does not translate well from environmental issues to security issues.

Not only does Beck fail to consider that when transnational security challenges are identified as risks they also become the subject of different interpretations and political agendas, Beck also fails to consider what one might call the cosmopolitanism of evil. In his analysis terrorism is oddly out of focus, as if it was not really a product of human agency subject to sociological analysis. Terrorism is presented as a phenomenon outside the sphere of the political which needs a political response in the same way a 'climatic catastrophe' would. In Beck's argument terrorism does not seem to influence or be influenced by political action any more than the weather. Beck does not seem to consider the possibility that terrorism is as much a part of globalisation as 'cosmopolitan multi-nation-states' are.[4] Actually, contrary to the cosmopolitan states, which Beck wishes for, the terrorists are actually here right now and not only a hope for the future. Furthermore, terrorism is widely regarded, also by Beck, as an ideal type for new enemies of a different rationality (states as well as non-state agents). It might be that cosmopolitanism is the logical conclusion to the risks that face late modern societies, but that does not mean that this is necessarily going to be so. Because Beck does not really weigh the actions of the terrorists into his equation he has great difficulties in dealing with the way states and non-state actors interact and how this interaction creates a completely different logic from the state-based cosmopolitan approach he describes with a clear reference to the EU.

For that reason Beck fails to acknowledge that the transnational cooperation against terrorism and the spread of WMD which indeed does occur is not so much the beginning of a cosmopolitan republic but rather an attempt to defend the states' monopoly of violence. From this perspective the 'war on terrorism' means exactly what it says. No matter

---

[4] Ibid., 267,

what inspires terrorists, President Bush and others regard terrorism as a doctrine that replaces politics with violence as a means of settling disputes within countries. But they do not worry so much about old-fashioned separatist movements. It is transnational organisations like al-Qaeda that present a challenge, because they reject the nation state as the unit of politics and replace loyalty to a state with loyalty to a faith. Or to put it another way, they reject the means-end rational logic of modern politics in favour of a value-based rationality. When choosing values over politics and their own version of a cosmopolitan community over the states' version they challenge the foundation of the state system itself. From this perspective states simply cannot 'live with terrorism' the way Didier Bigo suggests.

To live with terrorism is the kind of advice Dr Strangelove would have given policy-makers if Stanley Kubrick were to make the movie today. Few scholarly works have explained the logic of deterrence as well as Kubrick did in *Dr Strangelove* because it so happened that taken to its logical conclusion the means-end logic of deterrence in itself offered the text for absurd comedy.[5] In fact the views which Peter Sellers presents as Dr Strangelove were not all that different from what Herman Kahn – clearly the inspiration for the character, with an added twist of Wernher von Braun – was arguing in RAND reports at the time. The movie thus illustrates Phillip Windsor's point that 'deterrence became its own institution, its own form of rationality, its own bureaucracy'.[6] As such deterrence became that conceptual 'iron cage' which Weber believed was strangling modern society not able to think in other than means-end rational terms. The movie shows the American president and the Soviet leader struggling in an iron cage of deterrence from which they cannot escape. They had to live with nuclear weapons and de-terrence, and *Dr Strangelove* ends with the footage of nuclear bombs exploding to the tune of Vera Lynn's 'We'll Meet Again'.

In real life we escaped nuclear Armageddon. Instead deterrence came to be seen as a strategy that had worked miracles by delivering victory in the Cold War without the West having to pay the terrible price of a hot war. And suddenly the absurdity of it all faded away – all the assumptions of human nature, the ability to tightly manage crisis, the idea that not only would the 'Russians love their children too' they would also act in ways that fitted into game-theoretical matrixes, as indeed would the US chain of command. All of these highly contested

---

[5] Stanley Kubrick, *Dr Strangelove or: How I Learned to Stop Worrying and Love the Bomb* (Columbia Pictures, 1964).
[6] Windsor, *Strategic Thinking*, 169.

notions suddenly became the holy grail of strategy – often for the very people who had criticised them during the Cold War – because deterrence seemed as a moderate and sensible alternative to the new doctrines of risk management and pre-emption. Once again strategists argue in favour of living with the threat on its own terms rather than dealing with it. This time, however, politicians seem unwilling to get trapped in the iron cage of means-end rationality. One reason is that politicians like President Bush believe that the Cold War was not won by deterrence alone. He regards the Cold War in value-rational terms, believing that it was Western values that prevailed rather than Western arms. Furthermore, the assumptions of rationality on which deterrence was based are hard to maintain for a Western-government strategist reading the Chinese colonels' *Unrestricted Warfare* or studying al-Qaeda's operations. *Unrestricted Warfare* not only claims that globalisation and RMA introduce a new strategic paradigm, the book also shows that the ancient Chinese approach to strategy as a way to manage conflict fits a globalising world much better than Clausewitz' doctrines. Groups like al-Qaeda actively promote the idea that their struggle is a struggle for recognition rather than something the West would recognise as a means-end rational strategy.

The strategic challenges posed to the West do not straightforwardly fit the means-end rational bill, and the ways in which these issues are discussed outside the strategic community do not support a means-end rational approach either. Furthermore, today strategy is a practice performed by Dr Phil as well as Dr Strangelove.[7] Strategies on how to lose weight or organise family life compete with business strategies, strategies for crime prevention and military strategy to give meaning to the concept of strategy. The proliferation of strategy as a practice has broken the bars of the iron cage of means-end rationality because the non-military strategies often offer alternative approaches to strategy – and Western politicians are using these alternatives because they present them with opportunities for action rather than just advising them to learn to live with a problem.

It should be no surprise that politicians faced with strategic challenges such as terrorism, WMD, the developments of military technology, the rise of new powers and all the other issues discussed in this book seize any opportunity for action offered to them. The way the rationales of

---

[7] Dr Phillip McGraw is the host of an American television show in which he offers strategies for how to cope with the problems of modern family life – from weight problems to misbehaving children. Five of his books have made it to the *New York Times'* bestseller list. See www.drphil.com (11 May 2005).

nuclear deterrence were seriously challenged in public in the last decades of the Cold War illustrates how Western societies shed their means-end rational ways of thinking in terms of a more reflexive approach. This is the process Giddens and Beck describe as the creation of risk society; and the citizens of risk society are not prepared to live with pollution, crime or any other of the ills they see stemming from their own society. They demand risks to be managed and the proliferation of new risks to be pre-empted. One gets into government by promising to do this; so why should one not do the same thing when terrorism or WMD proliferation comes high on the political agenda?

Thus it turns out that it is the politicians rather than the professional strategists that are active in shaping the strategic agenda for the twenty-first century. 'Theory told us that NATO enlargement and a NATO–Russia relationship would be mutually exclusive goals. Practice proved otherwise,' Javier Solana (then NATO Secretary-General) argued in *The Economist* when NATO was enlarged with Poland, the Czech Republic and Hungary.[8] The theory Dr Solana is alluding to is the realist theories of alliances which predicted that any enlargement of the Alliance would provoke a hostile Russian reaction and assumed the eventual collapse of the Alliance in the absence of the Soviet threat.[9] These theories made the mistake of so many realist writings of strategy studies by assuming that the lessons of the twentieth century were applicable wholesale to the twenty-first century. These theories did not take into account that NATO governments redefined the nature of the security environment and that when doing so they came to regard NATO as a useful instrument in managing the risks of instability in post-Cold War Europe. NATO thus became a centrepiece of the Clinton administration's strategy for 'preventive defense', which in Secretary Perry's words was to ensure that the benign security conditions of the 1990s were to last. In the 1990s the security environment was regarded as much more plastic than realist strategic studies expect any security environment to be. One reason for this is that the study of strategy is still deeply rooted in the analysis of structural conditions like geography and enduring national interests at a time when globalisation is lifting many social, economic and political relationships out of a geographical setting and placing them in a global setting. Doing this globalisation changes the political horizon from one defined by the past into one defined by the

---

[8] Javier Solana, 'Growing the Alliance', *Economist*, 13 March 1999.
[9] Stephen M. Walt, 'Why Alliances Endure or Collapse', *Survival* 39 (1997), 156–80; Mearsheimer, 'Back to the Future'; Michael Mandelbaum, *The Dawn of Peace in Europe* (New York: The Twentieth Century Fund Press, 1996).

future. This presence of the future in political discourse means that politicians, for example, define NATO in terms of what it is going to become (a European security community) rather than what it was conceived as in 1948 (an alliance against the Soviet Union). This presence of the future in politics means that the role of the strategists is changing. Dr Strangelove argued in terms of game theory and history; risk society's strategists argue in terms of trends and probabilities. Their arguments have more in common with the weatherman on the morning news shows than with the scientists in their white coats that were the model for the researchers at RAND in the 1950s. If strategy is to take up its role as a 'guide to princes' again it will be like weathermen rather than Dr Strangelove. This means that politicians will ask for advice on what to do rather than accept to be told that they have to learn to live with security problems. The guidance which princes need is, now as always, a guide to judgement.

The dangers and opportunities which globalisation creates and the way risk societies respond to them present policy-makers with a wide range of choices. Having read all the quotes of President Clinton justifying bombing al-Qaeda training camps as well as Prime Minister Blair and President Bush arguing for going to war in Afghanistan and Iraq a reader of this book might be forgiven for having reached the conclusion that a risk frame of mind gives one an urge to launch cruise missiles or invade countries. Indeed, the increased number of military interventions by Western powers from the early 1990s reflects the challenges of globalisation and the way the governments of risk societies have interpreted them. However, the discussions in the previous chapters should also have demonstrated that the use of armed force is but one choice open to policy-makers. Where Dr Strangelove offered a set menu, the meteorologists allow governments to do strategy à la carte.

Risk strategy does not necessarily lead to war. In fact the focus on boomerang effects makes it impossible for any government in a risk society to regard war with the complacency and the belief in armed force's ability to produce a clear result which dominated the mind of the policy-makers that began the First World War. At the same time the presence of the future in policy-making means that a lot of scenarios that challenge the scenario that argues for war will be present. If the debate about whether to embark on the invasion of Iraq in 2002–3 shows anything it is that the use of armed force is highly contested.

It is not only political considerations which make the use of armed force highly contested. The bureaucratisation of war – what I have termed 'the UN approach to warfare' – means that lawyers will present policy-makers with fewer and fewer choices for how and when to use armed force. From this perspective globalisation is indeed creating a cosmopolitan community, and warfare has been replaced by the collective enforcement of global 'peace and security'. When the lawyers refer to armed conflict in their briefs, they are describing the type of warfare Clausewitz wrote about. States' use of armed force as a means of policy has been very tightly regulated since the adoption of the UN Charter and in this sense war has been outlawed. While the lawyers would be right in describing the use of armed force as governed by the UN approach, they would not present a complete picture. Regarding al-Qaeda as an ideal type for new rationalities for using armed force, strategists can add to the lawyers' description of armed force. As argued in Chapter 5, the boomerang effect of the bureaucratisation of war is that while international law regulates interstate warfare more tightly than perhaps ever before, these Clausewitzian wars are believed to account for fewer and fewer of the conflicts the West is to face. The UN approach is a way to safeguard the past from shaping the future, but strategists are focusing on the future, and the future presents plenty of strategic challenges in its own right.

Where law thus presents policy-makers with fewer and fewer choices for using armed force, strategy presents policy-makers with more and more choices for using armed force. Therefore politicians' judgement becomes crucial. Politicians can to a large extent choose whether to interpret a conflict in the terms of what their lawyers offer or in the terms of their strategists. They have very different arguments to offer their political masters. Where international law offers a firm ground on which to argue your case, a risk scenario offers no such certainty. If one's policy is successful then the risk one sets out to avert will never materialise. In that way policy in risk society echoes Sun Tzu's dictum that the greatest victories are won in battles that were never fought in campaigns no one has heard about.[10] While strategists may appreciate the dangers of the risks averted, and the notion of anonymous victories may appeal to any kind of poetic justice writers on strategy might entertain, not being able to demonstrate your victories and prove the value of your policy is not what politicians desire. The risk logic means that eliminating a future threat makes this threat 'unreal'. The only concrete result of a successful elimination of risk will thus be the boomerang effects of your action. One might have averted a great catastrophe, only to realise another one. Instead of being hailed for saving the country from the first risk, one will be expelled from office because of the second. In other

---

[10] Sun Tzu, *The Art of War* IV, 11.

circumstances, inaction may be the best thing considering the boomer-ang effects, but for a public demanding action that will not be good enough.

Operating under these terms the use of armed force cannot simply be a straightforward continuation of policy by other means. There is a continuous feedback between ends and means. We are dealing with a risk logic rather than a means-end rational logic.

For a risk society, strategy is all about judgement, but the politicians judging the strategic situation have no safe ground on which to argue their case. In other words, judgement is hard – and naturally politicians are tempted to make judgement more simple. One way of doing that is to base judgement on values – in effect to leave the means-end rational paradigm in favour of a value-rational paradigm.

Values make it possible for presidents and prime ministers to act, because acting on the basis of right and wrong one can invoke a purpose so great that weighing one risk against another seems petty. The value-based approach does not ignore the risks, but it makes it morally in-appropriate not to take the risks. President George Bush responded to 9/11 in this value-rational way. The President summed up his view in his second inauguration speech: 'America's vital interests and our deepest beliefs are now one.' The President then described the freedoms created in the American strive for a free society and went on: 'Advancing these ideals is the mission that created our Nation. It is the honorable achievement of our fathers. Now it is the urgent requirement of our nation's security, and the calling of our time.'[11] Of course the President's strategy for pursuing international terrorism, transforming the Middle East and waging war in Iraq has plenty of risks and boomerang effects, but, if one follows Bush's argument, these are the risks one must accept if one wants to answer 'the calling of our time'.

President Bush's argument conflates means and ends. The world is not only to be made safe for democracy; democracy is going to make the world safe for America. This makes it a reflexive strategy, but it is a reflection on history rather than on the values of democracy and the American experience with democracy itself. Bush concludes that the United States prevailed over fascism and communism in the twentieth century because of American values. Thus Americans have been repeat-edly told after 9/11 that their main contribution to the war on terrorism would be to uphold 'American values'. Defining the conditions for the conflict this way any dialogue or compromise with non-American views

---

[11] George W. Bush, *President Sworn-In to Second Term*, Capitol, 20 January 2005 (Wash-ington, DC: The White House, Office of the Press Secretary, 2005), §6.

is defeatism and any change in US foreign policy in response to terrorism is appeasement.

This is a rather strange interpretation of history. The President and his advisors are fond of comparing their challenge in meeting the new threat of terrorism with the challenge that faced President Truman's administration.[12] The response to the rise of Soviet power which Harry Truman, George Kennan and Dean Acheson formulated, however, was characterised by a fundamental reappraisal of the United States' values in a global context and a dramatic shift in US foreign policy. The Bush administration has toughened the United States' stand on security issues in general and terrorism in particular, but this book has demonstrated that the administration pursues no new strategic concepts. President Bush may be more ready to put these concepts into action than the two previous US presidents or indeed some of the United States' European partners, but the concepts of risk management and preemption have been around for some time. In other words, the Bush administration is so focused on values that it does not seriously consider rethinking US strategy.

It is probably the very focus on values that makes the Bush administration more ready to act than its allies and predecessors. The moral certainty of the administration makes it possible to silence other scenarios than the one the administration chooses to act on and the moral imperative dwarfs the boomerang effects. For example, believing that democracy is a good thing and that democracies are more peaceful than other types of government are great arguments for spreading democracy to the Middle East. But the possible boomerang effects of such export of democracy by force might make you think again. However, if democracy is believed to be a realisation of history's grand design, then you have no reason to doubt the cause because of the boomerang effects. One has a moral imperative for acting and the certainty that history will come down on one's side.

Moral certainty guarantees action, but it is the negation of strategy in a time where little is certain. A prince like George W. Bush basically does not want to be guided by strategists, because he has his values to guide him. Value-based strategy thus solves the problem of judgement only by turning the very values on which the strategy is based into a risk. Democracy becomes a theme and problem in itself when democracy is identified as the key to managing the risks of a globalising world.

---

[12] Condoleezza Rice, *Opening Remarks by Secretary of State Designate Dr Condoleezza Rice*, Senate Foreign Relations Committee, 18 January 2005 (Washington, DC: Department of State, 2005), §§10, 28–30.

Because of his moral certainty, however, President Bush does not reflect on the relationship between democracy and security. From ancient Greece onwards it has been debated whether democracy furthered peace or conflict. Most of the time the conclusion has been that democracy had a tendency to further confrontation and aggression. Athens conducted an aggressive foreign policy which in the end resulted in the Peloponnesian war that destroyed the power of the Greek city states. The republics of Renaissance Italy were, as Machiavelli pointed out, prone to internal conflict and weak in the face of outside interference. When promoted in societies very different from the Western ones where democracy in its modern form has taken root, these questions become of vital importance if one wants to assess whether the spread of democracy will in fact create more peace and security. However, President Bush seems not to reflect on these questions.

George Bush's presidency seems to confirm a common view among those schooled in means-end rationality: that either thought is means-end rational or it is irrational. Max Weber's great insight was that modern, means-end rationality was *not* the only kind of systematic thought – or not the only rational way of thinking, if one uses rational in the everyday sense of the term. A value-based approach to strategy, like the one President Bush employs, is rational too. And so is Osama bin Laden's or the Chinese colonels' approach to strategic questions. The modern paradigm of strategy based on Clausewitz' dictum on war is not the only alternative to an ideological approach to strategy. Analysing strategy in terms of risk, it becomes clear that there are many approaches to strategy. George Bush has solved the problem of judging risks in one way, the forty-fourth President of the United States will probably solve the problem of judgement in another way, just like the President of France today chooses to judge differently from President Bush. The differences in judgement confirm the risk paradigm rather than negating it. The challenges and risks of globalisation and the way risk society perceives them are open to political choice and judgement.

In meeting the challenges of risk society, policy-makers can do better than evading the boomerang effects of the policy choices by making judgement an ideological choice rather than a strategic choice. One reason why appealing to values is so attractive is that existing international law and state bureaucracies offer little scope for debating scenarios and boomerang effects in an open fashion and acting pre-emptively on risks.

International law has outlawed war at the risk of making itself irrelevant in the face of strategic issues that are not directly related to state–state confrontations. In fact it might always have been the case that international law dealt poorly with the issues of non-state agents, especially when it came to the use of force. This was of little consequence, however, when non-state agents were not believed to be very important for the conduct of strategy. Many, especially among those studying strategic studies, may still believe that non-state agents like al-Qaeda are not that important, but when Western publics and strategists do not share that view problems arise. In a political discourse shaped by the presence of the future, rules that seem to apply to yesterday's world of nation states rather than the globalised world of tomorrow can count on little respect. International law will need to take the new risks and the problems of judgement they entail into account if the new problems are not to put the old solutions at risk.

It is one of the paradoxes of strategy in the late modern age that Western armed forces are transforming on the technological and doctrinal level while remaining very much the same on the organisational level. They are simply not very well tuned to dealing with management, the presence of the future and the boomerang effects that characterise risk strategy. The civilian policy-making level is not much better. The civilian agencies are also bureaucracies which seek to externalise risks. They seek rules and predictability and do not want to admit responsibility for imperfect information or boomerang effects. When applied to strategic issues this means that the debate becomes a quest for certainty. But the problems of risk society offer no such certainty. In fact the best the civilian and military national security bureaucracy can hope for are actionable scenarios. By focusing on certainty, however, decision-making processes are probably filtering out many actionable scenarios because the information they are based on is not certain enough. Such scenarios become a risk in themselves in a bureaucratic decision-making process. The decision-making processes need to end the quest for certainty and instead be able to internalise risks. Decision-makers must be able to juggle multiple scenarios at the same time and, most importantly, they must be able to take account of different rationalities and risk cultures. It is on this count that strategic studies fails to guide princes, because it is in designing benchmarks and decision-making procedures as well as educating civil servants and officers in how to do strategy that strategic studies has perhaps its most important duty. If civil servants and officers still believe they act in a means-end rational world, they will make poor strategy. In fact most of them do not think they operate in such a world, but that leaves them with little guidance from scholarship and that is hardly advisable either.

On the political level the judgements of presidents and prime ministers are to be evaluated and the conduct of the defence establishment is to be controlled. Evaluation and control of the executive has proved difficult in recent conflicts because parliamentary checks and balances on the national security field is focused on giving authorisation to military action. Most Western constitutions carefully prescribe procedures for declaring war, but the bureaucratisation of warfare means that war is no longer declared. Parliaments get to vote on resolutions of action and appropriation bills, but when armed force is used as a management tool or as a pre-emptive measure parliamentary approval is very often post facto. So authorisation is often meaningless; and control is difficult because when armed force is used for management and pre-emption it is difficult to define the criteria for success by which the government's handling of a conflict should be evaluated. This shows that the problem of judgement is not just a problem for those deciding to act, but also a problem for those who are to evaluate the outcome of that action. Robert Kaplan argues that this means that democratic control of the use of force will gradually dwindle to the mere symbolical – the US Congress will control the use of the US armed forces no more than the Senate controlled the wars of the Roman emperor.[13]

It is not necessarily true, as Kaplan seems to believe, that globalisation produces threats which can be countered only by abandoning the existing democratic control of the strategic decision-making process. So arguing, Kaplan makes the mistake so often made within strategic studies: he assumes that a different way of doing strategy will mean the collapse of rationality. Some fear this possibility so much that any argument for a new strategy to fit a new security environment is regarded as a dangerously irresponsible kind of nihilism. People like Kaplan embrace changes, but because they accept that the choice stands between means-end rationality and irrationality they conclude that there will be no rules for the war on terrorism and other strategic pursuits of the twenty-first century. Both approaches ignore Weber's insights about the existence of different rationalities. One might speculate that the reason why they regard strategy as a choice between rationality and irrationality is that they ignore the fact that a new rationality is developing in society at large. Or perhaps they do not have much faith in the way the rest of society is changing and regard strategy as one last bastion of rationality. Strategy will be ill served, however, by being conducted on means-end rational terms in a risk society. Kaplan agrees with this point, but he does not believe that risk society produces a new rationality and thus fails to acknowledge that a new approach to strategy is possible.

[13] Robert D. Kaplan, *Warrior Politics: Why Leadership Demands a Pagan Ethos* (New York: Random House, 2002).

Instead, Kaplan turns to pre-modern ways of approaching the questions of war and peace. He concludes that strategy should be guided by a 'pagan ethos'. When one accepts Weber's notion of different rationalities, however, there is a much wider scope for strategic action and for democratic control with strategic action than suggested by the impossible choice between an irrelevant means-end rational approach and a 'pagan ethos'.

A 'pagan ethos' does not seem to be needed to manage the risks of crime or pollution. It is true that government in risk society is characterised by growing executive power. However, it is also true that much of this power is exercised under parliamentary scrutiny. Following the Vietnam war, American politicians are afraid to seem to 'tie the hand on the back' of the armed forces by micro-managing the conduct of military operations. This of course suits the military bureaucracy just fine, but when the authorisation to use armed force is becoming increasingly irrelevant then the elected representatives have little influence on the use of armed force if they do not scrutinise the way it is used during operations. Perhaps parliaments would be better served by defining benchmarks for military operations than by focusing on authorising these operations. If parliaments cannot control when and where operations are to be conducted, they can scrutinise how these operations are conducted and parliamentarians can question policy-makers on how best to achieve the strategic purposes the operations are to serve.

The benchmark approach might also be used to define certain procedures and estimates decision-makers are to present to parliament on national security issues requiring the use of armed force. Such estimates could include the assessment of competing scenarios. In fact the US government has moved along those lines by Congress's insistence on being presented with a presidential national security strategy and a quadrennial defence review. These reports are not just routine correspondence with Congress: they have turned into important policy-making tools. European governments have a lot to learn here. For European governments operating in coalition with US forces, benchmarking would be a vital tool for getting influence on strategy, but also for an opportunity for allied governments to explain their commitment precisely to their own parliament and public.

Strategy is increasingly guided by a risk rationality. Studied in the context of risk society, Western strategy in the post-Cold War world makes sense in a way it cannot possibly do when one expects strategy to be means-end rational. The question remains whether this analytical point is politically accepted. Parliaments cannot control strategy if parliamentarians do not understand the strategic challenges of globalisation. Publics, pundits and parliaments cannot evaluate the strategies of presidents and prime ministers if they do not appreciate the problem of judgement in risk society. The role of strategic studies should be to explain and analyse the new role of strategy in risk society, but strategic studies has largely rejected this opportunity to guide the prince as well as the demos. The result is debates dominated by old truths that do not fit new realities and are therefore all too easily made into a debate about subjects much more politically convenient than strategy, such as values.

Since the seventeenth century, strategy has been a central conceptual tool for forging security out of technological, social and political changes. It has been strategy that ensured that change did not overcome policy-makers, but instead gave them new tools to meet new challenges. At the beginning of the twentieth century many observers believed that modernity was a recipe for peace and thus that the advances in technology, economic growth and growing political liberty would make strategy redundant. As it turned out, modern strategy came into its own in order to rationalise the threats and the horrors the twentieth century actually offered. At the beginning of the twenty-first century, life in Western society is again characterised by technological progress and economic growth, and these developments seem intimately connected with a process of globalisation that apparently promises to make the world safe for democracy. However, today Western society has retained little of the optimism from the last turn of the century. Western societies have no illusions that globalisation is only a promise of progress. Being risk societies they also regard globalisation as a risk that needs to be managed. This view leads them to focus on the future and, as opposed to their optimistic forefathers, they are very conscious that, however hard they try to make a safer world, any action they take will invariably have a boomerang effect. Perhaps this focus on the risks is only for the best. It was a false belief in the inevitability of human progress that made decision-makers at the beginning of the twentieth century complacent about how much havoc war could still create. The First World War was one result of such complacency, whereas another was the militant belief in a certain way of human progress that led to the Second World War and the Cold War. So focusing on the risks might actually be a good idea, but it also means that the grand hopes and ambitious designs for a better future that characterised the beginning of the twentieth century are no longer. Even the promise of democracy as a recipe for peace and human freedom is today rather a way to manage risk than to realise a liberal utopia. We have stopped believing in lasting peace, what is left is only strategy – we had better be good at it.

Bibliography

Adams, John, *Risk* (London: Routledge, 1995).

Ahmed, Kamal and Ed Vulliamy, 'United They Stand: The "Odd Couple" Offensive', *Observer*, 8 September 2002.

Allison, Graham, T., *Essence of Decision: Explaining the Cuban Missile Crisis* (Boston: Little, Brown and Company, 1971).

Arend, Anthony Clark, 'International Law and the Preemptive Use of Military Force', *Washington Quarterly* 26 (Spring 2003), 89–103.

Aron, Raymond, 'The Evolution of Modern Strategic Thought', in *Problems of Modern Strategy*, The Institute for Strategic Studies (London: Chatto and Windus, 1970), 13–46.

'Reason, Passion, and Power in the Thought of Clausewitz', *Social Research: An International Quarterly of the Social Sciences* 39 (1972), 599–621.

Atkinson, Rick, *In the Company of Soldiers: A Chronicle of Combat in Iraq* (London: Little, Brown and Company, 2004).

Bacevich, Andrew J., 'Strategic Studies: In from the Cold', *SAIS Review* 13 (1993), 11–23.

American Empire: The Realities and Consequences of US Diplomacy (Cambridge, MA: Harvard University Press, 2002).

Barnett, Thomas P. M., *The Pentagon's New Map: War and Peace in the Twenty-First Century* (New York: Putnam, 2004).

Bartelson, Jens, 'Three Concepts of Globalization', *International Sociology* 15 (2000), 180–96.

Bartov, Omer, *The Eastern Front, 1941–45: German Troops and the Barbarisation of Warfare* (London: Macmillan, 1985).

Bauman, Zygmunt, *Modernity and the Holocaust* (Cambridge: Polity Press, 1989).

Globalization: The Human Consequences (Cambridge: Polity Press, 1998).

Society Under Siege (Cambridge: Polity Press, 2002).

Baylis, John and James Wirtz, 'Introduction', in John Baylis et al. (eds.), *Strategy in the Contemporary World: An Introduction to Strategic Studies* (Oxford: Oxford University Press, 2002), 1–14.

Beck, Ulrich, 'The Reinvention of Politics: Towards a Theory of Reflexive Modernization', in Ulrich Beck, Anthony Giddens and Scott Lash, *Reflexive Modernization: Politics, Tradition and Aesthetics in the Modern Social Order* (Cambridge: Polity Press, 1994), 1–55.

Risk Society, trans. Mark Ritter (London: Sage Publications, 1992).

World Risk Society (Cambridge: Polity Press, 1999).

What Is Globalization? (Cambridge: Polity Press, 2000).
'The Silence of Words: On Terror and War', *Security Dialogue* 34 (2003), 255–67.
Becker, Gavin de, *Fear Less* (Boston, MA: Little, Brown and Company, 2002).
Begg, David, Stanley Fischer and Rudiger Dornbusch, *Economics*, third edition (London: MacGraw Hill, 1991).
Beschloss, M. R. and S. Talbott, *At the Highest Levels. The Inside Story of the End of the Cold War* (Boston: Little, Brown and Company, 1993).
Betts, Richard K., 'Should Strategic Studies Survive?', *World Politics* 50 (1997), 7–33.
'Is Strategy an Illusion?', *International Security* 25 (2000), 5–50.
Bigo, Didier, *To Reassure, and Protect, After September 11*, www.ssrc.org/sept11/essays/ (1 December 2004).
Black, Jeremy, *War in the New Century* (London: Continuum, 2001).
Blair, Tony, *Prime Minister's Speech to Economic Club of Chicago*, Chicago, 23 April 1999 (London: Prime Minister's Office, 1999).
Prime Minister's Address to the Labour Party Conference, Brighton, 2 October 2001, www.labour.org.uk (17 October 2001).
PM Warns of Continuing Global Terror Threat, 5 March 2004 (London: Prime Minister's Office, 2004), www.number-10.gov.uk (7 October 2004).
'Blair: UK Terror Attack Inevitable', CNN, 21 January 2003, www.cnn.com (7 October 2004).
Blakely, Edward J. and Mary Gail Snyder, *Fortress America: Gated Communities in the United States* (Washington, DC: Brookings Institution Press, 1997).
Bond, Brian, *War and Society in Europe 1870–1970* (London: Fontana, 1998).
'Border Breach? Customs Fails to Detect Depleted Uranium – Again', ABC News, http://abcnews.go.com/sections/wnt/Primetime/sept11_uranium030910.html (9 October 2003).
Bourke, Joanna, *An Intimate History of Killing: Face-to-Face Killing in Twentieth-Century Warfare* (London: Granta Publications, 1999).
Bowden, Mark, *Black Hawk Down: A Story of Modern War* (New York: Penguin Books, 1999).
'The Kabul-ki Dance', *Atlantic Monthly*, November 2002, www.theatlantic.com (18 January 2005).
Boyd, Terry, 'Service Members Weigh Many Options in Deciding Whether to Re-enlist', *Stars and Stripes*, European Edition, 20 October 2003.
Brodie, Bernard, 'Strategy as a Science', *World Politics* 1 (1949), 467–88.
War and Politics (London: Cassell, 1974).
Bundy, McGeorge, *Danger and Survival. Choices about the Bomb in the First Fifty Years* (New York: Random House, 1988).
Burchell, Graham, Colin Cordon and Peter Miller (eds.), *The Foucault Effect: Studies in Governmentality* (London: Harvester Wheatsheaf, 1990).
Bush, George Herbert Walker, *Remarks at a White House Briefing on the National Drug Control Strategy*, 5 September 1990, George Bush Presidential Library, College Station, TX, http://bushlibrary.tamu.edu/ (1 March 2004).
Remarks at the Texas A&M University in College Station, Texas, 15 December 1992, The George Bush Presidential Library, College Station, TX.

Bush, George W., *A Period of Consequences*, The Citadel, Charleston, SC, 23 September 1999, www.vote-smart.org (12 April 2005).

Governor Bush Addresses American Legion, Milwaukee, Wisconsin, Wednesday 6 September 2000.

President Pledges Assistance for New York in Phone Call with Pataki, Giuliani, Remarks by the President in Telephone Conversation with New York Mayor Giuliani and New York Governor Pataki, 13 September 2001 (Washington, DC: The White House, Office of the Press Secretary, 2001).

Remarks by the President in Photo Opportunity with the National Security Team, The Cabinet Room, the White House, 13 September 2001 (Washington, DC: The White House, Office of the Press Secretary, 2001).

Remarks by the President on Arrival, 16 September 2001 (Washington, DC: The White House, Office of the Press Secretary, 2001).

Address to a Joint Session of Congress and the American People, 20 September 2001 (Washington, DC: The White House, Office of the Press Secretary, 2001).

President Bush Speaks to United Nations, Remarks by the President to United Nations General Assembly, UN Headquarters, New York, 10 November 2001 (Washington, DC: The White House, Office of the Press Secretary, 2001).

The President's State of the Union Address, 29 January 2002 (Washington, DC: The White House, Office of the Press Secretary, 2002).

President Thanks World Coalition for Anti-Terrorism Efforts, The South Lawn, 11 March 2002 (Washington, DC: The White House, Office of the Press Secretary, 2002).

President Bush Thanks Germany for Support Against Terror, Remarks by the President to a Special Session of the German Bundestag, The White House, 23 May 2002 (Washington, DC: The White House, Office of the Press Secretary, 2002).

Remarks by the President at 2002 Graduation Exercise of the United States Military Academy, West Point, New York, 1 June 2002 (Washington, DC: The White House, Office of the Press Secretary, 2002).

President Bush Discusses Iraq with Congressional Leaders, 26 September 2002 (Washington, DC: The White House, Office of the Press Secretary, 7 October 2002).

Remarks by the President at the Signing of HR 5005 the Homeland Security Act of 2002, 25 November 2002 (Washington, DC: The White House, Office of the Press Secretary, 2002).

President Bush Outlines Progress in Operation Iraqi Freedom, Boeing Integrated Defense Systems' Headquarters, St Louis, Missouri, 16 April 2003 (22 April 2004).

President Bush Announces Major Combat Operations in Iraq Have Ended, Remarks by the President from the USS *Abraham Lincoln* At Sea Off the Coast of San Diego, California, 1 May 2003 (Washington, DC: The White House, Office of the Press Secretary, 2003).

Remarks by the President at the United States Air Force Academy Graduation Ceremony, Falcon Stadium, United States Air Force Academy, 2 June

2004 (Washington, DC: The White House, Office of the Press Secretary, 2004).

President Sworn-In to Second Term, Capitol, 20 January 2005 (Washington, DC: The White House, Office of the Press Secretary, 2005).

Butterfield, Herbert, *History and Human Relations* (London: Collins, 1951).

Buzan, Barry et al., *Security: A New Framework for Analysis* (Boulder, CO: Lynne Rienner Publishers, 1997).

Carter, Helen, 'Eye Spy', *Guardian*, 1 August 2001.

Castells, Manuel, *The Rise of the Network Society* (Oxford: Blackwell, 1996).

Cheney, Richard B., *Remarks by the Vice President to the Veterans of Foreign Wars 103rd National Convention*, 26 August 2002 (Washington, DC: The White House, Office of the Press Secretary, 18 September 2002).

Churchill, Winston S., Sinews of Peace, 5 March 1946, Westminster College, Fulton Missouri, The Churchill Center, www.winstonchurchill.org (26 May 2000).

The Second World War, vol. I: *The Gathering Storm* (London: Cassell, 1948).

Clancy, Tom, *Executive Orders* (London: HarperCollins, 1996).

Clark, Wesley K., *Waging Modern War: Bosnia, Kosovo and the Future of Conflict* (New York: Public Affairs, 2001).

Clarke, Richard A., *Against All Enemies: Inside America's War on Terror* (New York: The Free Press, 2004).

Clausewitz, Carl von, *On War*, edited and translated by Michael Howard and Peter Paret (Princeton, NJ: Princeton University Press, 1976 (1832–4)).

Clinton, William Jefferson, *Address by the President to the 48th Session of the United Nations General Assembly*, The United Nations, New York (Washington, DC: The White House, Office of the Press Secretary, 1993).

Remarks by the President at Intervention for the North Atlantic Summit, NATO Headquarters, Brussels, Belgium (Washington, DC: The White House, Office of the Press Secretary, 1994).

Address to the Nation by the President, 20 August 1998 (Washington, DC: The White House, Office of the Press Secretary, 1998).

Statement by the President to the Nation, 24 March 1999 (Washington, DC: The White House, Office of the Press Secretary, 1999).

Remarks by President William Clinton to the Veterans of Foreign Wars on Kosovo, Eisenhower Hall, Fort McNair, 13 May 1999 (Washington, DC: The White House, Office of the Press Secretary, 1999).

Cohen, William S., *Remarks as Prepared for Delivery Secretary of Defense William S. Cohen National Defense University Joint Operations Symposium QDR Conference*, Fort McNair, Washington, DC, 23 June 1997 (Washington, DC: Office of Assistant Secretary of Defense (Public Affairs), 1997).

Coker, Christopher, *War and the 20th Century* (London: Brassey's, 1994).

Twilight of the West (Boulder, CO: Westview Press, 1998).

Globalisation and Insecurity in the Twenty-First Century: NATO and the Management of Risk, Adelphi Paper 345, International Institute for Strategic Studies (Oxford: Oxford University Press, 2002).

The Future of War: The Re-Enchantment of War in the Twenty-First Century (Oxford: Blackwell, 2004).

Conetta, Carl, The 'New Warfare' and the New American Calculus of War, Project on Defense Alternatives, Briefing Memo No. 26, 30 September 2002, www. comw.org/ (13 May 2004).

The Wages of War: Iraqi Combatant and Noncombatant Fatalities in the 2003 Conflict (Cambridge, MA: Commonwealth Institute, 2003).

Cordesman, Anthony H., The Iraq War: Strategy, Tactics, and Military Lessons (Westport, CT: Praeger, 2003).

Lessons and Non-Lessons of the Air and Missile Campaign in Kosovo (Washington, DC: Center for Strategic and International Studies, 2004).

The Ongoing Lessons of Afghanistan: Warfighting, Intelligence, Force Transformation, and Nation-building (Washington, DC: Center for Strategic and International Studies, 2004).

Cornwell, Rupert, 'Just Retribution or an Abuse of Human Rights? A Big Question, with Only One Answer in the US', Independent, 18 January 2002.

Cowell, Alan, 'Blair Hears Drumbeat of Dissent from Party', International Herald Tribune, 12 March 2003.

Creveld, Martin van, On Future War (London: Brassey's, 1991).

The Art of War: War and Military Thought (London: Cassell, 2000).

Cronin, Audrey Kurth, 'Behind the Curve: Globalization and International Terrorism', International Security 27 (2002), 30–58.

Crow, Graham, 'The Use of the Concept of "Strategy" in Recent Sociological Literature', Sociology 23 (1989), 1–24.

Crow, Sheryl, 'If It Makes You Happy', Sheryl Crow, A&M Records, 1996.

Dean, Mitchell, Governmentality: Power and Rule in Modern Society (London: Sage Publications, 1999).

Defense Technical Information Center, DOD Dictionary of Military and Associated Terms, www.dtic.mil/doctrine/jel/doddict/natoterm/d/00401.html (2 December 2004).

Deputy Secretary Wolfowitz, Interview with Sam Tannenhaus, Vanity Fair, 9 May 2003, transcript (Washington, DC: US Department of Defense, 2003).

Der Derian, James, 'The Art of War and the Construction of Peace', in Morten Kelstrup and Michael C. Williams (eds.), International Relations Theory and the Politics of European Integration: Power, Security and Community (London: Routledge, 2000), 72–105.

Efron, Sonni, Tyler Marshall and Bob Drogin, 'Powell's Talk of Arms Has Fallout', Los Angeles Times, 19 November 2004.

Elias, Norbert, The Civilizing Process (Oxford: Blackwell, 1978 (1939)).

Eminem, 'Without Me', The Eminem Show, Shady/Interscope Records, 2002.

Emsley, Clive, Arthur Marwick and Wendy Simpson (eds.), War, Peace and Social Change in Twentieth Century Europe (Buckingham: Open University Press, 1989).

Euben, Roxanne L., Enemy in the Mirror: Islamic Fundamentalism and the Limits of Modern Rationalism (Princeton, NJ: Princeton University Press, 1999).

Ewald, François, 'Insurance and Risk', in Graham Burchell, Colin Gordon and Peter Miller (eds.), *The Foucault Effect: Studies in Governmentality* (Hemel Hempstead: Harvester Wheatsheaf, 1991), 197–210.

Fallows, James, 'The Hollow Army', *Atlantic Monthly*, March 2004, www.theatlantic.com (18 January 2005).

Finnemore, Martha, *The Purpose of Intervention: Changing Beliefs About the Use of Force* (Ithaca, NY: Cornell University Press, 2003).

Fischer, Joschka, *Speech by Federal Foreign Minister Fischer in the German Bundestag on 20 March 2003 on the War against Iraq* (Berlin: German Foreign Ministry, 2003).

Foucault, Michel, 'Governmentality' in *Essential Works of Foucault 1954–1984*, vol. III: *Power*, ed. James D. Faubion (New York: The New Press, 2000), 201–22.

Freedman, Lawrence, 'Indignation, Influence and Strategic Studies', *International Affairs* 60 (1984), 207–19.

'The First Two Generations of Nuclear Strategists', in Peter Paret (ed.), *Makers of Modern Strategy: From Machiavelli to the Nuclear Age* (Oxford: Clarendon Press, 1998), 735–78.

The Revolution in Strategic Affairs, Adelphi Paper 318, International Institute for Strategic Studies (Oxford: Oxford University Press, 1998).

'The Third World War?', *Survival* 43 (2001), 61–88.

Deterrence (Cambridge: Polity Press, 2004).

Fukuyama, Francis, 'Their Target: The Modern World', *Newsweek*, Special Davos Edition (December 2001–February 2002), 58–63.

Gaddis, John Lewis, 'A Grand Strategy of Transformation', *Foreign Policy*, www.foreignpolicy.com (11 December 2002).

Surprise, Security, and the American Experience (Cambridge, MA: Harvard University Press, 2004).

'Grand Strategy in the Second Term', *Foreign Affairs* 84 (January/February 2005), 2–15.

German Marshall Fund, *Transatlantic Trends 2004 – Topline Data*, www.transatlantictrends.org (16 January 2005).

'German Prosecutor Refuses Rumsfeld Probe', *Washington Post*, 11 February 2005.

'German Prosecutor Rejects Investigation of Rumsfeld', *Los Angeles Times*, 11 February 2005.

Giddens, Anthony, *The Consequences of Modernity* (Cambridge: Polity Press, 1990).

Modernity and Self-Identity: Self and Society in the Late Modern Age (Cambridge: Polity Press, 1991).

'Risk Society: The Context of British Politics', in Jane Franklin (ed.), *The Politics of Risk Society* (Cambridge: Polity Press, 1998), 23–34.

Runaway World: How Globalisation is Reshaping Our Lives (London: Profile, 1999).

Gilbert, Felix, 'Machiavelli: The Renaissance of the Art of War', in Peter Paret (ed.), *Makers of Modern Strategy: From Machiavelli to the Nuclear Age* (Oxford: Clarendon Press, 1998), 11–31.

Goldstein, Jonah and Jeremy Rayner, 'The Politics of Identity in Late Modern Society', *Theory and Society* 23 (June 1994), 367–84.

Gore, Al, *Remarks by Vice President Al Gore, US Military Academy Commencement*, West Point, 27 May 2000, Clinton Presidential Materials Project, http://searchclinton.archives.gov/ (3 May 2004).

Iraq and the War on Terrorism, 23 September, 2002, www.commonwealthclub.org (13 October, 2004).

Gray, Colin, 'Villains, Victims, and Sheriffs: Strategic Studies and Security for an Interwar Period', *Comparative Strategy* 13 (1994), 353–69.

Gray, Colin S., *Explorations in Strategy* (Westport, CT: Greenwood, 1996).

Gray, Colin, 'Clausewitz Rules, OK? The Future is the Past – with GPS', *Review of International Studies* 25 (December 1999), 161–82.

'World Politics as Usual after September 11: Realism Vindicated', in Ken Booth and Tim Dunne (eds.), *Worlds in Collision* (London: Palgrave, 2002), 226–34.

Guehenno, J.-M., 'The Impact of Globalisation on Strategy', *Survival* 40 (Winter 1998–9), 5–19.

Gunaratna, Rohan, *Inside Al Qaeda: Global Network of Terror* (New York: Columbia University Press, 2002).

Guthrie, Charles, 'Why NATO Cannot Simply March in and Crush Milosevic', *Evening Standard*, 1 April 1999.

Hanson, Victor David, *Why the West Has Won: Carnage and Culture from Salamis to Vietnam* (London: Faber and Faber, 2001).

The Health and Safety Executive, *Reducing Risks, Protecting People*, Discussion Document (London: The Health and Safety Executive, 1999).

Heisbourg, François, 'A Work in Progress: The Bush Doctrine and Its Consequences', *Washington Quarterly* 26 (Spring 2003), 75–88.

Hersh, Seymour M., *Chain of Command: The Road from 9/11 to Abu Ghraib* (London: Allen Lane, 2004).

Herwig, Holger H., 'The Battlefleet Revolution, 1885–1914', in MacGregor Knox and Williamson Murray (eds.), *The Dynamics of Mildtary Revolution, 1300–2050* (Cambridge: Cambridge University Press, 2001), 114–31.

Herz, John, *Political Realism and Political Idealism* (Chicago, IL: Chicago University Press, 1951).

Hirst, Paul, *War and Power* (Cambridge: Polity Press, 2001).

Holbrooke, Richard, *To End A War*, revised edition (New York: The Modern Library, 1999).

Howard, Michael, *War and the Liberal Conscience* (New Brunswick, NJ: Rutgers University Press, 1978).

'Terrorism Has Always Fed Off its Response', *Times*, 1 September 2001.

Speech at the Conference New Policies for a New World, RUSI, unpublished, London, November 2001.

Hughes, Gordon, *Understanding Crime Prevention: Social Control, Risk and Late-Modernity* (Maidenhead: Open University Press, 1998).

Hulse, Carl, 'Pentagon Cancels Scheme for Wagering on Terror', *International Herald Tribune*, 30 July 2003.

Hundley, Richard O., *Past Revolutions, Future Transformations: What Can the History of Revolutions in Military Affairs Tell Us About Transforming the US Military?* (Santa Monica, CA: RAND, 1999).

Huntington, Samuel, *The Clash of Civilizations and the Remaking of World Order* (London: Touchstone Books, 1998).

'The Age of Muslim Wars', *Newsweek*, Special Davos Edition (December 2001–February 2002), 6–13.

Icasualties.org, http://icasualties.org/oif/ (13 April 2005).

Ignatieff, Michael, *Virtual War: Kosovo and Beyond* (London: Chatto and Windus, 2000).

Ikenberry, G. John, *After Victory: Institutions, Strategic Restraint and the Rebuilding of Order After Major Wars* (Princeton, NJ: Princeton University Press, 2001).

International Commission on Intervention and State Sovereignty, *The Responsibility to Protect* (Ottawa, ON: International Development Research Centre, 2001).

International Institute for Strategic Studies, *The Military Balance 2002–2003* (Oxford: Oxford University Press, 2003).

The Military Balance 2003–2004 (Oxford: Oxford University Press, 2004).

'It is Meaningless and Dangerous to Declare War Against Terrorism', Leading Article, *Independent*, 17 September 2001.

Jervis, Robert, *Perception and Misperception in International Politics* (Princeton, NJ: Princeton University Press, 1976).

John Kerry for President, http://johnkerry.com (3 May 2004).

Johnston, Les, *Policing Britain: Risk, Security and Governance* (London: Longman, 2000).

Joint Chiefs of Staff, *Joint Vision 2010* (Washington, DC: Chairman of the Joint Chiefs of Staff, 1997).

Joint Vision 2020 (Washington, DC: Chairman of the Joint Chiefs of Staff, 2000).

Joint Declaration by the British and French Governments on European Defence, Anglo-French Summit, London, Thursday 25 November 1999.

Joint Doctrine and Concepts Centre, *Strategic Trends* (Swindon: JDCC, 2003).

Kahn, Herman, *On Thermonuclear War* (Princeton, NJ: Princeton University Press, 1961).

Kalberg, Stephen, 'Max Weber's Types of Rationality: Cornerstones for the Analysis of Rationalization Processes in History', *American Journal of Sociology* 85 (1980), 1,145–79.

Kant, Immanuel, 'To Perpetual Peace: A Philosophical Sketch', *Kant's Political Writings*, trans. H. B. Nisbet and ed. H. Reiss (Cambridge: Cambridge University Press, 1970 (1795)).

Kaplan, Fred, *The Wizards of Armageddon* (New York: Simon and Schuster, 1983).

Kaplan, Robert D., *Warrior Politics: Why Leadership Demands a Pagan Ethos* (New York: Random House, 2002).

Keane, John, *Civil Society: Old Images, New Visions* (Cambridge: Polity Press, 1998).

Keegan, John, *The Face of Battle: A Study of Agincourt, Waterloo and the Somme* (London: Pimlico, 1991).

The Iraq War (London: Hutchinson, 2004).

Keller, Bill, 'The Fighting Next Time', *New York Times*, 10 March 2002.

Kemshall, Hazel, *Risk Assessment and Management of Known Sexual and Violent Offenders: A Review of Current Issues*, Police Research Series, Paper 140 (London: Home Office, 2001).

Kennan, George F., 'The Long Telegram', 22 February 1946, reprinted in Thomas Etzold and John Lewis Gaddis (eds.), *Containment: Documents on American Policy and Strategy, 1945–1950* (New York and London: Columbia University Press, 1978), 50–63.

Kennan, George F., alias X, 'The Sources of Soviet Conduct', *Foreign Affairs* 25 (July 1947), 566–82.

My Memoirs, 1925–1950 (London: Hutchinson, 1967).

Kerry, John, *Remarks by Senator John Kerry on New Strategies to Meet New Threats*, 1 June 2004, West Palm Beach, FL, www.johnkerry.com (4 June 2004).

Remarks of Senator John Kerry on Strengthening Our Military, 3 June 2004, Independence, MO, http://johnkerry.com (4 June 2004).

Kerry Lays Out Iraq Plan, 20 September 2004, New York, transcript *Washington Post*, www.washingtonpost.com (22 September 2004).

Remarks of Senator John Kerry on Security and Strength for a New World, Seattle, WA, 27 May 2005, www.johnkerry.com (4 June 2004).

Khalilzad, Zalmay et al., *The United States and a Rising China* (Santa Monica, CA: RAND, 1999).

Klein, Bradley S., 'After Strategy: The Search for a Postmodern Politics of Peace', *Alternatives* 13 (1988), 293–318.

Strategic Studies and World Order: The Global Politics of Deterrence (Cambridge: Cambridge University Press, 1994).

Knowlton, Brian, 'US Toll in Iraq War Starting to Hit Home', *International Herald Tribune*, 19 March 2005.

Knox, MacGregor and Williamson Murray (eds.), *The Dynamics of Military Revolution, 1300–2050* (Cambridge: Cambridge University Press, 2001).

Kubrick, Stanley, *Dr Strangelove or: How I Learned to stop Worrying and Love the Bomb* (Columbia Pictures, 1964).

The Labour Party, *Labour Looks Ahead*, abridged edition of *The Old World and the New Society* (London: The Labour Party, 1942).

Laird, Robbin F. and Holger H. May, *The Revolution in Military Affairs: Allied Perspectives*, McNair Paper 60 (Washington, DC: National Defense University, 1999).

Latham, Robert, *The Liberal Moment: Modernity, Security, and the Making of Postwar International Order* (New York: Columbia University Press, 1997).

Leonhard, Robert R., *The Principles of War in the Information Age* (Novato, CA: Presido Press, 1998).

Liang, Qiao and Wang Xiangsui, *Unrestricted Warfare* (Beijing: PLA Literature and Arts Publishing House, 1999). English translation by FBIS, www.c4i.org (12 June 2002).

Libicki, Martin, *The Mesh and the Net: Speculations on Armed Conflict in an Age of Free Silicon*, McNair Paper 28 (Washington, DC: National Defense University, 1994).

Liddell Hart, B. H., *Strategy* (London: Penguin, 1954).
Lifton, Robert Jay, 'Protean Man', *Partisan Review* (Winter 1968), 13–27.
Lincoln, Abraham, *First Inaugural Address*, 4 March 1861, www.libertyonline.
    hypermall.com/Lincoln/Lincoln-1.html (3 December 2004).
'The Litany and the Heretic', *Economist*, 31 January 2002.
Litwak, Robert S., 'The New Calculus of Pre-emption', *Survival* 44 (Winter
    2002–3), 53–80.
Lomborg, Bjørn, *The Sceptical Environmentalist* (Cambridge: Cambridge Univer-
    sity Press, 2001).
Luhmann, Niklas, *Risk: A Sociological Theory*, trans. Rhodes Barrett (New York:
    Walter de Gruyter, 1993).
Lupton, Deborah, *Risk* (London: Routledge, 1999).
Luttwak, Edward N., 'A Post-Heroic Military Policy', *Foreign Affairs* 74 (July/
    August 1996), 33–44.
Strategy: The Logic of War and Peace (Cambridge, MA: Belknap Press, 2001).
Machiavelli, Niccolò, *Discourses on Livy* (Oxford: Oxford University Press,
    1997).
The Prince (Chicago, IL: University of Chicago Press, 1998).
Art of War, ed. Christopher Lynch (Chicago, IL: University of Chicago Press,
    2003).
Mandelbaum, Michael, *The Dawn of Peace in Europe* (New York: The Twentieth
    Century Fund Press, 1996).
Marr, Andrew, 'Blair's Masochism Makes Great Television – But Is It a Good
    War Strategy?', *Daily Telegraph*, 12 March 2003.
Marshall, Andrew W., *Some Thoughts on Military Revolutions*, Second Version,
    Office of the Secretary of Defense, Director of Net Assessment, Washing-
    ton, DC (1993).
Mazower, Mark, *Dark Continent: Europe's Twentieth Century* (London: Allen
    Lane, 1998).
Mearsheimer, John J., 'Back to the Future: Instability in Europe after the Cold
    War', *International Security* 15 (1990), 5–56.
Mearsheimer, John J. and Stephen M. Walt, 'An Unnecessary War', *Foreign
    Policy* (January/February 2003), 50–9.
Metz, Steven, *Armed Conflict in the 21st Century: The Information Revolution and
    Post-Modern Warfare* (Carlisle, PA: Strategic Studies Institute, US Army
    War College, 2000).
'The Next Twist of the RMA', *Parameters* (Autumn 2000), 40–53.
Mills, C. Wright, *The Sociological Imagination* (New York: Oxford University
    Press, 1959).
'Misguided Math About the Earth', *Scientific American* (January 2002), 61–71.
Moore, Michael, *Fahrenheit 9/11* (Columbia, 2004).
A More Secure World: Our Shared Responsibility, Report of the Secretary-General's
    High-Level Panel on Threats, Challenges and Change (New York: United
    Nations, 2004).
Morgan, D. H. J., 'Strategies and Sociologists: A Comment on Crow', *Sociology*
    23 (1989), 25–9.

Morris, Julian, 'Defining the Precautionary Principle', in Julian Morris (ed.), *Rethinking Risk and the Precautionary Principle* (Oxford: Butterworth-Heinemann, 2000), 1–21.

Morton, Oliver, 'The Softwar Revolution: A Survey of Defence Technology', *Economist*, 10 June 1995.

Moskos, Charles C., 'Toward a Postmodern Military: The United States as a Paradigm', in Charles C. Moskos, John Allen Williams and David R. Segal (eds.), *The Postmodern Military: Armed Forces After the Cold War* (Oxford: Oxford University Press, 2000), 14–31.

Murray, Williamson and MacGregor Knox, 'Thinking About Revolutions in Warfare', in Knox and Murray (eds.), *The Dynamics of Military Revolution, 1300–2050* (Cambridge: Cambridge University Press, 2001), 1–14.

Murray, Williamson and Robert H. Scales Jr, *The Iraq War* (Cambridge, MA: The Belknap Press, 2003).

Naim, Moises and Michael O'Hanlon, 'Reinventing War', *Foreign Policy* (November/December 2001), 30–47.

National Security Council, 'A Report to the National Security Council by the Executive Secretary on United States Objectives and Programs for National Security', 14 April 1950, reprinted in D. Merrill (ed.), *Documentary History of the Truman Presidency*, vol. VII: *The Ideological Foundations of the Cold War – the 'Long Telegram,' the Clifford Report, and NSC 68* (Lanham, MD: University Publications of America, 1996), 324–59.

The National Security Strategy of the United States of America, 17 September 2002 (Washington, DC: The While House, 2002).

NATO, *The Alliance's Strategic Concept*, Agreed by the Heads of State and Government participating in the meeting of the North Atlantic Council in Rome on 7–8 November 1991 (Brussels: NATO Handbook, NATO Office of Information and Press, October 1995).

Allied Joint Doctrine, September 1998.

The Alliance's Strategic Concept, Approved by the Heads of State and Government participating in the meeting of the North Atlantic Council in Washington, DC, on 23 and 24 April 1999, reprinted in NATO Handbook – Documentation (Brussels: NATO Office of Information and Press, 1999).

'NATO Chiefs Test Readiness for Terror Crisis', *International Herald Tribune*, 9 October 2003.

NATO, *Prague Summit Declaration*, Issued by the Heads of State and Government participating in the meeting of the North Atlantic Council in Prague on 21 November 2002 (Brussels: NATO, 2003).

Neumann, John von and Oskar Morgenstern, *Theory of Games and Economic Behaviour* (Princeton, NJ: Princeton University Press, 1944).

Nevin, Thomas, 'Ernest Jünger: German Stormtrooper Chronicler', in Hugh Cecil and Peter H. Liddle (eds.), *Facing Armageddon: The First World War Experienced* (London: Leo Cooper, 1996), 269–77.

Nye, Joseph S. and Sean M. Lynn-Johns, 'International Security Studies: A Report of a Conference on the State of the Field', *International Security* 12 (1988), 5–27.

Nye Jr., Joseph S. and William A. Owens, 'America's Information Edge', *Foreign Affairs* 75 (1996), 20–36.

OECD, *Security in Maritime Transport: Risk Factors and Economic Impact* (Directorate for Science, Technology and Industry, Maritime Transport Committee, July 2003).

Owens, Bill (with Ed Offley), *Lifting the Fog of War* (New York: Farrar, Straus and Giroux, 2000).

Pace, General Peter, Interview with Hannah Storm, CBS, *Early Show*, 5 May 2004, transcript (Washington, DC: US Department of Defense, 2004), www.defenselink.mil (6 April 2005).

Parker, Geoffrey, *The Military Revolution: Military Innovation and the Rise of the West, 1500–1800* (Cambridge: Cambridge University Press, 1996).

Perle, Richard, 'Thank God for the Death of the UN', *Guardian*, 21 March 2003.

Perry, William J., 'Desert Storm and Deterrence', *Foreign Affairs* 70 (1991), 66–82.

Perry, William and Ashton Carter, *Preventive Defense: A New Security Strategy for America* (Washington, DC: The Brookings Institution, 1999).

Pollack, Kenneth, 'Next Stop Baghdad', *Foreign Affairs* 81 (March/April 2002), 32–47.

Posen, Barry, *Sources of Military Doctrine: France, Britain, and Germany between the World Wars* (Ithaca, NY: Cornell University Press, 1984).

Posen, Barry R., 'The Struggle Against Terrorism: Grand Strategy, Strategy and Tactics', *International Security* 26 (2001), 39–55.

Priest, Dana, 'A Decisive Battle That Never Was', *Washington Post*, 19 September 1999.

'Private Contractors in Iraq', *Economist*, 7 April 2004.

Promfret, John, 'China Looks Beyond Old Rules', *International Herald Tribune*, 9 August 1999.

Quadrennial Defense Review Report, May 1997 (Washington, DC: Department of Defense, 1997).

30 September 2001 (Washington, DC: Department of Defense, 2001).

Rapoport, David C., 'The Fourth Wave: September 11 in the History of Terrorism', *Current History* (December 2001), 419–24.

Rasmussen, Mikkel Vedby, 'The Prisoner's Reflection: Identity and Detainees in the "War on Terrorism"', in Mikkel Vedby Rasmussen, Sten Rynning, Kristian Søby Kristensen and Bertel Heurlin (eds.), *The Revolution in Military Affairs* (Copenhagen: Institute for International Studies, 2003), 213–28.

The West, Civil Society and the Construction of Peace (London: Palgrave, 2003).

Reimer, Jeffrey W., 'Durkheim's "Heroic Suicide" in Military Combat', *Armed Forces and Society* 25 (Fall 1998), 103–20.

Rice, Condoleezza, 'The Making of Soviet Strategy', in Peter Paret (ed.), *Makers of Modern Strategy: From Machiavelli to the Nuclear Age* (Oxford: Clarendon Press, 1998), 648–76.

Opening Remarks by Secretary of State Designate Dr Condoleezza Rice, Senate Foreign Relations Committee, 18 January 2005 (Washington, DC: Department of State, 2005).

Riddell, Bob, 'Doom Goes to War', *Wired* (April 1997), www.wired.com (21 July 2000).

Risk: Improving Government's Capability to Handle Risk and Uncertainty, Strategy Unit Report, November 2002 (London: Cabinet Office, 2002).

Rogers, Clifford J., '"As If a New Sun had Arisen": England's Fourteenth-Century RMA', in MacGregor Knox and Williamson Murray (eds.), *The Dynamics of Military Revolution, 1300–2050* (Cambridge: Cambridge University Press, 2001), 15–34.

Rosenberg, Justin, *The Follies of Globalisation Theory* (London: Verso, 2000).

Rothenberg, Gunther E., 'Maurice of Nassau, Gustavus Adolphus, Raimondo Montecuccoli, and the "Military Revolution" of the Seventeenth Century', in Peter Paret (ed.), *Makers of Modern Strategy: From Machiavelli to the Nuclear Age* (Oxford: Clarendon Press, 1998), 32–63.

Rousseau, Jean-Jacques, *On Social Contract or Principles of Political Right*, in *Rousseau's Political Writings*, trans. Julia Conaway Bondanella, ed. Alan Ritter and Julia Conoway Bondanella (New York: W. W. Norton, 1988), 84–117.

Rumsfeld, Donald, *21st Century Transformation of US Armed Forces*, Remarks as Delivered by Secretary of Defense Donald Rumsfeld, National Defense University, Fort McNair, Washington, DC, Thursday 31 January 2002 (Washington, DC: Department of Defense, 2002).

Sanger, David E. and Thom Shanker, 'War Planners Begin to Speak of War's Risks', *New York Times*, 18 February 2003.

Schelling, T. C., 'The Retarded Science of International Strategy', *Midwest Journal of Political Science* 4 (May 1960), 107–37.

Schiesel, Seth, 'On the Ground in Iraq, the Best Compass is in the Sky', *New York Times*, 17 April 2003.

Schröder, Gerhard, *The Terrorist Attacks in the United States and the Decisions Taken by the United Nations Security Council and NATO* (Berlin: Bulletin der Bundesregierung, No. 61/1, 19 September 2001).

Searle, John R., *The Construction of Social Reality* (London: Penguin Books, 1995).

The Security Policy Conditions for Danish Defence, August 2003, Royal Danish Ministry of Foreign Affairs, www.um.dk (30 September 2003).

Shaw, Martin, 'Strategy and Social Process: Military Context and Sociological Analysis', *Sociology* 24 (1990), 465–73.

'The Development of "Common Risk" Society: A Theoretical Overview', in Jürgen Kuhlmann and Jean Callaghan (eds.), *Military and Society in 21st Century Europe: A Comparative Analysis* (London: Transaction Publishers, 2000), 13–26.

Risk Transfer Militarism and Legitimacy of War after Iraq, www.theglobalsite.ac.uk/press/402shaw.htm (31 October 2004).

The New Western Way of War: Risk-Transfer War and Its Crisis in Iraq (Cambridge: Polity Press, 2005).

Shearer, David, *Private Armies and Military Intervention*, Adelphi Paper 316 (Oxford: International Institute of Strategic Studies, Oxford University Press, 1998).

Shy, John, 'Jomini', in Peter Paret (ed.), *Makers of Modern Strategy: From Machiavelli to the Nuclear Age* (Oxford: Clarendon Press, 1998), 143–85.

Soja, Edward W., *Postmetropolis: Critical Studies of Cities and Regions* (Oxford: Blackwell, 2000).

Solana, Javier, 'Growing the Alliance', *Economist*, 13 March 1999.

The Development of a Common European Security and Defence Policy: The Integration Project of the Next Decade (Berlin: EU-Commission/Institut für Europäische Politik, Press Release, 17 December 1999).

A Secure Europe in a Better World, European Council, Thessaloniki, 20 June 2003 (Brussels: EU High Representative for the Common Foreign and Security Policy, 2003).

Sterling, Bruce, 'War is Virtual Hell', *Wired* (March–April 1993), www.wired.com (21 July 2000).

Sun Tzu, *The Art of War*, trans. and with an introduction by Samuel B. Griffith (Oxford: Oxford University Press, 1963).

Swidler, Ann, 'The Concept of Rationality in the Work of Max Weber', *Sociological Inquiry* 43 (1973), 35–42.

Tama, Jordan, 'Is Europe Too Cautious?', *Foreign Policy* (January/February 2004), 88–90.

Tilly, Charles, *Coercion, Capital and European States: AD 990–1990* (Oxford: Basil Blackwell, 1990).

Townsend, Mark and Paul Harris, 'Security Role for Traffic Cameras', *Observer*, 9 February 2003.

Transcript: First Presidential Debate, 30 September 2004, from Coral Gables, FL. Text from FDCH E-media, www.washingtonpost.com (7 October 2004).

Tuchman, Barbara W., *The Guns of August* (New York: Macmillan, 1962).

UN Charter, www.un.org/aboutun/charter (26 January 2005).

United States Army, *White Paper: Concepts for the Objective Force* (2002).

The United States Commission on National Security/21st Century, *New World Coming: American Security in the 21st Century*, Phase I Report on the Emerging Global Security Environment for the First Quarter of the 21st Century (September 1999).

'United States: Vulnerable to Cyber Attack', *Stratfor*, 31 March 2001, www.stratfor.com/europe/commentary/0103302345 (1 April 2001).

US Department of Defense, *News Briefing, Army Brig. General Robert W. Crone*, Washington, DC, 2 October 2003 (Washington, DC: US Department of Defense, 2003).

Van Loon, Joost, *Risk and Technological Culture: Towards a Sociology of Virulence* (London: Routledge, 2002).

Villepin, Dominique de, Interview given during the *Complément d'enquête* programme on France 2, Paris, 24 March 2003, www.special.diplomatie.fr (27 March 2003).

BBC Dimbleby Lecture, BBC News, www.bbc.co.uk (6 November 2003).

Virilio, Paul, 'Military Space', in James Der Derian (ed.), *The Virilio Reader* (Malden, MA: Blackwell, 1998), 22–8.

Wæver, Ole, 'Securitization and Desecuritization', in Ronnie D. Lipschutz (ed.), *On Security* (New York: Columbia University Press, 1995), 46–86.

'Security: A Conceptual History for International Relations', unpublished paper presented at the 12th Nordic Political Science Congress, Uppsala, 19–21 August (1999).

Walker, R. B. J., 'The Subject of Security', in Keith Krause and Michael C. Williams (eds.), *Critical Security Studies* (Minneapolis, MN: University of Minnesota Press, 1997), 61–81.

Wallace, Claire, 'Reflections on the Concept of "Strategy"', in David Morgan and Liz Stanley (eds.), *Debates in Sociology* (Manchester: Manchester University Press, 1993), 94–117.

Walsh, Nick Pation, 'Putin Puts £6m Price on Rebels' Heads', *Guardian*, 9 September 2004.

Walt, Stephen M., 'Why Alliances Endure or Collapse', *Survival* 39 (1997), 156–80.

'Beyond Bin Laden: Reshaping US Foreign Policy', *International Security* 26 (2001), 57–78.

Waltz, Kenneth N., 'The Continuity of International Politics', in Ken Booth and Tim Dunne (eds.), *Worlds in Collision* (London: Palgrave, 2002), 348–53.

Warden, John, 'Air Theory for the Twenty-first Century', in Barry R. Schneider and Lawrence E. Grinter (eds.), *Battlefield of the Future: 21st Century Warfare Issues*, The Air War College Studies in National Security (Maxwell Air Force Base, AL: Air War College, 1995).

Weber, Max, *From Max Weber: Essays in Sociology*, ed. H. H. Gerth and C. Wright Mills (London: Routledge, 1997).

Weiner, Tim, 'Drive to Build High-Tech Army Hits Cost Snags', *New York Times*, 28 March 2005.

Weldes, Jutta, *Constructing National Interests: The United States and the Cuban Missile Crisis* (Minneapolis, MN: University of Minnesota Press, 1999).

Wildavsky, Aaron, 'Trial and Error Versus Trial Without Error', in Julian Morris (ed.), *Rethinking Risk and the Precautionary Principle* (Oxford: Butterworth-Heinemann, 2000), 22–45.

Williams, Cindy (ed.), *Holding the Line: US Defense Alternatives for the Early 21st Century* (Cambridge, MA: The MIT Press, 2001).

Willmott, H., *The Great Crusade: A New Complete History of the Second World War* (New York: The Free Press, 1989).

Windsor, Phillip, *Strategic Thinking: An Introduction and Farewell*, ed. Mats Bredal and Spyros Economides (Boulder, CO: Lynne Reinner, 2002).

Wolfowitz, Paul, *Building a Military for the 21st Century*, Prepared Statement for the House and Senate Armed Services Committees, 3–4 October 2001 (Washington, DC: US Department of Defense, 2001).

Remarks Prepared for Delivery by Deputy Secretary Paul Wolfowitz, World Affairs Council, Monterey, CA, Friday 3 May 2002 (Washington, DC: US Department of Defense, 2002).

Woodward, Bob, *Bush at War* (New York: Simon and Schuster, 2002).

Wright, Quincy, 'The Outlawry of War and the Law of War', *American Journal of International Law* 47 (July 1953), 365–76.

www.operations.mod.uk, www.operations.mod.uk/telic/index.htm (14 May 2004).

Zizek, Slavoj, *Welcome to the Desert of the Real!*, The Global Site, 16 September 2001, www.theglobalsite.ac.uk/times/109zizek.htm (18 February 2002).

Index